Business Information

Finding and Using Data In the Digital Age

The McGraw-Hill/Irwin Series: Operations and Decisions Sciences

Business Information

Finding and Using Data In the Digital Age

Jay L. Zagorsky
Ohio State University and
Boston University

Boston   Burr Ridge, IL   Dubuque, IA   Madison, WI   New York   San Francisco   St. Louis
Bangkok   Bogotá   Caracas   Kuala Lumpur   Lisbon   London   Madrid   Mexico City
Milan   Montreal   New Delhi   Santiago   Seoul   Singapore   Sydney   Taipei   Toronto

McGraw-Hill Higher Education

A Division of The McGraw-Hill Companies

BUSINESS INFORMATION: FINDING AND USING DATA IN THE DIGITAL AGE
Published by McGraw-Hill/Irwin, a business unit of The McGraw-Hill Companies, Inc., 1221 Avenue of the Americas, New York, NY, 10020. Copyright © 2003 by The McGraw-Hill Companies, Inc. All rights reserved. No part of this publication may be reproduced or distributed in any form or by any means, or stored in a database or retrieval system, without the prior written consent of The McGraw-Hill Companies, Inc., including, but not limited to, in any network or other electronic storage or transmission, or broadcast for distance learning.
Some ancillaries, including electronic and print components, may not be available to customers outside the United States.

This book is printed on acid-free paper.

1 2 3 4 5 6 7 8 9 0 DOC/DOC 0 9 8 7 6 5 4 3 2

ISBN 0-07-250770-5

Publisher: *Brent Gordon*
Senior sponsoring editor: *Scott Isenberg*
Editorial assistant: *Lee Stone*
Senior marketing manager: *Zina Craft*
Project manager: *Laura Griffin*
Production supervisor: *Gina Hangos*
Coordinator freelance design: *Mary L. Christianson*
Producer, media technology: *Todd Labak*
Cover designer: *Jenny El-Shamy*
Cover image: © *Rafael Lopez Studio*
Senior digital content specialist: *Brian Nacik*
Typeface: *10.5/13 Times Roman*
Compositor: *GAC/Indianapolis*
Printer: *R. R. Donnelley & Sons Company*

Library of Congress Cataloging-in-Publication Data
Zagorsky, Jay L.
    Business information: finding and using data in the digital age/by Jay L. Zagorsky.
      p.cm.
    Includes index.
    ISBN 0-07-250770-5 (alk. paper)
    1. Information technology—Management. 2. Data mining. I. Title.
HD30.2.Z337 2003
658'.05—dc21   2002025453

The author and publisher of this book have used their best efforts in preparing this material. The author and publisher make no warranty of any kind, expressed or implied, with regard to the programs, data, or documentation described or referenced in this book. The author and publisher shall not be liable in any event for any damages caused by using these programs, data, or documentation.

www.mhhe.com

Brief Contents

Contents

Preface

We currently live in the information age. So much information is given to us so fast that many individuals complain they are overloaded. Yet, while we live in a time of extremely easy access to primary information sources, few people in business know where to find this information, know how the underlying data are collected, or understand successful techniques for using this information. This book explains these topics by looking at the world's primary information on three different levels: personal, industrial, and national/international.

Personal data, discussed in the first part, are useful for marketing products and services, locating a new store, or targeting a mailing campaign. Data examined in this section include demographic information on how many people live in a targeted area, what their income is, and how much they spend on various products and services.

Industry- and company-level data described in the middle of the book, such as sales, profit, capitalization, staffing levels, inventory changes, and growth prospects, help you understand how your company fits into an industry. Understanding industrial data provides you with the numbers needed to write an effective business plan, map out new strategies, or analyze a business sector before investing. Two chapters in this section deal with human resource questions such as determining how much other companies are paying workers with similar skills.

The final third of the book examines key economic indicators that affect businesses and the financial markets. These chapters explain key indicators such as inflation, interest rates, GDP and unemployment, which often impact business decisions. Last, an entire chapter guides you through the myriad sources of import and export data, because more and more companies are expanding beyond their country's borders.

Each section of the book is important because information from all three levels is often used to solve business problems. Hence, current and future business managers in marketing, financial management, sales, or personnel and those planning on starting their own company will all benefit from reading this book.

The chapters are designed to stand alone, so some information is repeated. Each chapter follows the same pattern. The first part discusses the data that are available, how the data are collected, and the information's strengths and weaknesses. The second part shows you first what simple tables are available. The last part then shows you where more complex prepared tables and analyses exist and how to access the most precise information by creating custom tabulations. Inserted throughout every chapter are practice problems for assessing and extending your understanding. The answers to these problems are found at the end of the book.

I would like to acknowledge my students at Boston University's School of Management who took QM830: Business Information. Their help in reading and commenting on the early drafts of this book provided much useful guidance. Thanks to Randy Olsen and the staff at the Ohio State University's Center for Human Resource Research who taught me the inner workings of both the National Longitudinal Surveys and many other national data collections.

Thank you to the professors who reviewed this work in various stages, including Martha Valentine-Rossing of Regis University, Antonia Espiritu of Hawaii Pacific University, David Hays of Central Michigan University, and Gregory Fleet of University of New Brunswick at St. John. Thanks also to Barry Keating of University of Notre Dame, J. Holton Wilson of Central Michigan University, Pamela Schindler of Wittenberg University, Donald Cooper of Florida Atlantic University, and Nancy Weida of Bucknell University.

A special thanks goes to my editor at McGraw-Hill, Scott Eisenberg, and his assistant Lee Stone. Lee's efforts smoothed the long path from rough manuscript to a finished book. I also want to thank the production staff, headed by Laura Griffin, for all their work.

A special thanks to Steve McClaskie at Ohio State, who showed me the need for this book by forwarding many e-mails from individuals needing data to answer their business problems. Inspiration for many practice questions and scenarios was taken from these e-mails. I appreciate the efforts of Amanda McClain whose editing greatly improved my writing. Finally, and most important, I would like to thank my wife, Kim Meyers, for her support and encouragement.

Jay L. Zagorsky

Acknowledgments

Internet screen images are reprinted with permission from the following companies and organizations:

Dun and Bradstreet

American Society of Association Executives

Thomas Register of American Manufacturers

Bank of Canada

Center for Human Resource Research, The Ohio State University

Institute of Social Research, The University of Michigan

International Monetary Fund

Statistics Canada

Statistics Canada information is used with the permission of the Minister of Industry, as Minister responsible for Statistics Canada. Information on the availability of the wide range of data from Statistics Canada can be obtained from Statistics Canada's Regional Offices, its World Wide Web site at **http://www. statcan.ca**, and its toll-free access number 1-800-263-1136. All Statistics Canada information and screen images were extracted in fall 2001.

To my wife Kim

Chapter 1

Introduction

Every day there are thousands of important business meetings where questions like these are discussed:

"How big is our target audience?"

"How much do our competitors produce?"

"Are the pay raises we are giving enough?"

"What do people generally spend on these products?"

"Which location is a better site for our new store?"

Unfortunately, often no one knows the answers to the meeting's key questions. When this happens, either someone makes a rough guess and that rough guess is accepted as fact or outside consultants are called in and an answer arrives weeks after it was needed. This book shows you how to answer these and many other key business questions quickly with publicly available information and gives you the tools for becoming any company's information consultant. Then the next time key business questions arise, you can provide answers, not guesses.

Unanswered questions are a paradox in the Information Age. The paradox arises because, while the amount and quality of information is growing exponentially, few business managers know what information is available and how to get that information. If you are a business manager, business student, or someone who needs to answer quantitative questions, this book will help you understand:

- What sources of information exist

- Where to find information

- How this information is collected

- What the limitations are of this information

- How to process this information

- How to interpret this information

Information is the most vital commodity in business today. In the past, businesses that controlled raw materials like iron, steel, coal, and oil were king, but today businesses that produce, control, and disseminate information rule the market. The goal of this book is simply to help you become part of the information royalty.

Until now, no book has existed to teach business managers and students how to answer their own quantitative questions.[1] While almost all the data sources discussed in this book have existed for decades, until the mid-1990s finding and accessing these data sources was extremely difficult. Prior to the mid-1990s almost all data were released on massive 9-track tapes, suitable only for mainframe computer processing. To use those data you needed to access and understand mainframe computers, statistical processing languages like SAS or SPSS, and survey methodology.

In the past five years, however, a major transformation has occurred. Every major public data collection in the United States has become available either online via the Internet or on CD-ROM. Moreover, many of these data sets now come with simple-to-use table creation software. This means that to use these data sets today all you need is a question to answer, a personal computer, an Internet connection, and the ability to read instructions.

This transformation from mainframes to personal computers has revolutionized the process of researching your own questions. Today, you no longer need the help of expensive outside consultants or overworked inside consultants to answer many quantitative business questions. More important, learning research skills makes you an invaluable resource at your company, boosting your pay and opportunities.

Even if you are a business manager or student who is working or planning to work outside the United States, this book is relevant. Every major country in the world runs census and other surveys that are similar in scope, questions, and timing to those in the United States. These similarities occur not because the United States is the best model, but instead because statistical agencies from various countries constantly meet, with the goal of standardizing the world's statistical programs. This standardization means business

---

[1]There are a number of business books, discussed in the conclusion, that teach research methods. These books are primarily designed for managers who need to create, implement, and analyze custom surveys, which is far beyond the needs of most business professionals.

professionals outside the United States can find in their country many of the same types of information discussed in this book. The biggest difference between countries is not the amount of information collected but ease of access. While currently the United States provides much easier access both on- and offline, improvements in data dissemination are constantly occurring in other countries.

This book is also relevant for individuals interested in countries beyond the United States since many chapters include the key Internet locations of international information. Canadian data are especially highlighted because my academic research extensively uses these sources.

Three philosophies guide this book. First, the book is written for individuals without a technical background. To understand the sources, examples, and methods used in the following chapters, you do not need any special statistical, quantitative, or research skills.

Second, all the sources of information used are publicly available, either free or for a nominal charge. While there are a large number of excellent commercially available data sources, such as Compustat®, ABI-Inform®, and Lexis-Nexis®, few people in business know about the extensive amount of free data disseminated by the United States government, academic institutions, and other organizations. If you spend all of your time searching for information, try the commercially available sources.[2] If your research needs do not justify spending tens of thousands of dollars a month on commercial database subscription fees, then this book will show you a cheaper way to find information. More important than saving money, most sources discussed in this book allow you to specify exactly what data to analyze. This means that instead of pulling general articles out of a commercial database, you create custom answers that deal specifically with your situation.

The third philosophy is that the best way to learn how to do research is by practice and experimentation. You will get much more from this book if you read it while sitting at a computer connected to the Internet. While you are reading, extract data from a website, look up a prepared table, or follow a link to another place on the World Wide Web. These techniques will broaden your understanding of what information is available and how to use it. The book contains many detailed business examples that are discussed in an easy-to-understand step-by-step format. Replicate each example, and then think about a similar question that your business faces and try to answer it. Interspersed throughout each chapter are a number of practice questions. Try to answer

---

[2]If you use these commercial sources Paula Berinstein's book, **Finding Statistics Online** published by Information Today Inc., contains many tips for effectively searching the commercial databases.

them and then check your results with answers found at the book's end. In addition to practice problems in the book, there are supplemental materials available online at the book's McGraw-Hill website (**http://www.mhhe.com** and type Zagorsky into the search box). Supplemental files include items such as the forms, questionnaires, instructions, and reference materials used to create many of the data sets discussed in the following chapters. These supplemental materials provide details for individuals interested in going beyond the information in this book. If you really want to understand a topic, download and fill in the underlying survey, census, or form.

The book's website also contains a set of electronic bookmarks linking you to the key places discussed. Downloading these bookmarks to your computer provides a quick chapter-by-chapter method of navigating business information on the Internet.

The key to success in business today is knowledge. After mastering the material in this book you will understand the most important sources of business information, making you part of the information royalty.

Chapter  2

Information Basics

Before diving into what information exists, where to find it, and how it will help your business, it is important to understand some of the basic points. To give you this background, the chapter first overviews the primary sources of business information. It then discusses two simple but key techniques used to manipulate business data. The chapter concludes with a common mistakes checklist, which if followed helps you avoid making errors.

Where Does Business Data Come From?

Why do managers care where business data come from? Because knowing the origin lets you decide *Do I trust my source*? Until you trust the source, don't use the information. Only trustworthy sources of business information are discussed in this book. Nevertheless, even the trustworthiest data have limitations. Knowing how business data are generated helps you understand how far to trust the data. Business information primarily comes from four places:

1. Complete enumerations (census, inventory, profit/loss statements)

2. Surveys (cross-sectional and longitudinal)

3. Estimates (forecasts, predictions, guesses)

4. Marketing studies (surveys, experiments, focus groups, scanner data)

Complete enumeration means methods that count everything or everyone. For example, no company creates a quarterly profit and loss statement by randomly selecting sales and expenses to report. Instead every sale and expense is included. Surveys are a random selection of a complete enumeration. Well-known surveys, like the Gallup Poll, interview around 1,000 people to tell us what the entire nation is thinking instead of interviewing all 285 million residents. Almost all the sources of information in the next chapters are based on either censuses or surveys.

Estimates are forecasts and predictions that come from "experts." While some experts use very sophisticated techniques to predict, others just provide an intuitive guess. Nevertheless, no matter how the estimates are made, even the best guesses about the future are just guesses. Estimates from experts are not covered in this book, since the goal is to reduce your reliance on others by making you the expert. Finally, marketing studies include market surveys, experiments, focus groups, and scanner data, which are all designed to provide feedback on a particular business or product line. Since most marketing studies and focus groups provide information specific to a single company, this information is also not covered in the book.

Because understanding how censuses and surveys are conducted is the key way to decide if they are trustworthy, the book contains an appendix entitled "Census and Survey Details." If you have the time, read this appendix to broaden your understanding. If you do not have time, there are four main ideas to remember when using census and survey information:

1. You do not need a census or complete enumeration to get accurate information. Information from a well-designed and executed survey is just as good as, and sometimes better than, a complete census. Just because the information is from a sample does not mean it is less precise. For example, many people in and out of government have argued that sampling the United States population would provide a more accurate and cheaper count of the populace than the current method of asking every family to fill out a form during the decennial census.

2. To a certain point, the more people interviewed for a survey, the more accurate the answers. However, the level of accuracy does not increase one-for-one with the sample size. For many types of information, a randomly selected sample of 1,000 residents provides a good idea as to what an entire nation is thinking. Increasing the sample size to 10,000 does **not** make the answers 10 times more accurate.

3. Never trust information that comes from a nonrandom sample. Some sources of business information, such as salary surveys, are based on a convenient set of companies, not on a random sample. Would you use information from an inventory that counted only items on easy-to-see shelves? No, because this method of taking an inventory results in a distorted picture. Treat surveys that track only businesses, customers, or people that are conveniently available with the same mistrust as a badly done inventory.

4. Finally, understand that not all information from a census or survey is accurate. All information described in this book ultimately comes from

people's answers. Since humans are imperfect, so is the information. For example, in the 2000 presidential election between George Bush and Al Gore, a complete count was done of all votes in Florida. Nevertheless, many people stated the state's election results were wrong. In Palm Beach County, a confusing ballot caused many individuals to vote for a candidate different from the one they wanted. In other counties, the vote count changed because additional chads would fall off every time the ballots were fed through the counting machine. This election clearly showed that even results from a complete enumeration or census of paper ballets have a measurable margin of error.

Keep these four ideas in the back of your mind when reading the rest of the book.

Key Formulas

There are two very simple mathematical formulas used over and over with business data. They are both easy to learn, even if the last math course you took was decades ago. The first formula is the percentage change formula, which shows how much something is growing or shrinking. When the formula's result is a positive number, the data are growing, while a negative result from the formula means the data are shrinking. For example, if you sold $200 million of product last year and $225 million this year, the percentage change formula tells you the sales growth rate. The most common percentage change formula, and the only one used in this book, is:[1]

$$\text{Percentage change} = \frac{(\text{New Value} - \text{Old Value})}{\text{Old Value}} \times 100\%$$

To calculate how much sales grew over the last year, plug $200 into the formula as the old value and $225 as the new value. The equation shows that sales grew by 12.5 percent last year.

$$12.5\% = \frac{(\$225 \text{ million} - \$200 \text{ million})}{\$200 \text{ million}} \times 100\%$$

Practice Question

While three years ago your staff numbered 64 people, today you have just 52. What is the percentage change in your staff's size?

[1]For those who are curious, the other two formulas are: [ln(New Value) − ln(Old Value)] × 100% where ln stands for the natural logarithm (base e), and [(New Value − Old Value)/New Value] × 100%. For small changes, they all give about the same answer; for large changes, the formulas provide quite different answers.

The other key formula used constantly is the inflation adjustment. Chapter 10, entitled "Prices," goes into much more detail about adjusting for inflation, but the intuition and math are both very simple. A dollar today is worth much less than a dollar 50 years ago. Because a dollar does not buy the same amount, you must adjust all money figures to account for this change. The government keeps track of what a dollar is worth using the Consumer Price Index. Recent values from this index are listed in Table 2.1.

Once you know the values, you can adjust old prices into current terms using this formula:

$$\text{Inflation Adjusted Price} = \text{Original Price} \times \frac{\text{Value of CPI Currently}}{\text{Value of CPI Originally}}$$

For example, when I went to baseball games during the early 1980s, bleacher seats cost $4. To determine how much that is in today's (2001) dollars, you can use the inflation formula. First, put the average 1982 CPI value of 96.5 in as the value of CPI originally, then put the 2001 CPI value of 177.1 in as the value of CPI currently, and finally, put $4 in as the original price. Inserting these values into the formula gives:

$$\$7.34 = \$4 \times \frac{177.1}{96.5}$$

If baseball ticket prices rose only as fast as general inflation, bleacher seats should have cost slightly more than $7 in 2001, instead of the higher price I currently pay. It is important to adjust for price changes even in a low inflation environment. Currently United States inflation is running around

TABLE 2.1
United States Consumer Price Index from 1970 to 2001

Year	Avg. CPI	Year	Avg. CPI	Year	Avg. CPI
1970	38.8	1981	90.9	1992	140.3
1971	40.5	1982	96.5	1993	144.5
1972	41.8	1983	99.6	1994	148.2
1973	44.4	1984	103.9	1995	152.4
1974	49.3	1985	107.6	1996	156.9
1975	53.8	1986	109.6	1997	160.5
1976	56.9	1987	113.6	1998	163.0
1977	60.6	1988	118.3	1999	166.6
1978	65.2	1989	124.0	2000	172.2
1979	72.6	1990	130.7	2001	177.1
1980	82.4	1991	136.2		

Note: The complete table containing all the CPI numbers from 1913 to present is located at **http://www.bls.gov/cpi.**

3 percent per year. Even at this low rate, prices roughly double every 24 years. Unless inflation is zero, always adjust monetary figures for general price changes.

Practice Question

In 2001 a gallon of gas costs $1.60. Adjusting only for inflation, how much should a gallon of gas have cost back in 1975? (Hint: Rearrange the formula.)

Common Mistakes and Problems Checklist

Before diving into specific sources of information, it is important to have a good checklist to prevent common mistakes and handle common problems. Why use a checklist? It is simpler to correct mistakes and problems early in the process than late. While using a checklist before analyzing and reporting your findings does not catch every error, catching problems early in the process results in more trustworthy answers. The following checklist is not meant to be all-inclusive. After you gain experience, begin adding and subtracting items to create your own personal checklist.

- Does the information make sense?

- Does the information need a time or price adjustment?

- Do I need to think about seasonal adjustment issues?

- Are size adjustments important?

- Did the data jump or change over time?

- Do I need to update old information?

- Did I check the answer from another source?

Sensible Data

The reason most managers want hard numbers is to make better decisions. Providing the wrong numbers means not only that people make worse decisions but also that their image of your trustworthiness falls. It is hard to be part of the information royalty if mistakes make you look like the court jester. The simplest way to prevent most mistakes is to **STOP** and come up with a rough estimate or range before beginning. If you are expecting numbers between $5 and $25 and you come up with $10,000, back up and recheck your work. Having a rough idea before starting is the best way to save time, money, and maybe your career.

Beyond having a rough estimate, you should also check whether the results are sensible. For example, if you are looking at males and females the results should contain just two categories, and finding three or more indicates a severe problem. Even the most experienced researchers make simple mistakes. One mistake I often make is looking up or tabulating information for just males or just females when I want both sexes. To catch this mistake I now write down how many people I expect to find before starting. If I see only half the expected number it is time to start over.

Another common mistake arises when dealing with large numbers. Instead of printing excessively large numbers, information is often reported after dividing all numbers by 1,000, 10,000, or 1,000,000. Financial data on individual companies are many times reported in millions. Most industry data are reported in billions and most data on the United States economy are reported in trillions. Accidentally forgetting which adjustment factor is used can make it seem that a company is larger than the entire industry. Once again, having a rough idea ahead of time how big the number should be eliminates adjustment factor problems.

Time and Price Adjustments

One important issue that often traps new researchers is confusion about time frequency. Some data are provided in daily form (financial market information), others monthly (retail sales), some quarterly (GDP, exports, and imports), and a few in yearly terms (population). When using information with different time units, you should ensure that everything is adjusted to a common time frame. Do not report in a single paragraph weekly, monthly, and annual figures. Instead use a common time frame, such as quarterly figures, which makes comparisons easy and eliminates confusion when presenting results.

It bears repeating, that you should adjust prices for inflation. My grandfather constantly talked about the "good old days" when a cup of coffee was a dime. Today, the cheapest cup of coffee at the local Starbucks is $1.30. While the price of coffee has changed, so have all other prices including wages and income. The real comparison is not 10¢ versus $1.30 for a cup of coffee but instead 10¢ times the inflation adjustment factor versus $1.30. After seeing this adjustment, even Grandpa admitted that the "good old days" were not as good as they first appeared.

Seasonal Adjustment

When seeking out business information, you will constantly need to decide between seasonally adjusted and ***not*** seasonally adjusted data. Which one should you use? Seasonal adjustment techniques smooth out spikes or short-falls that occur normally during the year. For example, hiring shoots up every summer as both construction and warm-weather businesses expand their staff. Hiring also falls every January, when retail outlets lay off temporary Christmas workers. The graph in Figure 2.1 shows the difference in United States monthly employment before and after seasonal adjustment. Overall, the solid, seasonally adjusted line climbs relatively smoothly while the dashed unadjusted line fluctuates.

Which type of data should you use, seasonally adjusted or unadjusted? The answer depends on the problem you are trying to solve. The financial markets react daily to changes in economic indicators. If you are trying to understand or predict financial market behavior, use *adjusted* data since they contain less long-term noise. If you are dealing with a short duration product or problem, like staffing for the Christmas season, use *unadjusted* data since they provide better information on short-term fluctuations. If your problem does not fit either case, start with **unadjusted** data. While most media stories report only adjusted information, more business data are available in unadjusted form.

Size Adjustment

Another important check is to see if any size adjustments are needed. One of the most common size adjustments corrects for changes in population. For example, if you are interested in comparing air travel by Canadians and United

FIGURE 2.1

Monthly Employment in the United States before and after Seasonal Adjustment

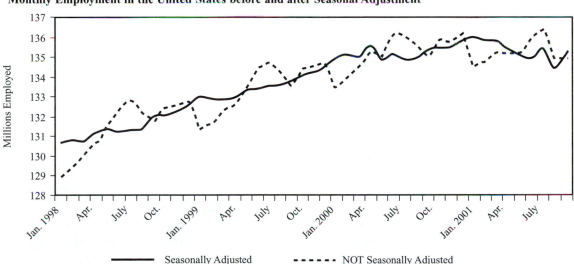

Source: Various issues of U.S. Bureau of Labor Statistics' *Employment and Earnings.*

States residents, do not simply look at total air miles flown in both countries. While Canada's land area is huge, its population is one-tenth the size of the United States. Hence, any direct comparison of the totals between the two countries is skewed because one country's population is so much bigger than the other. To compare air travel or any other factor, divide total air miles by total population to arrive at air travel per person.

While this air travel example is fairly straightforward, there are many less obvious examples. Few retail stores are built in inner cities. The standard reason executives give is that residents of inner cities have below average incomes and do not have the purchasing power of families in the suburbs. Size adjustment is important here also. For many retail establishments, sales are driven not by average family income but instead by total area income. Hence, retail executives should multiply average family income by the number of families living in the area. When properly adjusted for density, many inner city neighborhoods actually represent a better market for some retailers than sparsely settled, richer suburban neighborhoods.

Finally, you need to correct for size when examining financial variables. For example, the total profits of a company are rarely reported in the financial news. Instead profits per share are reported. Per share data make it easier to compare companies of unequal size, like Coca-Cola and Pepsi. Other industries, like banking, often report profit per dollar of capital so that the profits of large national banks like Chase Manhattan or Bank of America are directly comparable to smaller regional and local banks.

Do the Data Jump?

When data are compiled over more than one year, sometimes the graph of the data series will break and show a sudden upward or downward jump. When a series has a break or sudden jump, it is very important to figure out why. Never ignore jumps. For example, when you are tracking financial data, a jump in share prices often signals major corporate events like acquisitions or major sales. When you are tracking business information derived from a census or survey, a jump often signals a change in the underlying questions or definitions.

Surveys and census questionnaires are not static. They regularly change over time as questions and definitions are refined. For example, prior to 1967 the Current Population Survey, which tracks the nation's unemployment rate, asked questions to randomly chosen individuals 14 years of age or older. After 1967, however, the survey was administered only to individuals age 16 years or older. The definitional shift in ages occurred because of increases in the minimum age for leaving school and the steady decrease in the number of children working.

Whenever a series jumps, investigate why. When you present your findings, people will ask you why the sudden change occurred. If the jump is due to a questionnaire or definitional change, it is often easy to adjust the data so that the numbers are consistent over time. For example, you can remove all 14- and 15-year-olds from Current Population Survey data prior to 1967. This ensures you have both a consistent series and one that has no unexplained changes. Sometimes, there is no simple explanation. Even if you cannot explain the jump, simply describing your search for an explanation increases other managers' perceptions of your trustworthiness.

Do I Need to Update Old Information?

In business, you often want newer data than what are currently available. While not all data are released slowly, some government items, like tax information, are two or three years old by the time they are released. When faced with old information you have three choices. You can ignore all sources that are not current. The problem with this approach is that you still need information to make your decision. The second choice is to just update all numbers for inflation. For example, if salary numbers are two years old and inflation has increased by 6 percent over this period, you can increase all salary numbers by 6 percent.[2] This simple trick is easy to implement and generally provides a good current estimate.

If you have extra time or the information is very important, find data for previous years. Let's say you are trying to set the salary for computer programmers and these workers make up most of your costs. Do not get just the most current salaries. Instead examine computer programmers' salaries over the past 10 or 15 years, and you will find computer salaries have risen faster than those for most other occupations. Using this information, you can include the extra premium received by this group of workers when adjusting older data to produce current estimates.

In business there is a strong tendency to believe that old or historic information is useless because the industry is changing so rapidly. In general this is nonsense. The technological frontier is progressing very rapidly. However, while the latest and greatest technology is announced with great fanfare, this technology spreads or diffuses very slowly throughout the business community. Older data are not useless because change is not instantaneous; instead it occurs slowly. One simple example of the difference between technological

---

[2]Just multiply all numbers by 1.06 to increase salaries by 6%.

change and technological diffusion is the music business. Currently, digital music files are being swapped, bought, and traded on the Internet. While everyone agrees digital music is technologically superior to everything before it, there are still two stores in my neighborhood currently selling vinyl records. Digital music might be superior, but customers and businesses still exist for the old technology.

Did I Check the Answer from Another Source?

One way to ensure your answers are correct is to check the answers from another source. While in business it is rare to have two sets of information that cover exactly the same data, you can often find another data set that can confirm or deny whether your answer is roughly correct. For example, a cross-check for census answers is done by comparing data from the annual March Demographic Supplement to the Current Population Survey. Sometimes there is no comparable survey. In these cases use a previous year of the same survey to check the answers. The more sources confirming your findings, the more confidence you and others will have in the results.

The above issues are not an exhaustive checklist. As you answer business questions you will encounter problems. When this happens, write them down and create an expanded checklist. Using your personalized checklist before doing any analysis or presentation improves the quality of your work and reduces the chance of mistakes that could damage your career or reputation.

Summary

Remember several basic ideas during any search for information. First, you do not need a census or complete enumeration to get accurate information. Information from a well-designed and executed survey is just as good as and sometimes better than information from a complete census. Second, there are some very simple mathematical formulas used over and over with business data. The most common is the percentage change formula, shown below, which quantifies growth or shrinkage.

$$\text{Percentage change} = \frac{(\text{New Value} - \text{Old Value})}{\text{Old Value}} \times 100\%$$

Third, and most important, as you examine specific sources of information you should review a checklist to prevent mistakes. The checklist I recommend is:

- Does the information make sense?

- Does the information need a time or price adjustment?

- Do I need to think about seasonal adjustment issues?

- Are size adjustments important?

- Did the data jump or change over time?

- Do I need to update old information?

- Did I check the answer from another source?

This list is not all-inclusive. After you gain experience in using and finding data, add your own items to the list. Using a checklist cannot catch every mistake, but it will minimize the number of times errors occur.

Chapter 3

Quick Information: Statistical Compendia

Frequently in business there is no time for a thorough analysis. All too often the boss, a customer, or another manager calls and needs an answer instantly or even sooner. When you need information quickly, the best source is statistical compendia. While the rest of this book contains pointers to an amazing amount of information, it takes time and effort to use these more detailed sources. This chapter, however, is designed for those moments when you do not have time for a complete analysis but need to find preprocessed answers quickly.

Currently there exist numerous compendia, in both physical and electronic form. If you expect to answer important questions with little or no notice, learn how to use these resources ahead of time. Periodically browse the compendia to understand the types of business information they contain and refresh your memory. Then, when asked for an instant answer, you will show everyone you are king of information.

This chapter considers two scenarios. First, your boss calls from the middle of an advertising agency meeting. The agency is proposing a radio campaign to promote your company's new product, which is aimed at the elderly market. While her question is simple, "Do the elderly listen to the radio?" the pressure is not, since a conference room full of people is waiting for your answer. Second, you have been asked to invest in a golf course. Before investing you want to know answers to some basic questions like: How many golfers are there? Is golf a growing game? How many golf courses exist in the United States?

To answer these and other common business scenarios you need to know that almost every major country in the world periodically issues a thick book filled with table upon table of information about all facets of that country.[1] Moreover, if these books do not have the exact figures you need, the compendia contains at the bottom of each table and in the front of each chapter detailed notes that point to sources of more information. While a few years ago these books only existed in printed form, many countries are now putting the books on CD-ROM and the Internet. With a digital version you can directly cut and paste information into reports, e-mails, and spreadsheets. Countries that have posted their compendia on the Internet make looking up information easy no matter where you are in the world.

Statistical Abstract of the United States

If you are serious about becoming a king of information, buy a statistical compendia and look at it frequently. In the United States the statistical compilations, which began in 1878, are produced yearly by the Commerce Department and are called the *Statistical Abstract of the United States.* While these books are found in the reference section of almost every library, you can purchase your own copy for around $40 from the United States Government Printing Office (**http://bookstore.gpo.gov**) and from any major bookseller. The CD-ROM version of the *Statistical Abstract* comes out a few months after the book and sells for around $10 more than the print version.

Given the amount of information available in each volume, this book is an incredible bargain and the single most useful resource available for quickly answering most general business questions. Beyond the data and references, the front of each *Statistical Abstract* lists many telephone numbers and Internet addresses for finding more information. Table 3.1 lists the chapters and key contents of a typical *Statistical Abstract.*

The online version is found on the Census Bureau's website (**http://www. census.gov**) shown in Figure 3.1. The "Statistical Abstract" link is located near the bottom of the page in the section marked "Special Topics."

Picking the "Statistical Abstract" link brings up the *Abstract*'s homepage, shown in Figure 3.2. To download one of the chapters just pick the link labeled "Adobe Acrobat PDF (Portable Document Format) files." A list of chapters that looks similar to Table 3.1 will then appear. It is important to note that while PDF files are available back to 1995, online chapters do *not* have every table contained in the printed version. The missing tables are primarily those

---

[1] The best place to see the books discussed in this chapter is the reference room of a major research library. The Library of Congress Business Reference room (5th floor Adams building) contains one of the largest sets of compendia in the United States.

TABLE 3.1
Typical Contents of the United States Statistical Abstract

Note: Some section titles are abbreviated. Depending on the year, different material is included.

Title	Contains Information About
Population	Number of people in U.S. by age, race, sex
Vital Statistics	Births, deaths, marriage, and divorce
Health and Nutrition	Medical care, insurance, doctors, hospitals
Education	Grade schools, test scores, students, colleges
Law Enforcement, Courts	Crime, drug use, police, prisons, fires
Geography and Environment	Pollution, trash/recycling, weather by city
Parks, Recreation, Travel	Books, music, sports, arts, leisure, tourism
Elections	Voting, politicians, political contributions
State and Local Government	Spending, income, debt, taxes, lotteries
Federal Government	Spending, income, debt, taxes, employment
National Defense and Veterans	Military spending, manpower, VA programs
Social Insurance and Human Services	Social Security, welfare, pensions, charity
Labor Force and Employment	Wages, benefits, hours worked, unions
Income, Expenditures, and Wealth	GDP, spending, poverty, net worth
Prices	Consumer, producer, export, and import prices
Banking, Finance, and Insurance	Credit cards, mortgages, bonds, stock, IRAs
Business Enterprises	Payroll, bankruptcy, mergers, patents, profits
Communications and Technology	Media usage, phones, TV, books, mail, ads
Energy	Fuel prices, utilities, solar, gas, electricity
Science and Technology	R&D spending, number of scientists, NASA
Land Transportation	Trucks, cars, commuting, highways, deaths
Air and Water Transportation	Aerospace industry, shipyards, merchant fleet
Agriculture	Farms, crops, prices, exports, meat, milk
Natural Resources	Timber, paper, fish, mining, oil, coal, gas
Construction and Housing	Home sales, homeownership, office space
Manufacturers	Alcohol, clothes, shoes, steel, computers
Domestic Trade and Services	Supermarkets, catalogs, mail order, lodging
Foreign Commerce and Aid	Foreign investment, exports, imports
Outlying Areas	Puerto Rico, Guam, Virgin Islands, Samoa
Comparative International Statistics	Population, spending, taxes, income, patents
Industrial Outlook	Business trends

copyrighted by private companies or industry associations, which are often the very tables you need. While editions prior to 1998 are missing quite a few tables, since 1998 the online edition looks very close to the printed version.

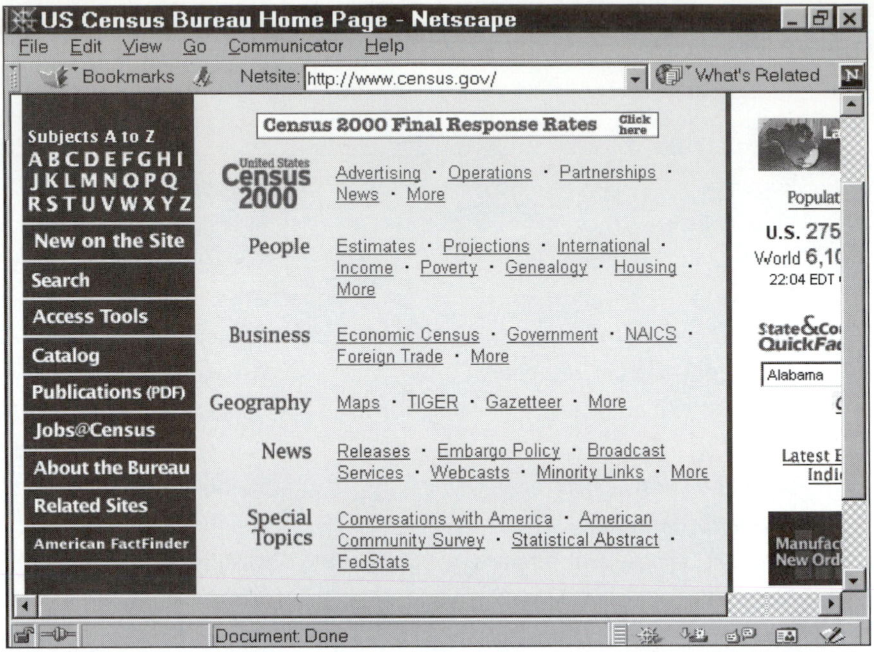

FIGURE 3.1
United States Census
Bureau Homepage

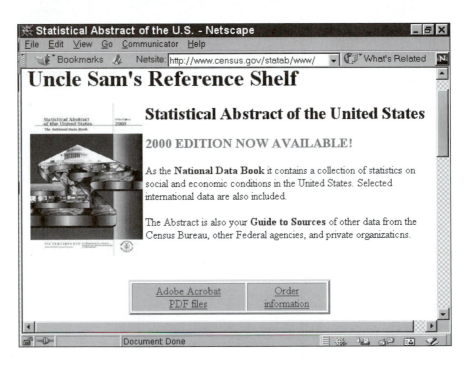

FIGURE 3.2
United States
Statistical Abstract
Homepage

Now that you know about the *Statistical Abstract,* let's answer the first scenario, which asked, "Do the elderly listen to the radio?" Download

FIGURE 3.3

United States Statistical Abstract Table on Multimedia Audiences

Acrobat Reader - [StatAbs2000Sec18.pdf]
File Edit Document View Window Help

No. 911. Multimedia Audiences—Summary: 2000

[In percent, except total (199,438 represents 199,438,000). As of spring. For persons 18 years old and over. Represents the percent of persons participating during the prior week, except as indicated. Based on sample and subject to sampling error; see source for details]

Item	Total population (1,000)	Television viewing	Television prime time viewing	Cable viewing [1]	Radio listening	Newspaper reading	Accessed Internet [2]
Total	199,438	93.5	82.1	71.3	84.0	79.3	45.4
18 to 24 years old.	25,691	92.2	73.8	68.6	90.6	73.3	58.7
25 to 34 years old.	39,066	92.4	81.3	71.1	90.6	77.0	53.3
35 to 44 years old.	44,791	92.4	81.1	71.9	89.7	80.5	53.8
45 to 54 years old.	34,774	93.7	83.5	74.7	87.5	83.5	54.8
55 to 64 years old.	22,711	94.7	85.6	76.4	80.8	82.4	35.1
65 years old and over	32,404	96.5	86.7	65.4	61.1	78.1	10.7
Male.	95,691	94.3	82.3	72.0	85.3	79.3	47.1
Female	103,747	92.8	81.8	70.6	82.8	79.2	43.8
White	167,002	93.4	82.0	72.6	84.4	80.0	46.8
Black	23,628	95.9	84.9	67.3	84.1	77.3	33.1
Asian	5,507	92.2	77.4	49.8	74.6	68.3	53.5
Other	3,301	88.3	74.4	68.2	78.1	72.0	46.4
Spanish speaking	21,359	93.5	81.6	55.9	84.6	66.3	34.1
Not high school graduate	35,260	94.8	82.7	56.6	73.0	60.0	11.6
High school graduate	66,360	94.5	84.6	71.8	82.7	78.8	31.0
Attended college	52,878	93.6	80.6	76.2	89.3	83.7	59.5
College graduate	44,940	91.1	79.4	76.1	88.1	89.7	76.5
Employed:							
Full time	113,259	92.7	81.0	74.6	91.1	82.0	56.8
Part time	17,176	92.2	78.7	70.9	89.2	82.1	55.1
Not employed.	69,003	95.3	84.6	65.9	71.0	74.1	24.2
Household income:							
Less than $10,000. . . .	14,292	93.6	81.6	47.7	68.0	58.7	14.6
$10,000 to $19,999 . . .	24,406	95.3	84.2	55.8	71.2	68.6	14.2
$20,000 to $29,999	25,327	94.8	84.3	63.8	79.7	73.9	24.5

175% | 5 of 18 | 5.76 x 9.18 in

Figure caption:
United States Statistical Abstract Table on Multimedia Audiences

the *Abstract*'s "Communications" chapter[2] and jump to the table labeled Multimedia Audiences, which is shown in Figure 3.3. This table, which summarizes media audiences, shows that listening to the radio declines rapidly by age. While over 90 percent of teenagers surveyed had listened to the radio in the past week, only 61 percent of those over 65 listened. Either television or newspaper advertising better fits your product's needs since among those over 65, almost 80 percent read a newspaper the previous week and over 96 percent watched TV. Quickly providing this kind of information helps not only your company, but also your career.

When you need to find something quickly, look in the index found at the end of the *Statistical Abstract*. The index often pinpoints the exact table you need. To become proficient at using this book, try answering two more questions. First, your company is thinking of marketing a new pet product. How many households in the United States own a dog or cat? How many dogs and cats are there?

To answer this question, open the *Statistical Abstract*'s index and search for "Pets."[3] The 2000 edition's index, for example, shows pet ownership data are located in Table 424, in the middle of the "Parks, Recreation and Travel" chapter. Then either download or open the *Abstract* to Table 424. This table,

[2]Renamed "Information and Communications" starting in the 2001 edition.
[3]The Pet Ownership table was not included in the 2001 edition.

FIGURE 3.4

United States Statistical Abstract Table on Pet Ownership

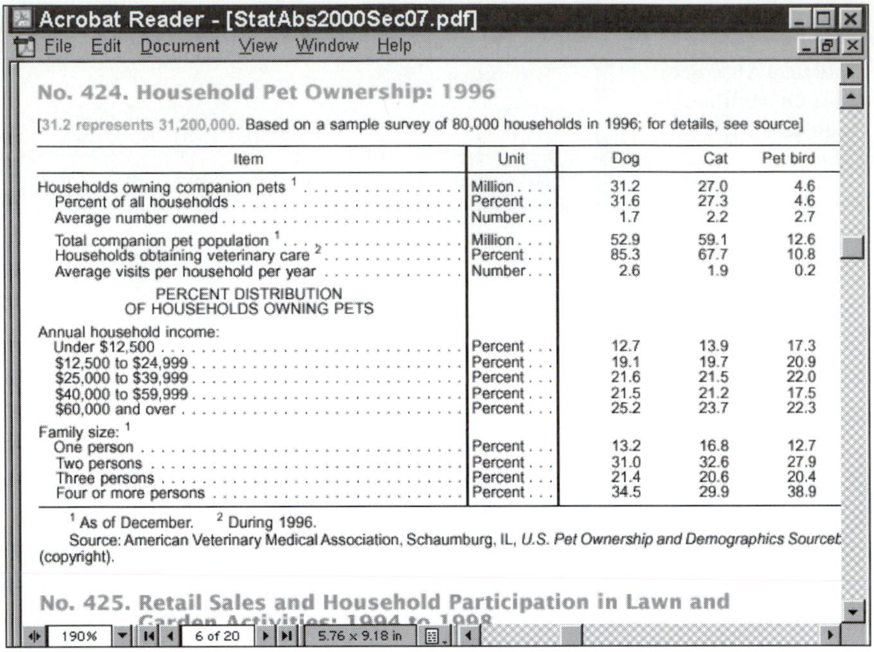

Acrobat Reader - [StatAbs2000Sec07.pdf]				
File Edit Document View Window Help				

No. 424. Household Pet Ownership: 1996

[31.2 represents 31,200,000. Based on a sample survey of 80,000 households in 1996; for details, see source]

Item	Unit	Dog	Cat	Pet bird
Households owning companion pets [1]	Million	31.2	27.0	4.6
Percent of all households	Percent . . .	31.6	27.3	4.6
Average number owned	Number . . .	1.7	2.2	2.7
Total companion pet population [1]	Million	52.9	59.1	12.6
Households obtaining veterinary care [2]	Percent	85.3	67.7	10.8
Average visits per household per year	Number . . .	2.6	1.9	0.2
PERCENT DISTRIBUTION OF HOUSEHOLDS OWNING PETS				
Annual household income:				
Under $12,500	Percent . . .	12.7	13.9	17.3
$12,500 to $24,999	Percent . . .	19.1	19.7	20.9
$25,000 to $39,999	Percent . . .	21.6	21.5	22.0
$40,000 to $59,999	Percent . . .	21.5	21.2	17.5
$60,000 and over	Percent . . .	25.2	23.7	22.3
Family size: [1]				
One person	Percent . . .	13.2	16.8	12.7
Two persons	Percent . . .	31.0	32.6	27.9
Three persons	Percent . . .	21.4	20.6	20.4
Four or more persons	Percent . . .	34.5	29.9	38.9

[1] As of December. [2] During 1996.
Source: American Veterinary Medical Association, Schaumburg, IL, *U.S. Pet Ownership and Demographics Source* (copyright).

No. 425. Retail Sales and Household Participation in Lawn and Garden Activities: 1994 to 1998

| 190% | 6 of 20 | 5.76 x 9.18 in | |

reproduced as Figure 3.4, shows that 31.2 million households have a dog and 27.0 million households have a cat. The table also shows there are 52.9 million dogs and 59.1 million cats in United States households.

To gain more practice, let's answer the second scenario where you have been asked to invest in a golf course. Before investing you want to know answers to some basic questions about the popularity of the game and the number of golf courses already built.

To answer this, look in the *Abstract's* index for "Golf." In a typical year the United States *Abstract* lists six different tables of information. The best one to look at is the table entitled Selected Recreational Activities. This table from the 2000 edition, reproduced as Figure 3.5, shows that the number of golfers rose from a mid-1970s level of 13 million, peaked in 1990 at almost 28 million golfers, fell in the early 1990s but lately is on the upswing with about 26 million golfers by 1998. While the number of golfers in 1997 was below the 1990 peak, those participating in 1998 played 528 million rounds of golf, 26 million more than in 1990. The number of golf courses is also increasing, from 12,846 courses in 1990 to 14,900 in 1998. Overall, the numbers suggest both steady growth and more active involvement in the sport by many participants.

Practice Question

Your department's projected budget is due today. You want to give all your employees a cell phone to improve communication. Unless you have

FIGURE 3.5
United States
Statistical Abstract
Table on
Recreational
Activities

No. 434. Selected Recreational Activities: 1975 to 1998

[26 represents 26,000,000]

Activity	Unit	1975	1980	1985	1990	1995	1996	1997	1998
Softball, amateur: [1]									
Total participants [2]	Million.	26	30	41	41	42	42	41	41
Youth participants	1,000	450	650	712	1,100	1,350	1,416	1,440	1,500
Adult teams [3]	1,000	66	110	152	188	187	183	178	168
Youth teams [3]	1,000	9	18	31	46	74	79	80	81
Golfers (one round or more) [4][5]	1,000	13,036	15,112	17,520	27,800	25,000	24,737	26,474	26,427
Golf rounds played [4][5]	1,000	308,562	357,701	414,777	502,000	490,200	477,400	547,200	528,500
Golf facilities [4]	Number.	11,370	12,005	12,346	12,846	14,074	14,341	14,602	14,900
Classification:									
Private	Number.	4,770	4,839	4,861	4,810	4,324	4,306	4,257	4,251
Daily fee	Number.	5,014	5,372	5,573	6,024	7,491	7,729	7,984	8,247
Municipal	Number.	1,586	1,794	1,912	2,012	2,259	2,306	2,361	2,402
Tennis: [6]									
Players	1,000	[7]34,000	(NA)	13,000	21,000	17,820	19,499	19,500	(NA)
Courts	1,000	130	(NA)	220	220	240	245	245	(NA)
Indoor	1,000	8	(NA)	14	14	15	15	15	(NA)
Tenpin bowling: [8]									
Participants, total	Million.	62.5	72.0	67.0	71.0	79.0	91.0	91.0	91.0
Male	Million.	29.9	34.0	32.0	35.4	36.3	41.8	41.8	41.8
Female	Million.	32.6	38.0	35.0	35.6	42.6	49.2	49.2	49.2
Establishments	Number.	8,577	8,591	8,275	7,611	7,049	6,880	6,688	6,542
Lanes	1,000	141	154	155	148	139	136	133	131
Membership, total [9]	1,000	8,751	9,664	8,064	6,588	4,925	4,662	4,405	4,156
American Bowling									
Congress	1,000	4,300	4,688	3,657	3,036	2,370	2,261	2,135	2,027
Women's Bowling									
Congress	1,000	3,692	4,187	3,714	2,859	2,036	1,917	1,798	1,678
Young American									
Bowling Alliance [10]	1,000	759	789	693	693	519	484	472	451
Motion picture theaters [11]	1,000	15	18	21	24	28	30	32	34

an accurate cost estimate, the accounting department automatically eliminates the item from your request. How much is the typical cell phone bill? How long is the typical cell phone call?

Practice Question

You are thinking of opening a chain of small kiosks in every major United States airport and want to target the largest airport first. What are the five busiest airports?

Other Countries' Data Compilations

Business today is more and more internationally focused. While a few decades ago, knowing about just the United States market was enough to succeed; today you need to look outside those borders. Fortunately, statistical compendia are published not only for the United States but also for almost every other major country. Using these other countries' compendia and associated websites enables you to evaluate markets and countries before starting or becoming heavily involved in a business deal abroad.

To help you find information about foreign countries quickly, the next three tables (Tables 3.2–3.4) provide sources for Europe, the Americas, and Asia and Africa. For each country listed, the table contains the name of its statistical compendium with the compendium's languages in parentheses, the name of

TABLE 3.2
Information on European Countries

Note: Italy publishes an English language supplement to *Annuario Statistico Italiano* entitled the *Italian Statistical Abstract.* Unfortunately, the English version contains less than half the information of the Italian version.

Country	Name of Statistical Compendium (Language)	Main Government Statistical Organization
France	*Annuaire Statistique de la France* (French) **http://www.insee.fr/en/home/home_page.asp**	National Institute of Statistics and Economic Studies (INSEE)
Germany	*Statistisches Jahrbuch für die Bundesrepublik Deutschland* (German) **http://www.statistik-bund.de/e_home.htm**	Federal Statistical Office Germany
Ireland	*Statistical Abstract* (English) **http://www.cso.ie**	Central Statistics Office
Italy	*Annuario Statistico Italiano* (Italian) **http://www.istat.it/homeing.html**	National Statistical Institute
Netherlands	*Statistisch Yearbook* (English) **http://www.cbs.nl/en**	Statistics Netherlands
Russia	*Russia and Eurasia Facts and Figures Annual by Academic International Press* (English Compilation) **http://www.gks.ru/eng**	State Committee of the Russian Federation on Statistics
Spain	*Anuario Estadístico de Espana* (Spanish) **http://www.ine.es/welcoing.htm**	Spanish Statistical Institute (INE)
Switzerland	*Statistisches Jahrbuch der Schweiz* (German and French) **http://www.statistik.admin.ch/eindex.htm**	Swiss Federal Statistical Office
United Kingdom	*Annual Abstract of Statistics* (English) **http://www.statistics.gov.uk**	Office of National Statistics

the country's primary statistical agency and that agency's website address. If you cannot find or access a compendium, try the website for information.

Once again, look through the relevant foreign compendia **before** you need the information. Then when a question or crisis arises you will know what information is available and where to find it.

The statistical compendia found in these tables vary widely in their business usefulness. Some books, like *Yearbook Australia,* are amazing, with information spanning a large variety of subjects from the climate to the political structure. Others, like the French *Annuaire Statistique de la France,* are massive tomes filled with very detailed information about a smaller number of subjects. Some books, like the *China Statistical Yearbook,* provide only a few tables on which to base business decisions.

TABLE 3.3

Information on Countries in North and South America

Note: UCLA's (University of California at Los Angeles) Latin America Center annually publishes the *Statistical Abstract of Latin America*. For those who do not read Spanish or Portuguese, this English-only edition provides a quick method of examining data for the entire continent.

Country	Name of Statistical Compendium (Language)	Main Government Statistical Organization
Argentina	*Anuario Estadístico* (Spanish) **http://www.indec.mecon.ar/í_default.html**	National Institute of Statistics and Census (INDEC)
Brazil	*Anuá rio Estadístico do Brasil* (Portuguese) **http://www.ibge.gov.br/english**	Brazil Institute of Geography and Statistics (IBGE)
Canada	*Canada Yearbook* (English and French) **http://www.statcan.ca/start.html**	Statistics Canada
Mexico	*Anuario Estadístico de los Estados Unidos Mexicanos* (Spanish) **http://www.inegi.gob.mx**	National Institute of Statistics, Geography and Information (INEGI)
United States	*Statistical Abstract of the United States* (English) **http://www.census.gov**	United States Census Bureau
Venezuela	*Anuario Estadístico de Venezuela* (Spanish) **http://www.ocei.gov.ve**	Central Office of Statistics and Information (OCEI)

The amount of information found in the statistical websites listed in the previous tables also varies widely. Some countries, like the United Kingdom, offer a large amount of data, but the data are widely scattered among different web servers and URLs. Other countries, such as Canada and Spain, put all on-line statistics in a single database.[4] Some countries like the United States have a tremendous amount of information freely available while others, like India and Russia, currently provide only a rough indication of the data they collect but have almost no facts or figures available via the Internet. One problem when accessing many of these international websites is that many of the sites are not available in English. Without a translator it is very hard to navigate places like the main Russian and Chinese statistical sites.

To understand what is available outside the United States let's answer a simple question. What is the population of greater Montréal? To find the population of Montréal, which is the largest French-speaking city in North

[4]Canada's data are grouped into a giant set of statistical tables called CANSIM. Spain's collection is called INEbase. While both data sets are easily located and used, Spanish data are free but Canada imposes a charge of a few dollars for every data series extracted.

TABLE 3.4
Information on Countries in Asia and Africa

*One excellent resource for Western readers who are interested in Japan but cannot translate Kanji or Katakana characters is to read the **DIR Guide to Japanese Economic Statistics** by Mikihiro Matsuoka and Brian Rose (1994 Oxford University Press). This book explains in English many major Japanese data collections and also discusses their good and bad points.

Country	Name of Statistical Compendium (Language)	Main Government Statistical Organization
Australia	*Yearbook Australia* (English) **http://www.abs.gov.au/**	Australian Bureau of Statistics
China	*China Statistical Yearbook* (English and Chinese) **http://www.stats.gov.cn/english/index.htm**	National Bureau of Statistics
Indonesia	*Statistical Yearbook of Indonesia* (English and Indonesian) **http://www.bps.go.id/**	Statistics Indonesia
India	*Statistical Abstract of India* (English and Hindi) **http://www.nic.in/stat/**	Ministry of Statistics and Programme Implementation
Israel	*Statistical Abstract of Israel* (English and Hebrew) **http://www.cbs.gov.il/engindex.htm**	Central Bureau of Statistics
Japan*	*Japan Statistical Yearbook* (English and Japanese) **http://www.stat.go.jp/english/index.htm**	Statistics Bureau
Korea	*Korea Statistical Yearbook* (English and Korean) **http://www.nso.go.kr/eng/**	National Statistical Office
New Zealand	*New Zealand Official Yearbook* (English) **http://www.stats.govt.nz/**	Statistics New Zealand
South Africa	*South African Statistics* (English and Afrikaans) **http://www.statssa.gov.za/**	Statistics South Africa

America, first find the URL for Canada's statistical website in the previous set of tables.[5] Then go to Statistics Canada's English homepage, which looks like Figure 3.6.

To find the population of Montréal pick the "Canadian statistics" link in the upper portion of the screen to bring up the information choices seen in Figure 3.7.

The size of various Canadian cities is found in "Population," under the heading "The People." To get a specific city, pick "Population" again followed by "Population, census metropolitan areas." This brings up a table, partially

[5]You should have found **http://www.statcan.ca/start.html**.

FIGURE 3.6
**Statistics Canada's
Internet Homepage**

Copyright Statistics Canada.
Reprinted with permission.

FIGURE 3.7
**Top Level Screen for
Canadian Statistics**

Copyright Statistics Canada.
Reprinted with permission.

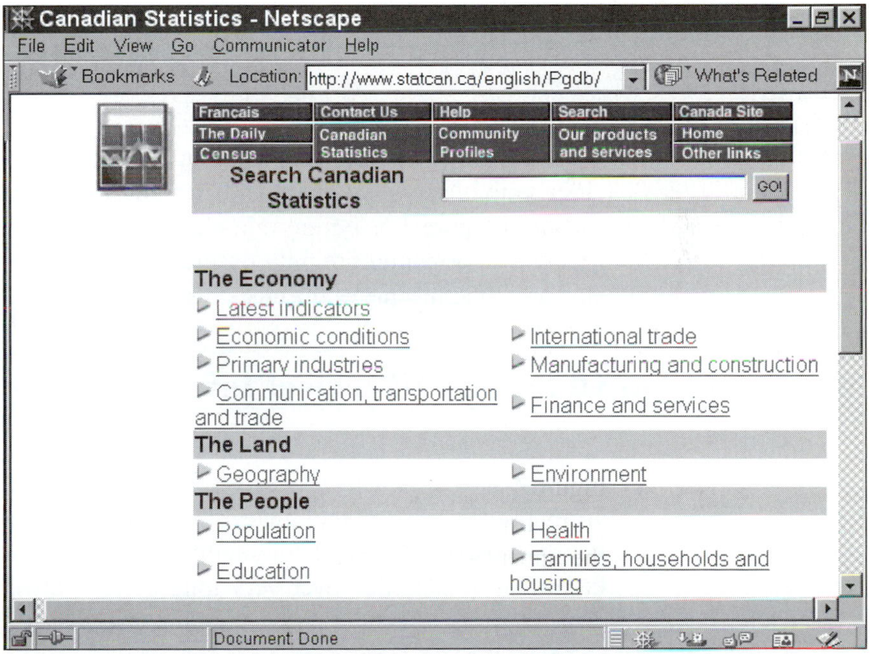

shown in Figure 3.8, that lists the population of every major Canadian city, from the largest (Toronto) to the smallest (Saint John in New Brunswick). The second line shows that greater Montréal has about 3.5 million inhabitants.

FIGURE 3.8
Population of Canadian Cities

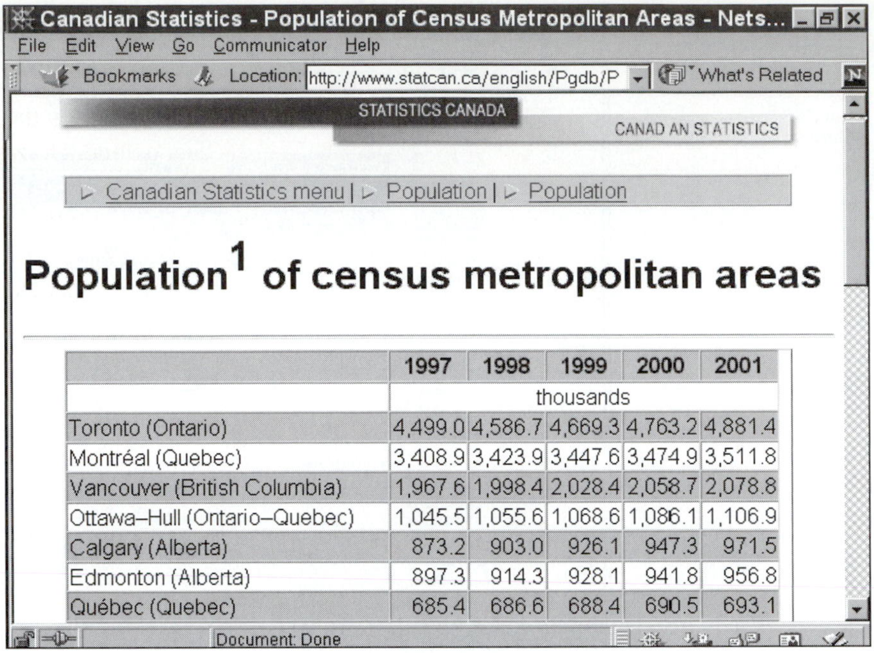

Population[1] of census metropolitan areas

	1997	1998	1999	2000	2001
	thousands				
Toronto (Ontario)	4,499.0	4,586.7	4,669.3	4,763.2	4,881.4
Montréal (Quebec)	3,408.9	3,423.9	3,447.6	3,474.9	3,511.8
Vancouver (British Columbia)	1,967.6	1,998.4	2,028.4	2,058.7	2,078.8
Ottawa–Hull (Ontario–Quebec)	1,045.5	1,055.6	1,068.6	1,086.1	1,106.9
Calgary (Alberta)	873.2	903.0	926.1	947.3	971.5
Edmonton (Alberta)	897.3	914.3	928.1	941.8	956.8
Québec (Quebec)	685.4	686.6	688.4	690.5	693.1

Practice Question

How much has the population of the Canadian town of Halifax, Nova Scotia, grown or shrunk over the past five years?

Practice Question

What is the population of Dublin, Ireland?

An alternative method for finding information about specific Canadian cities is to pick "Community Profiles" on the Statistics Canada homepage shown in Figure 3.6. Typing in a place name in the search box (not shown) provides information not only on the population but also on the education, land area, and income of the city's residents.

Where to Find Older and Historical Information

While the above sources provide a quick way to accurately assess the current business situation, many times historical data are also needed. Historical data are important because they reveal long-term trends affecting your business. For example, the financial community has used historical data on stock market prices to state that over very long periods of time buying and holding stocks outperforms all other types of investments.

More important, businesses not only need current data but also forecasts of the future. How do you arrive at future estimates or projections? The easiest method is to extrapolate based on historical trends. Gathering and graphing a data series over long time periods visually shows you not only where your industry, occupation, or product line has been but also where it is probably going.

The extent of historical information depends on the country. Few countries match Brazil in how far back their data extend. Brazil publishes *Estatísticas Históricas do Brasil: Séries Econômicas, Demográficas e Sociais de 1550 a 1988,* which translated means *Historical Statistics of Brazil: Economic, Demographic and Social Time Series from 1550 to 1988.* Given that only a handful of companies have a corporate history that extends beyond 100 years, few businesses need information as far back as Brazil's goes. Most industrialized countries began to seriously collect statistical data during the period between the First and Second World Wars.

In the United States the standard reference book for historical information is the *Historical Statistics of the United States from Colonial Times to 1970.* This two-volume set, published by the Commerce Department, provides detailed historical data for tracking many key business trends. The books are available both in hard copy and on CD-ROM, but currently not on the Internet.[6]

Historical Statistics is useful even if history for your product or industry is measured in months instead of decades. A current problem for many managers is trying to predict the Internet's impact on their business. Examining the historical impact of television on radio is one useful method for forecasting the impact of Internet on television. Where is information on television's impact on radio? Chapter R in *Historical Statistics* (volume 2, pages 792–800) contains data on the number of stations, sets owned, and the amount of advertising. These data show that the explosive growth of commercial television clearly undermined the radio industry's profitability by impacting radio advertising. However, the data also show that television had no impact on other radio business measures such as the number of stations or sets owned.

Another example from *Historical Statistics* shows business managers how prices change over time. Chapter E (volume 1, pages 183–214) tracks wholesale, retail, and consumer prices over time. The data from this chapter are graphed in Figures 3.9 and 3.10 on the next page. Figure 3.9 shows how consumer prices changed from 1800 till World War I while Figure 3.10 shows how prices changed from World War I until the present. The first graph shows that, contrary to what most business managers expect today, prices in the United States

---

[6]The parallel Canadian book, entitled *Historical Statistics of Canada,* is available online for free. This book contains over 1,000 tables that track Canadian society from the start of Confederation in 1867 until the mid-1970s. To access this information go to Statistics Canada's website (**http://www.statcan.ca/start.html**) and use the search button to find publication 11-516-XIE.

FIGURE 3.9

Pre-World War I Consumer Prices (1967 = 100)

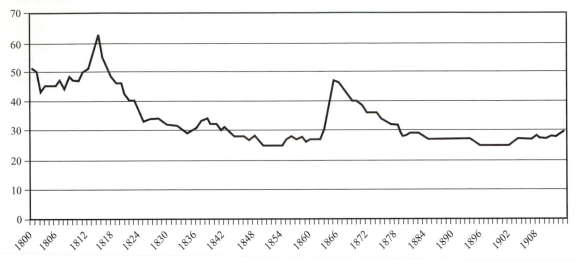

FIGURE 3.10

Post-World War I Consumer Prices (1967 = 100)

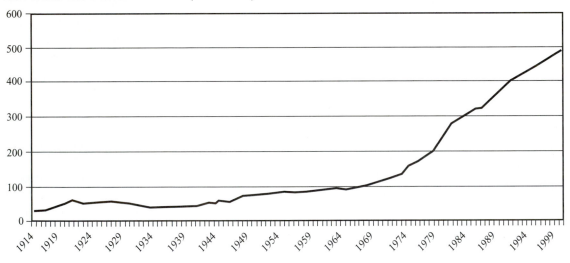

do not always go up. Prior to World War I most business managers worried more about deflation, which is when prices consistently go down. The two short periods of United States inflation experienced prior to World War I were both tied to wartime problems. The first spike was during the War of 1812 and the second occurred during the Civil War. Outside of these two periods, consumer prices tended to fall steadily not rise.

Figure 3.10 shows that immediately after World War I prices rose slightly, but most of the large consumer price increases occurred in the 1970s and 1980s. This two-hundred-year perspective shows that a long-term strategy based on constantly increasing prices does not always work.

Other General Sources of Quick Information

Statistical abstracts are also published by many states in the United States. These abstracts provide detailed information on the city and county level about subjects as diverse as the number of people and food stamp usage. Like country abstracts, the quality, timeliness, and usefulness of the information varies widely. Some states are just beginning to provide useful information for business needs, while others have huge databases. For example, Hawaii not only regularly publishes a statistical summary but also has compiled and printed a massive tome entitled *Historical Statistics of Hawaii*. Two good representatives of state-level books and their associated websites are the *Kansas Statistical Abstract*[7] (**http://www.ku.edu/pri/ksdata/ksdata.shtml**) and the *Indiana Fact Book*[8] (**http://www.stats.indiana.edu**). The complete list and contact information for all 50 state abstracts is printed midway through Appendix I in the *Statistical Abstract*.

Additionally, the United States government and a number of international agencies have published a variety of subject-related sources of information. One example is the Bureau of Justice Statistics' *Sourcebook of Criminal Justice Statistics*. Published each year, this book provides a wealth of facts and figures for businesses connected to law enforcement, the court system, or prisons. The United States Department of Agriculture annually publishes *Agricultural Statistics,* which contains data for farmers, food wholesalers, and supermarket executives. The Bureau of Labor Statistics produces the *Handbook of Labor Statistics*[9] containing information needed to answer human resource questions. The Bureau of Transportation Statistics annually produces *National Transportation Statistics*. Each year the OECD (Organization for Economic Co-operation and Development) publishes the *Insurance Statistics Yearbook,* which provides data on the insurance industry for all OECD countries. This list is just a small sample of subject compendia available.

The primary drawback for all compendia is that much of the information is slightly out of date. For example, many *Statistical Abstract* tables refer to data

---

[7]*Kansas Statistical Abstract,* 34th edition, September 2000, Thelma Helyar, editor, Institute for Public Policy and Business Research, The University of Kansas.
[8]*The Indiana Fact Book 1998–99,* Terry Creeth, editor, Indiana University Press, Bloomington, Indiana.
[9]The *Handbook* is now published by Bernan Press (**http://www.bernan.com**).

that are two or three years old when the book is published. While using current numbers is best, having some facts available instantly is better than having no facts at all. Moreover, comparing older compendia with later editions shows that information on most subjects is very similar from year to year.

Summary

For most broad topics there currently exists a book or website, which compiles summary information. The most useful compendium for United States business use is the *Statistical Abstract of the United States*. This book is published yearly and contains a host of national, international, and historical facts. The current online version can be found by picking the "Statistical Abstract" link at the bottom of the Census Bureau's homepage (**http://www.census.gov**). Then download the relevant chapters.

If you expect to answer important questions with little or no notice, buy or print out the relevant national, international, state, or subject area compendium ahead of time. Then, do not let the book gather dust. Look through the book to see what types of business information it contains. Do it periodically, because over time it is easy to forget what is in a compendium, and opening the book refreshes your memory. These books have so much information that you will notice something new every time you browse through it. Doing this ensures you are always ready to quickly answer key business questions.

Chapter  4

Demographic Information

How do business managers find information about the 286 million people living in the United States? What data can you use to understand the country's 112 million households? Most information on demographic characteristics of the United States population comes from the Census Bureau. Census Bureau data let business managers answer questions like:

- How many individuals live in a neighborhood, city, state, or region?

- Which areas are growing the fastest?

- How many people are a particular age, or are members of a particular ethnic or racial group?

The Census Bureau gathers demographic data two ways. First, every 10 years the Bureau conducts a census of the entire country. Unfortunately, that provides a profile of the entire country only at decade-long intervals. To remedy this problem, every March the Census Bureau runs a smaller survey with a bigger name, the March Current Population Survey Demographic Supplement, usually called just the *March CPS*. Using this smaller but more frequently run survey, the bureau fills in the missing parts of the picture.

To gain a better understanding of census demographic data, let's first answer a scenario where you are a magazine publisher targeting young women ages 20 to 24. How much bigger would your audience be if you broadened the magazine's focus to serve 18- to 26-year-olds? In the second scenario, you are responsible for picking new store locations. You need to choose one site in Georgia to open the next store. Your company's product mix does best in areas with lots of retirees. How can you find out where in Georgia is the highest density of people over age 65?

Where Does United States Demographic Information Come From?

The primary source of United States demographic data is the population census. The population census is done once each decade in the spring of all years that are evenly divisible by 10, such as 1990, 2000, and 2010. The goal is to collect information about all people residing in the country on April 1st, whether they are citizens or not. While the original intention of the first census in 1790 was just to distribute seats fairly in the House of Representatives, today the census is used for many more purposes. The census not only affects a state's congressional representation, but it also determines how the federal government distributes about $100 billion dollars in aid. At the state and local level, the census is also used for zoning, planning, and situating public services. For the business manager, the census provides the raw data needed for planning, marketing, production, and distribution decisions.

The census does all these things by tracking down almost every single person in the country. Most people answer the census by filling in and mailing back a simple form.[1] For people without a permanent address and for those individuals who do not return the form, the Census Bureau attempts to fill out the form either by telephone calls or by sending interviewers out for face-to-face visits. In large urban areas, census staff and homeless advocates even tally the number of individuals living on the streets. On census day, staff are also sent to mobile home parks, campgrounds, and boat marinas to ensure that people who are traveling are included in the tally. The census, using help from the military, also counts United States citizens stationed overseas or on active duty ships.[2] The key point for business managers and students is that the census goes to extraordinary lengths to give you a complete picture of the entire population, not just those who are conveniently reachable.

Beyond tracking the general population, the census also breaks information down into special subgroups. For example, the census is very useful for businesses selling products and services to college students since it separately tracks people living in group situations. The census considers as home any place an individual is currently spending two or more months, no matter what the circumstances. This means the census is a simple but accurate source for

---

[1] The Census Bureau does the mailing using the country's most accurate and complete mailing list, called the Master Address File. Unfortunately, the entire list is confidential under Title 13 of the Federal Code and is unavailable to bulk mailers.
[2] Citizens who are living abroad but not working for the United States government or military are excluded from the Census count.

FIGURE 4.1

Short Form
for the 2000
United States Census

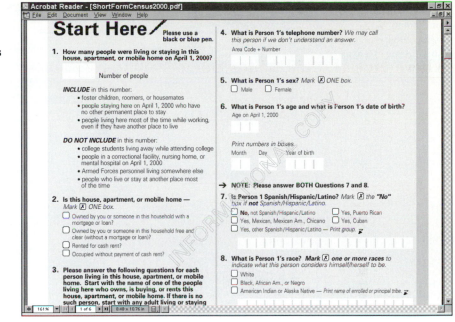

detailed information not only about college students but also people living in institutional settings like nursing homes, prisons, and jails.

The United States census provides a detailed picture of the population by combining the results from two different surveys, commonly called the *short* and *long forms*. Most people (five out of every six households) fill in the census short form, which is also called the 100 percent data. The key page of this form is reproduced in Figure 4.1. The short form first asks how many people are in the household and whether the house or apartment is owned, rented, or lived in for free. Then the short form asks the name, relationship to the person filling out the form, sex, age, birth date, ethnicity, and race for each person in the household.

Approximately one out of every six households, or 17 percent of the nation's residents, is sent a much more detailed survey called the long form, or census sample data.[3] One section of this 12-page questionnaire is shown in Figure 4.2. The long form includes all the questions contained in the short form and then adds 46 more.

The first 26 additional questions, which are repeated for every person in the household, provide extensive demographic details about each individual. These detailed demographic profile questions ask each person's marital status,

[3]Copies of both the long and short forms are located on this book's website.

FIGURE 4.2
Long Form
for the 2000
United States Census

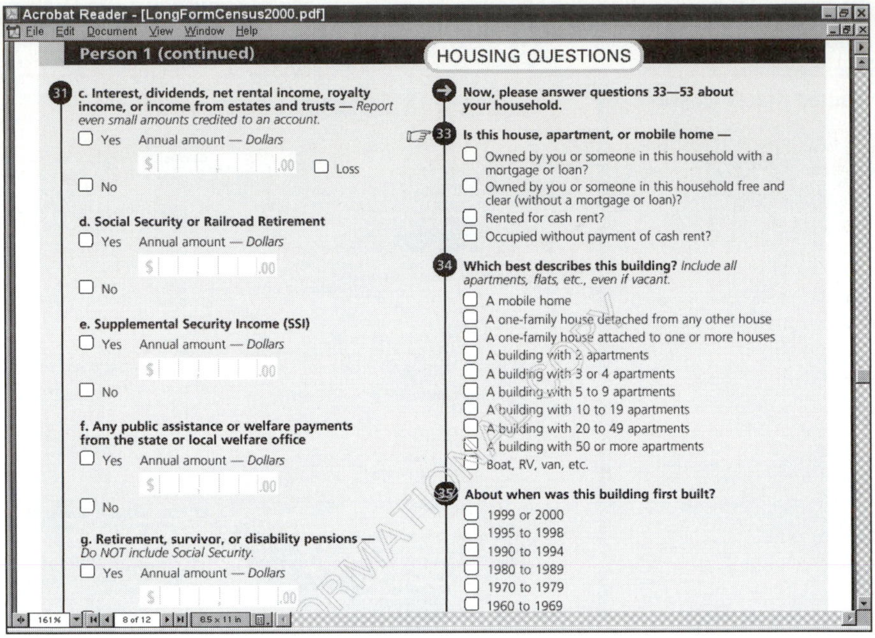

current school attendance status, current grade, and the highest level of schooling the person ever completed. The questionnaire also asks if the person speaks a language other than English at home and how well the person speaks English. Questions then ask if the person is a citizen, when the person came to this country, and if the person lived at the same address five years ago. The household member who fills out the form reports each person's health status as well as whether the person has living grandchildren. The census then asks a number of labor market questions, which determine each person's employment status, industry, occupation, and commuting habits. The demographic questions end by recording how much income the person received in the prior calendar year.

Then the next section of the long form asks 20 questions about the family's housing. The first question determines the home's ownership status, using the same categories as the short form. Information is collected about the type of building, when the dwelling was built, number of rooms and number of bedrooms. The housing section records whether the residence has complete plumbing services, complete kitchen facilities, and telephone service.

Questions are then asked about the type of fuel used to heat the home, the cost of utilities, the amount of land associated with the home and if any businesses are located in the building. The survey concludes by asking for the cost of rent or mortgage payments each month and finally for an estimate of the property's current market value. While business managers cannot get all this information for a particular family, all this information is available from nationwide summaries down to very small geographic areas. If you really want to understand what information is available, print out both the short and long forms and fill in each with information on your own household's situation.

While the census provides a tremendous amount of information, there are two drawbacks to using these data for business purposes. First, United States census data are collected only once every 10 years. Given that it takes years to process and release the summaries from the millions of surveys, many businesses feel census information is neither timely nor currently accurate.

To remedy this problem the Census Bureau has begun a new program called the American Community Survey to replace the long form. This new survey was tested in a small number of cities starting in 1996 and will run nationwide beginning in 2003. The idea behind the American Community Survey is simple. Beginning with 2010, the census will focus only on counting the nation's population via the short form. The long form will be sent randomly every year to a small number of households. Hence, long form information will be available yearly instead of at 10-year intervals. This ensures that businesses get details about the demographic, housing and income makeup of the United States population on a more continual basis and census staff have their work spread out more evenly.

The second problem with the current census is that it undercounts poor urban minorities, especially young males. Because young Hispanic and African-American males are missed, the "official" populations of cities like New York City, Chicago, and Los Angeles, which have large numbers of poor residents, are smaller than their actual populations. This means these large cities get both less federal funding and less congressional representation. The Census Bureau proposed for both the 1990 and 2000 censuses to fix the undercount by doing an additional survey of areas that contain large numbers of hard-to-reach individuals. Using this additional survey, the Census Bureau would statistically adjust the official census count for missing individuals.

While many researchers agree that statistical adjustment would improve the official census count, there is considerable disagreement among politicians over using this correction. Since poor minority districts often vote for Democratic candidates, anything that would boost the influence of these areas is bitterly fought by the Republican Party. To date, the Supreme Court has barred the Census Bureau from using statistical sampling to adjust the official population figures.[4] Nevertheless, it is important for business managers who hire

---

[4]A detailed view of the politics surrounding statistical sampling and the 1990 Census is found in Margo Anderson and Stephen Fienberg's **Who Counts? The Politics of Census-Taking in Contemporary America** (Russell Sage Foundation, 1999).

or market products to young urban minorities to understand that more of these individuals exist than census data report.

Other Countries' Demographic Information

Almost every country in the world periodically runs a census. Some, like England, count the population every decade, while others like Ireland, Australia, and Canada count the population once every five years. Most English-speaking countries ask similar questions and use similar procedures to collect these data. For example, Canada, like the United States, has two forms: a short questionnaire containing 7 questions that is sent to 80 percent of all households and a long form sent to the remaining 20 percent containing the short form's questions plus 52 more.

Many of the questionnaires used in other English-speaking countries are quite similar to each other. For example, all countries ask about the age, sex, and education of each person living in the home. Nevertheless, there are slight differences between countries and some of the forms have interesting questions asking about a person's religion (England), native language (Canada), and access to the Internet (Ireland) that are not tracked by the United States Census Bureau. To see census forms from Australia, Canada, Ireland, and England look at this book's website.

Geographic Classifications

Before searching for demographic data it is important to understand the concepts behind the geographic classifications used by the Census Bureau. The Census Bureau uses two different methods to divide the country. The first is a hierarchy based on legal boundaries, shown in Table 4.1, while the second is based on cities' effective boundaries.

In the hierarchy method, the entire country is first divided into four census regions: the West, Midwest, Northeast, and South. These regions are then broken down into nine divisions. For example, the West region is broken into two

TABLE 4.1
Geographical Hierarchy of the United States

United States	1 country
Census regions	4 regions: West, Midwest, Northeast, South
Census divisions	9 divisions, i.e. Pacific, Mountain, Middle Atlantic, etc.
States	50 states
Counties	3,098 legal subdivisions of states
Census tracts	Areas with at least 4,000 people
Census blocks	Over 8 million blocks

divisions, the Pacific and Mountain. Each division comprises between three to eight different states. The 50 states are further divided into over 3,000 areas called counties.[5] Counties are broken down into census tracts, which are areas containing at least 4,000 people. Finally the smallest level of detail is called the block. In urban areas blocks correspond to a small collection of streets, and often directly match a neighborhood. In suburban and rural areas, blocks cover much more land but still often match the neighborhood concept. In the 2000 census, there were over 8 million distinct blocks.

While the hierarchy is primarily based on legal boundaries, the city method understands that business opportunities do not stop at political boundaries. Many major cities have grown beyond their political boundaries and now overlap multiple counties and states. For example, the nation's capital, Washington D.C., now covers parts of Maryland and Virginia as well as the District of Columbia. The Census Bureau recognizes this fact and groups cities based not on political boundaries but on population. To reflect these nonpolitical boundaries, the census puts one of three acronyms after an urban area's name: MSA, PMSA, and CMSA. MSA stands for Metropolitan Statistical Area and is a city or urban area with 50,000 or more inhabitants. PMSA stands for Primary Metropolitan Statistical Area and is the name given to even larger urban areas. CMSA stands for Consolidated Metropolitan Statistical Area; these are collections of PMSAs and MSAs, and they comprise the nation's biggest cities.

The greater Chicago area is a good example of how cities are classified. The Census Bureau calls greater Chicago the Chicago-Gary-Kenosha CMSA. This huge metropolitan area covers parts of three states (Indiana, Illinois, and Wisconsin), contains 9 million people, and comprises four PMSAs. Other areas, like greater El Paso, Texas, with a population under three quarters of a million, are much smaller than Chicago. El Paso is classified as an MSA and has an urban area border that extends only to the edge of El Paso County. Appendix II of each *Statistical Abstract* contains a more detailed description of how these areas are defined and has a complete list of all United States metropolitan areas. Understanding these three labels is important because tracking a broadly defined metropolitan area compared to a city's inner core produces very different information.

Basic Demographic Information

The quickest way to find basic demographic information from the census is to look in the *Statistical Abstract of the United States* (pick the Statistical Abstract link on the Census Bureau's homepage **http://www.census.gov**). The

---

[5]Counties are called parishes in Louisiana.

FIGURE 4.3
United States
Population by
Age and Sex

Acrobat Reader - [StatAbs2000Sec01.pdf]

File   Edit   Document   View   Window   Help

No. 13. Resident Population by Sex and Age: 1999

[In thousands, except as indicated (272,691 represents 272,691,000). As of July 1. For derivation of estimates, see text of this section]

Age	Total	Male	Female	Age	Total	Male	Female
Total	272,691	133,277	139,414	50 to 54 yrs. old	16,446	7,998	8,448
Under 5 yrs. old	18,942	9,683	9,259	50 yrs. old	3,649	1,781	1,868
Under 1 yr. old	3,820	1,952	1,868	51 yrs. old	3,502	1,707	1,795
1 yr. old	3,757	1,920	1,837	52 yrs. old	3,728	1,818	1,910
2 yrs. old	3,758	1,921	1,837	53 yrs. old	2,732	1,322	1,410
3 yrs. old	3,755	1,920	1,835	54 yrs. old	2,835	1,371	1,464
4 yrs. old	3,853	1,970	1,882	55 to 59 yrs. old	12,875	6,183	6,693
5 to 9 yrs. old.	19,947	10,208	9,739	55 yrs. old	2,750	1,323	1,427
5 yrs. old	3,895	1,994	1,901	56 yrs. old	2,935	1,413	1,522
6 yrs. old	3,944	2,020	1,924	57 yrs. old	2,581	1,238	1,343
7 yrs. old	4,030	2,059	1,972	58 yrs. old	2,285	1,094	1,191
8 yrs. old	3,909	1,999	1,910	59 yrs. old	2,325	1,115	1,210
9 yrs. old	4,170	2,137	2,033	60 to 64 yrs. old	10,514	4,968	5,546
10 to 14 yrs. old	19,548	10,012	9,537	60 yrs. old	2,232	1,054	1,177
10 yrs. old	4,036	2,070	1,966	61 yrs. old	2,147	1,020	1,127
11 yrs. old	3,896	1,994	1,902	62 yrs. old	2,029	958	1,071
12 yrs. old	3,846	1,967	1,879	63 yrs. old	2,022	958	1,065
13 yrs. old	3,878	1,985	1,893	64 yrs. old	2,084	977	1,106
14 yrs. old	3,892	1,996	1,896	65 to 69 yrs. old	9,447	4,337	5,111
15 to 19 yrs. old	19,748	10,151	9,597	65 yrs. old	1,909	889	1,021
15 yrs. old	3,820	1,962	1,858	66 yrs. old	1,879	869	1,010
16 yrs. old	3,924	2,022	1,902	67 yrs. old	1,877	861	1,015
17 yrs. old	4,017	2,074	1,943	68 yrs. old	1,880	856	1,025
18 yrs. old	3,875	1,989	1,886	69 yrs. old	1,902	862	1,040
19 yrs. old	4,111	2,104	2,007	70 to 74 yrs. old	8,771	3,862	4,909
20 to 24 yrs. old	18,026	9,183	8,843	70 yrs. old	1,841	828	1,014
20 yrs. old	3,898	1,999	1,900	71 yrs. old	1,843	822	1,021
21 yrs. old	3,705	1,897	1,808	72 yrs. old	1,771	783	988
22 yrs. old	3,564	1,817	1,746	73 yrs. old	1,661	719	942
23 yrs. old	3,378	1,714	1,664	74 yrs. old	1,656	710	945
				75 to 79 yrs. old	7,329	3,057	4,272

175%   14 of 62   5.76 x 9.18 in

first section, Population, contains facts and figures based primarily on short and long form answers. The table entitled Population and Area (Table 1 in every edition) lists the total resident population counted in every census since 1790.

While few people need to know the population in 1820, two parts of this chapter are particularly interesting for business uses. The first part of the chapter contains tables that break the current population down by categories like age, race, ethnicity, and immigrant status. These breakdowns are needed in retail marketing to understand the target audience's size. For example, the table labeled Resident Population, by Sex and Age (partly shown in Figure 4.3 is the 2000 edition's table) divides all residents by age into single year categories enabling you to know facts like exactly how many 57-year-old men are currently living in the United States (1.238 million in 1999).

While not many products are aimed just at 57-year-old men, let's answer the first scenario where you are a publisher printing a magazine focusing on young women ages 20 to 24. This table shows that you are currently targeting 8.8 million women as readers. What happens if you expand the editorial focus to serve 18- to 26-year-old women? The table shows potential readership grows by 7.3 million women, to approximately 16 million. The table does not show if changing your editorial focus is a good or bad idea, but it does provide a detailed measure of your audience's size.

FIGURE 4.4
United States
Projected Population
by Age and Sex

Acrobat Reader - [StatAbs2000Sec01.pdf]

File   Edit   Document   View   Window   Help

No. 14. Resident Population Projections by Sex and Age: 2000 to 2050

[In thousands, except as indicated (275,306 represents 275,306,000). As of July. Data shown are for middle series; for assum...

Age	2000			2005			2010			2015	2020
	Total	Male	Female	Total	Male	Female	Total	Male	Female		
Total	275,306	134,554	140,752	287,716	140,698	147,018	299,862	146,679	153,183	312,268	324,927
Under 5 years	18,865	9,639	9,227	19,212	9,815	9,397	20,099	10,272	9,827	21,179	21,951
5 to 9 years.	19,781	10,122	9,659	19,122	9,774	9,348	19,438	9,936	9,502	20,321	21,403
10 to 14 years	19,908	10,196	9,712	20,634	10,564	10,069	19,908	10,183	9,724	20,229	21,146
15 to 19 years	19,897	10,227	9,670	20,990	10,788	10,202	21,668	11,132	10,536	20,892	21,224
20 to 24 years	18,518	9,433	9,085	20,159	10,269	9,889	21,151	10,776	10,375	21,748	21,020
25 to 29 years	17,861	8,876	8,984	18,351	9,144	9,207	19,849	9,901	9,948	20,765	21,384
30 to 34 years	19,580	9,682	9,898	18,582	9,146	9,436	19,002	9,385	9,617	20,484	21,410
35 to 39 years	22,276	11,071	11,205	20,082	9,927	10,155	19,039	9,380	9,659	19,442	20,938
40 to 44 years	22,618	11,218	11,400	22,634	11,222	11,412	20,404	10,069	10,334	19,346	19,773
45 to 49 years	19,901	9,776	10,125	22,230	10,965	11,264	22,227	10,967	11,260	20,057	19,034
50 to 54 years	17,265	8,398	8,867	19,661	9,578	10,082	21,934	10,739	11,195	21,929	19,804
55 to 59 years	13,324	6,397	6,927	16,842	8,101	8,741	19,177	9,248	9,929	21,400	21,412
60 to 64 years	10,677	5,046	5,631	12,848	6,086	6,762	16,252	7,725	8,528	18,519	20,696
65 to 69 years	9,436	4,334	5,102	10,086	4,661	5,425	12,159	5,640	6,520	15,410	17,598
70 to 74 years	8,753	3,876	4,877	8,375	3,757	4,618	8,995	4,066	4,929	10,897	13,864
75 to 79 years	7,422	3,103	4,319	7,429	3,172	4,257	7,175	3,110	4,065	7,772	9,484
80 to 84 years	4,913	1,866	3,047	5,514	2,157	3,356	5,600	2,247	3,353	5,484	6,024
85 to 89 years	2,705	883	1,821	3,028	1,046	1,982	3,476	1,242	2,234	3,612	3,611
90 to 94 years	1,179	319	861	1,402	404	998	1,625	497	1,128	1,930	2,074
95 to 99 years	364	81	283	442	104	338	556	139	417	678	844
100 years and over .	65	12	53	96	18	77	129	26	103	177	235
5 to 13 years	35,775	18,309	17,465	35,475	18,144	17,331	35,321	18,056	17,265	36,497	38,361
14 to 17 years	15,734	8,096	7,637	16,931	8,709	8,222	16,681	8,583	8,098	16,437	16,839
18 to 24 years	26,596	13,572	13,023	28,498	14,543	13,956	30,163	15,388	14,774	30,254	29,593
16 years and over . .	212,810	102,573	110,237	224,447	108,336	116,111	236,301	114,175	122,126	246,455	256,230
18 years and over . .	204,932	98,509	106,423	216,098	104,030	112,068	227,761	109,768	117,993	238,155	247,776
10 to 49 years	160,558	80,479	80,079	163,661	82,026	81,635	163,247	81,794	81,453	162,961	165,929
16 to 64 years	177,974	88,100	89,874	188,077	93,017	95,059	196,586	97,208	99,377	200,496	202,498
55 years and over . .	58,836	25,916	32,920	66,060	29,505	36,555	75,145	33,939	41,206	85,878	95,841

175%   15 of 62   9.18 x 5.76 in

Beyond age, other tables in this part of the *Statistical Abstract* break down the population by race, Hispanic origin, immigrant status, location, and even religion. If you need to quickly evaluate the potential size of a market the Population chapter of the *Statistical Abstract* provides fast information.

The second part of the chapter provides population projections. Many editions of the *Abstract* provide each set of population projections three times, because the Census Bureau demographers have three sets of assumptions regarding life expectancy, births, and immigration trends. Projections using the most pessimistic set of assumptions are called the lowest series, the most optimistic assumptions produce the highest series, and the one most people in business should use is called the middle series.

The key *Statistical Abstract* table for businesses needing estimates of future populations is labeled Resident Population Projections by Sex and Age. This table, taken from the 2000 edition and partly reproduced in Figure 4.4, projects the number of people living in the United States until 2050. The middle series calculates that the United States population will grow from 275 million to about 400 million within 50 years. Most of this growth does not occur among children, since the number of children under age 5 is projected to grow from 19 million to 27 million, a gain of just 42 percent. Instead, most of the growth is projected to occur among the elderly. For example, the very oldest, those 85 years and over, are projected to grow from 4.3 million to over 19 million, a gain of 340 percent.

The bottom of the table shows that while the 34.8 million elderly individuals over age 65 constituted 12.7 percent of the population in the year 2000, the number of these elderly is expected to grow to 82 million, or 20 percent, by the year 2050. The implications for business are clear; market demographics are shifting away from children's goods and services and toward the old.

Practice Question	You are the editor of a brand new magazine aimed at active older men ages 55 to 65. How big is the current market for your product? How big will this market be in 2010?
Practice Question	Your boss wants to know whether there are more Asians or Hispanics living in the Greater San Francisco Area. Which population is larger?

Detailed Information Available from the Census

Beyond the *Statistical Abstract* tables, the Census Bureau continually produces more detailed demographic reports and documents. Many of these reports are massive but contain very little text to read. Instead, most are filled with giant tables that break down the report's subject into tiny slices of information. While this section lists only the reports available online, most reference libraries contain decades' worth of the printed reports for businesses needing information for the 1980s and earlier. For individuals interested in where the raw data came from, how the results were calculated, and the statistical precision of the results, appendices in most reports answer all these questions.

There are two main types of reports business managers should know about. First, after the census is completed, the Census Bureau publishes reports with titles like *2000 Census of Population: United States* and the *2000 Census of Housing, Residential Finance.* In addition to reports for the whole nation, similar reports are available by state. To read the 1990 and 2000 census documents online go to the Census Bureau's homepage (**http://www.census.gov**), which is shown in Figure 4.5. On the left side pick the word Publications. Then pick Census of Population and Housing from the list of categories that appears.

Until just a few years ago wading through these reports was the only way to get detailed census information. Today, business managers who are pressed for time do not have to look at these reports. For most business purposes the FactFinder website, described in the next section, is much better than searching for numbers in these massive books.

The population projection series, called P25, is the second important set of demographic reports that business managers should be familiar with. This series periodically produces five different reports that contain the government's best guess about how the population will grow at both the national and state

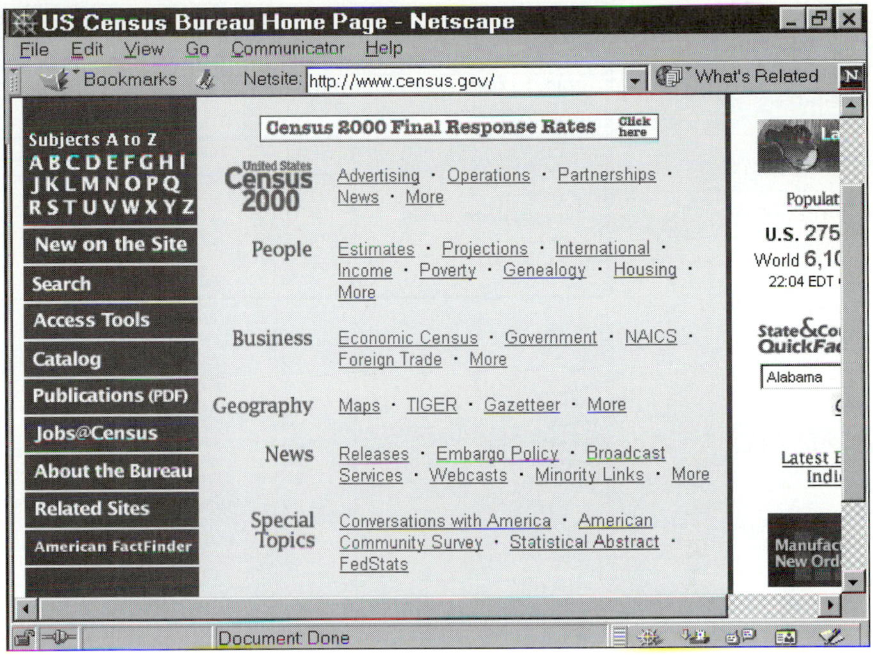

FIGURE 4.5
United States Census
Bureau's Internet
Homepage

TABLE 4.2
Titles in the
Population
Projection, or the
P25 Series

National and State Population Estimates

Projections of the Number of Households and Families in the United States

Population Projections of the U.S. by Age, Sex, Race, and Hispanic Origin

Population Projections, States

Projections of the Voting-Age Population for States

levels. The titles of these five reports are shown in Table 4.2. Accurate population projections are extremely important for business managers making costly long-term decisions, for example, decisions regarding infrastructure elements such as power plants, telecommunication equipment, roads, and utility lines that are expensive to install and will be in service for decades.

To read a P25 document, return to the Census Bureau's homepage (**http://www.census.gov**) and again pick the word Publications. The P25 reports are under the Population heading. Using P25 documents is very straightforward. Let's say you manage a large chain of stores and try to situate them so about 25,000 people surround each store. For planning purposes you need to know how many more stores are needed in New York State between 2000 and 2005. To answer this question, download the P25 volume "Population Projections, States." Table 1 of this document is partly reproduced in Figure 4.6. The table projects the number of residents by state at five-year intervals. New York

FIGURE 4.6
Population and
Projected Population
by State

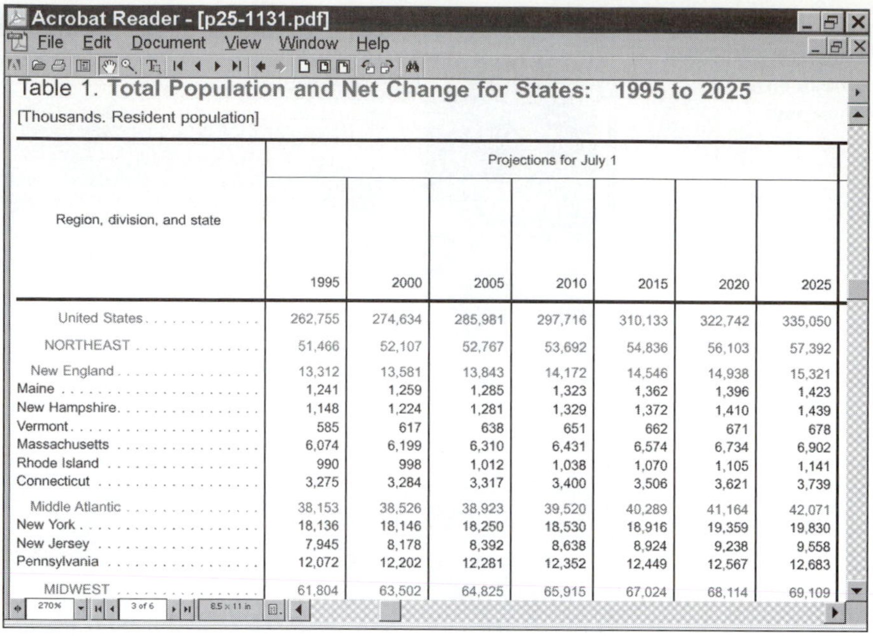

Acrobat Reader - [p25-1131.pdf]

File   Edit   Document   View   Window   Help

Table 1. Total Population and Net Change for States: 1995 to 2025
[Thousands. Resident population]

Region, division, and state	Projections for July 1						
	1995	2000	2005	2010	2015	2020	2025
United States............	262,755	274,634	285,981	297,716	310,133	322,742	335,050
NORTHEAST.............	51,466	52,107	52,767	53,692	54,836	56,103	57,392
New England...............	13,312	13,581	13,843	14,172	14,546	14,938	15,321
Maine.................	1,241	1,259	1,285	1,323	1,362	1,396	1,423
New Hampshire.............	1,148	1,224	1,281	1,329	1,372	1,410	1,439
Vermont.................	585	617	638	651	662	671	678
Massachusetts..............	6,074	6,199	6,310	6,431	6,574	6,734	6,902
Rhode Island	990	998	1,012	1,038	1,070	1,105	1,141
Connecticut................	3,275	3,284	3,317	3,400	3,506	3,621	3,739
Middle Atlantic.............	38,153	38,526	38,923	39,520	40,289	41,164	42,071
New York.............	18,136	18,146	18,250	18,530	18,916	19,359	19,830
New Jersey	7,945	8,178	8,392	8,638	8,924	9,238	9,558
Pennsylvania	12,072	12,200	12,281	12,352	12,449	12,567	12,683
MIDWEST	61,804	63,502	64,825	65,915	67,024	68,114	69,109

270%   3 of 6   8.5 x 11 in

is expected to increase its population by 154,000 people (18,250,000 −
18,146,000) from 2000 to 2005. This means over the next five years your
company needs to build approximately six additional stores in New York.

If the P25 volumes have almost, but not exactly, the information you need,
pick the letter P in the Subjects A to Z area of the Census Bureau's homepage.
Then click on the Projections link under the Population title. This link brings
up the Population Projection Program's homepage, which contains many additional tables not included in the P25 volumes. For example, the P25 table
shown in Figure 4.6 projects state residents using five-year time intervals
while the online tables provide projections using one-year intervals.

**Practice
Question**

You are offered the exclusive franchise rights for the next 10 years to either
North Dakota or South Dakota. This franchise typically generates more
sales in faster-growing areas than slower-growing ones. To choose wisely,
determine which state has the faster-growing population.

Using the FactFinder Website To Create
Custom Demographic Tables

The problem with the preprinted reports or *Statistical Abstract* tables is that
many times they have almost, but not exactly, what you want. Moreover, some
of the reports contain giant tables covering tens and sometimes hundreds of

FIGURE 4.7
American FactFinder
Homepage

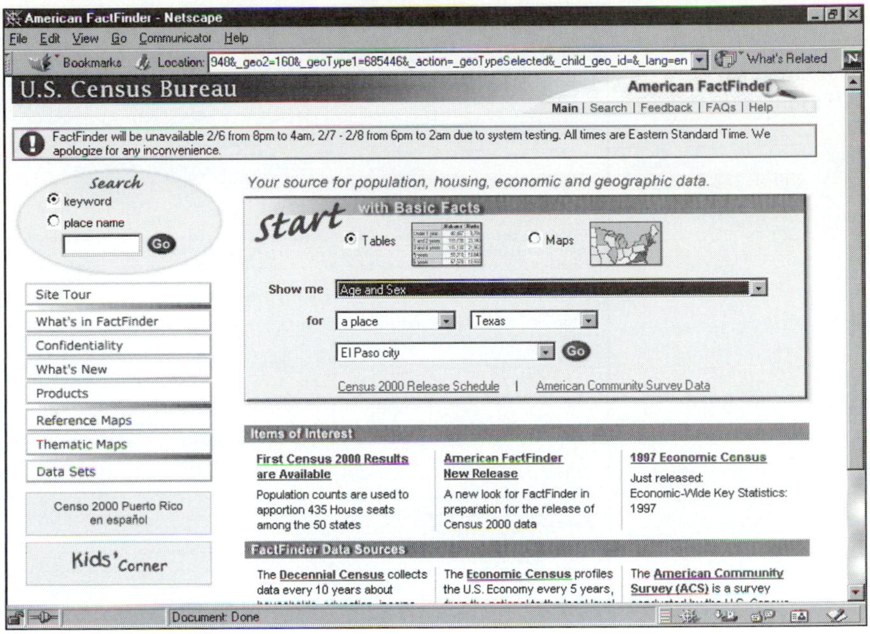

pages. Finding a specific piece of information in a huge preprinted table is often very difficult. To make accessing census data easier, the Bureau has designed a new website that enables anyone to create custom tables. The site, called the *American FactFinder*, is located at **http://factfinder.census.gov** and the top-level screen looks like Figure 4.7.

To quickly find information for a city, county, or state use the Start with Basic Facts box located in the top right corner of the FactFinder homepage. As an example, let's find information about El Paso's population. The first step is to select the type of information needed by picking the Tables button and then pulling down the "Show me" menu. The "Show me" menu has a variety of selections ranging from individuals' place of birth to the length of time they spend commuting. For our example, select the tables labeled "Age and Sex (1990 QT)."[6]

The second step is to pick the physical area of interest. For most tables the Start with Basic Facts allows you to choose one of four types of areas; the entire United States, a state, a county, or a place. For this example in the first box select "a place." This will produce a list of states. Use this list to put Texas in

---

[6]Some of the tables end in *QT* while others end in *GCT*. *QT* stands for Quick Table and provides data on a single place, like the city of El Paso. *GCT* stands for Geographic Comparison Table and provides data on all similar places, like a table of all Texas cities.

FIGURE 4.8
American FactFinder Population of El Paso, Texas

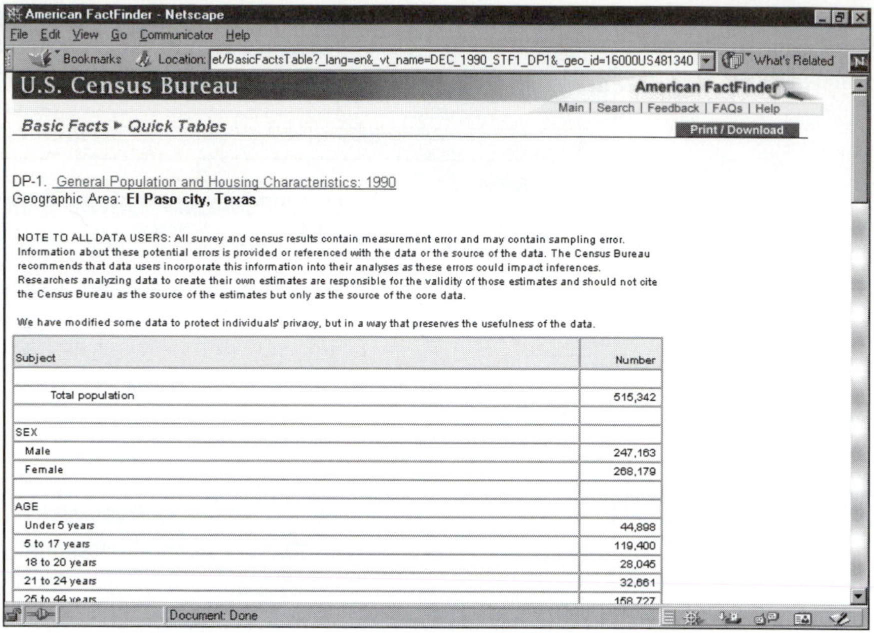

DP-1. General Population and Housing Characteristics: 1990
Geographic Area: **El Paso city, Texas**

NOTE TO ALL DATA USERS: All survey and census results contain measurement error and may contain sampling error. Information about these potential errors is provided or referenced with the data or the source of the data. The Census Bureau recommends that data users incorporate this information into their analyses as these errors could impact inferences. Researchers analyzing data to create their own estimates are responsible for the validity of those estimates and should not cite the Census Bureau as the source of the estimates but only as the source of the core data.

We have modified some data to protect individuals' privacy, but in a way that preserves the usefulness of the data.

Subject	Number
Total population	515,342
SEX	
Male	247,163
Female	268,179
AGE	
Under 5 years	44,898
5 to 17 years	119,400
18 to 20 years	28,046
21 to 24 years	32,661
25 to 44 years	158,727

the second box. Filling in the state causes a list of cities and towns to automatically appear. From this new list select the city of El Paso so that your boxes look similar to Figure 4.7.

Picking Go produces the results, which are partly shown in Figure 4.8. The results show that relatively few elderly people live in El Paso since only about 10 percent of its residents were age 65 or older. Instead of older people, El Paso is full of children, with about one-third of the population under 18 years old. The bottom of the table reveals that the typical person in El Paso is Hispanic, since over two-thirds of the population claim Spanish or Latino ancestry.[7] Using other "Show me" tables a very detailed picture of El Paso, or any other place, is quickly produced.

Sometimes you do not want facts on a single place, but instead need to compare information from different areas in a state. One way to get this kind of information is to use the maps button in the Start with Basic Facts area on FactFinder's homepage. The map selection provides a slightly different list of subjects than the selections found when creating the table for El Paso. Examples of map information topics are: education, poverty, and population density.

Let's answer the chapter's second scenario in which you wanted to find the area in Georgia with the most retirees. At the FactFinder homepage (**http://factfinder.census.gov**), pick the circle beside the word Maps in the Start with

[7]Hispanics comprised 355,669 out of 515,342 people in 1990.

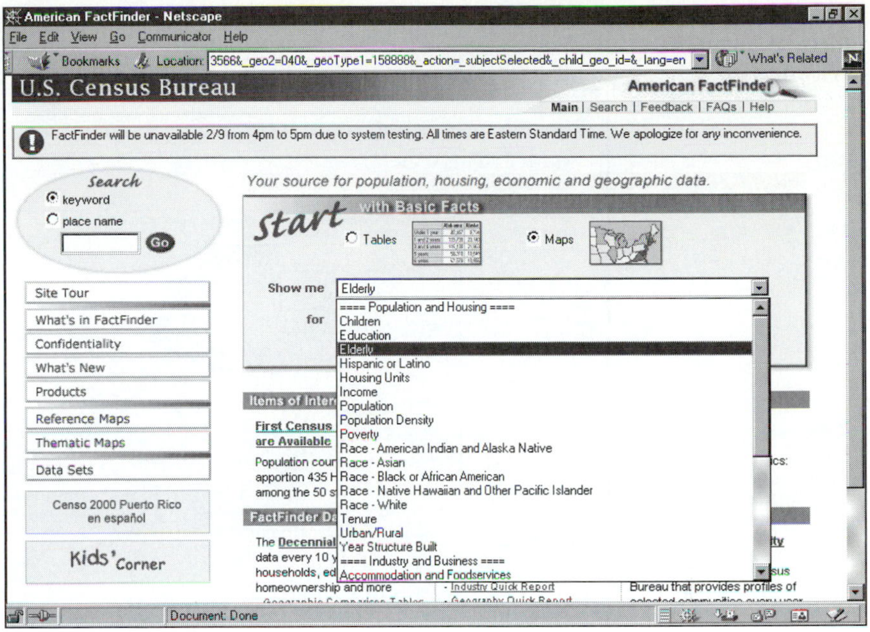

FIGURE 4.9
American FactFinder
List of Maps

Basic Facts area. Then select the table labeled Elderly under the "Show me" pull-down menu, seen in Figure 4.9.

The second step is to pick the physical area of interest. For this example start by selecting State by County in the first box and then select Georgia in the second box. When the state is filled in, pick the Go button to see the results, or look at Figure 4.10. The darkest counties, like those in the northeastern part of the state, have the highest concentration of elderly while the lightest counties, like those around Atlanta, have the least.

If you already know the names of counties in the northeast corner of Georgia, this map is all you need. If you do not know the names, FactFinder has a simple method of finding them out. Go to the FactFinder homepage and select the Reference Maps button on the left side. This brings up a map of the United States. By zooming in on Georgia, a map comes up which shows the county names for different parts of the state. Figure 4.11 shows the zoomed in reference map for Georgia and reveals that Union, Towns, and Rabun counties are the locations meeting your store locating criteria. Zooming in further on the reference map shows major roads and cities, which help in refining site locations.[8] At the finest zoom level, you can see the boundaries of specific census tracts and block groups.

---

[8]When choosing a location, consider both the absolute number of people as well as the percentage meeting the criteria before making a decision.

FIGURE 4.10
Elderly Population of Georgia

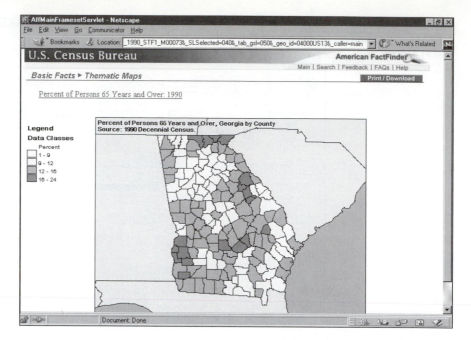

FIGURE 4.11
FactFinder Reference Map for Northeast Georgia

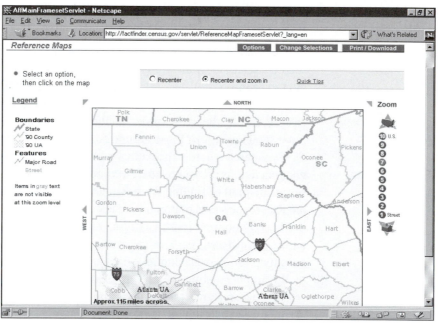

Another way to see a map is to directly type in an address. Go to the FactFinder homepage and again select the Reference Maps button on the left side. At the bottom of the page are boxes that allow you to reposition the map, to any address or zip code. To find the census tract and census block of Boston

FIGURE 4.12
FactFinder Quick
Tables Geographic
Selections

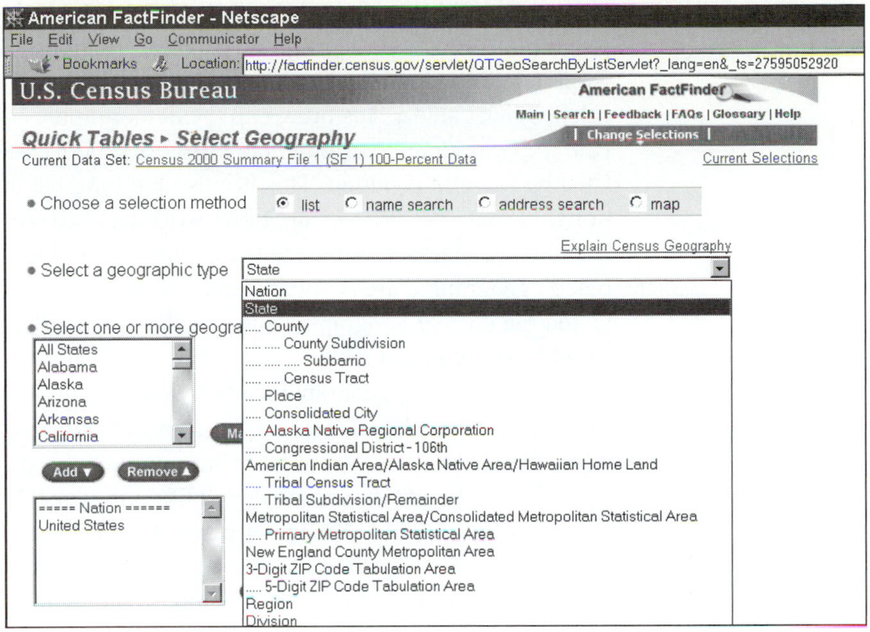

University (B.U.) Business School, type 595 Commonwealth Avenue in the street address box, Boston in the city box, and Massachusetts in the state box. The resulting map shows that detailed data on the demographics of the area around the business school are found by requesting information on census tract 101.02 and block 2001 in Suffolk county.

Once you know the specific state, county, or tract, you can quickly find more detailed information than what is available under Start with Basic Facts. To see more specific information, under the Decennial Census entry on the FactFinder homepage select the link entitled Quick Tables. This entry provides very detailed information from both the census short and long forms for a variety of geographic areas. Tables are available not only on major topics like age, race, and sex but also on more unique items such as the number of people living in group quarters, such as dormitories and prisons. Additionally, users can pick data from either the 2000 or 1990 census to track how an area changed over the decade.

Most important, Quick Tables expands the range of geographic selections. As Figure 4.12 shows, Quick Tables information is available not only for states, counties, and places but also for MSAs, PMSAs, and even specific census tracts.[9] Moreover, Quick Tables allows picking multiple geographic areas, which removes Basic Fact's limitation of viewing data from just one location.

---

[9]For 2000 census data, users can also retrieve data by zip code.

As a simple example of the power of Quick Tables, let us determine the demographics of people living around B.U. Business School. First go to the FactFinder homepage and under the Decennial Census entry select the link entitled Quick Tables. This brings up the demographics of the entire country. To find the demographics around the business school, pick Geography under the Change Selections button. This brings up a long list of geographic specifications. Change the type of area box to "...........Census Tract." Change the state box to Massachusetts and the county box to Suffolk. Last, in the box labeled "geographic areas" pick Census Tract 101.02. To ensure you have selected the correct geographic specifications push the Map It button and you should see Figure 4.13.

Once the correct geographic area is selected, use the Add button to include that area in the table. Then use the Remove button to eliminate the default table. Finally, push the Show Table button to see the specific demographics for this neighborhood. On census day 2000, out of the 3,938 people living near B.U. Business School, almost 94 percent were between ages 15 and 24. The table shows only 4 individuals were children under 10 years old and 40 individuals were 65 years or older. Demographic details show that 94 people of Korean descent and 2 people of Hawaiian descent live in this neighborhood. The table also provides information on housing use and shows that 86 percent of the housing stock is occupied by renters. This level of detail is available not only for Boston, but also for any other portion of the United States selected.

FIGURE 4.13
FactFinder Reference Map of Area around B.U. Business School

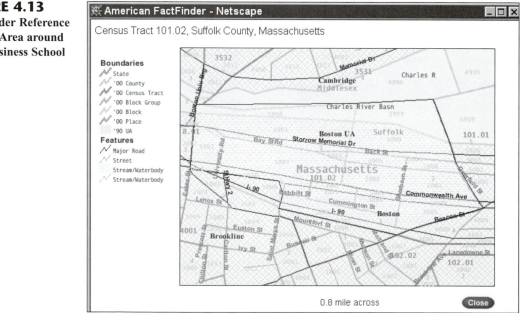

The best way to see how Quick Tables works and its usefulness is to sit down and test out the FactFinder website. No description in this book can replace the experience of trying the site yourself. Experiment by using a variety of options under Change Selections at the top of each Quick Tables page.

Practice Question

Your Boston-based health club is located at 39 Dalton Street, in Suffolk County. Your best clients are young professionals ages 25 to 34 who are eager for exercise. You are thinking of mailing out flyers to this market. How many flyers do you need printed?

Practice Question

How many renters live in your neighborhood? If you live outside the United States, answer this question for the city of Upper Arlington, which is on the edge of Ohio State's campus.

Summary

Periodically all major countries collect information from almost every person living in the nation via a population census. This census happens every 5 years in countries like Canada and Australia and occurs every 10 years in the United States and England.

These census data provide business managers with a very detailed view of the demographic makeup of the population. Just as important, these censuses also show you the population's income, racial composition, education, and housing characteristics. When wisely used, census data let you either examine the specific makeup of an area or find an area that has specific attributes. Using this information business managers have key data for making better marketing, production, and distribution decisions.

Anyone needing to quickly access United States census data should use the American FactFinder website located at **http://factfinder.census.gov**. This site allows you to create custom tables or graphs from either the 1990 or 2000 Census. This website's demographic information ranging from the entire country to a particular neighborhood is freely available.

Chapter 5

Income

How much money do people earn? Answering this question is key for many businesses because the more money people earn, the more they spend. In this chapter you will learn to answer questions like: Where do high-income people live? How much does a person with particular age, marital status, or educational characteristics earn? What is the average income for a particular area? These questions, while simple, are crucial for many sales, marketing, and site decisions. This chapter answers these questions by describing the two most commonly used sources of information about United States household incomes: the census long form and the March Current Population Survey (CPS).

To help you understand income data, let's assume for the first scenario that you need income information to complete marketing profiles. Every item that is sold comes with a form asking the new owner to register the product. The information on these forms is crucial to your business because it is used to fine-tune your marketing and pricing plans. While overall response rates are good, many buyers leave the household income section blank. Is there any way to get a rough estimate of income based solely on the demographic information provided on the forms?

In the second scenario you are a financial planner. Your company provides plenty of information about stocks, bonds, life insurance, and other investment options that you sell. However, before discussing where to invest, clients often want to know how their income compares to others'. Where do you get this kind of information?

Income Information from the Census Long Form

There are two primary sources for United States income information. The census long form, discussed in the previous demographics chapter, provides income data for very precise geographic areas of the country. Businesses using this information can target groups of city blocks that have the income and demographic characteristics of likely customers.

The long form, which is filled out by 17 percent of United States households, asks a series of eight questions about money earned in the calendar year before the census (1989, 1999, 2009, etc.). The same set of questions is asked about each adult in the household. Totaling the responses provides a good estimate of total family income. The eight questions specifically ask about:

- Wages, salary, commissions, bonuses, or tips from all jobs.

- Self-employment income, after business expenses.

- Interest, dividends, net rental, royalty, estates, or trust income.

- Social Security or Railroad Retirement Income.

- Supplemental Security Income (SSI).

- Any public assistance or welfare payments.

- Retirement, survivor, or disability pensions.

- Any other income regularly received like child support or alimony.

To quickly find income information from the census go to the FactFinder homepage (**http://factfinder.census.gov**), shown in Figure 5.1. Use the Start

FIGURE 5.1
American FactFinder Internet Homepage

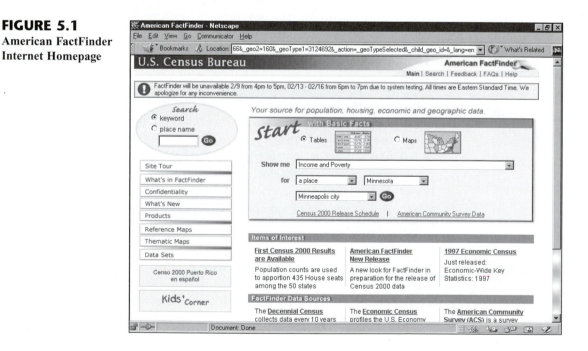

with Basic Facts box located in the top right corner and begin by picking the Tables button. Then pull down the "Show me" menu and select the table entitled Income and Poverty.

Let's say you need to know how many very high-income households exist in the city of Minneapolis. To find information on Minneapolis, start by selecting "a place" in the box labeled "for." This will produce a list of states. Use this list to put Minnesota in the second box. After the state is filled in, a list of places automatically appears. From the place list select the city of Minneapolis so that your screen looks similar to Figure 5.1.

The final step is to pick Go. The 1990 results, which are shown in Figure 5.2, divide households in Minneapolis into 10 different income levels. The top of the list shows that in the 1990 census slightly more than 10,000 Minneapolis households had annual incomes of less than $5,000. Since you are interested in very high-income families, instead of looking at the top of the list check the bottom, which shows the number of families earning $150,000 or more. FactFinder data show that about 1.2 percent of Minneapolis households (1,888 out of 160,531) in 1990 met this very high-income criterion.

If you need information different from what is available under Basic Facts, select the link entitled Quick Tables, which is found under the heading Decennial Census on FactFinder's homepage. Since only the census long form tracks income data, first use the Change Selections button to ensure this data

FIGURE 5.2
Household Income in Minneapolis

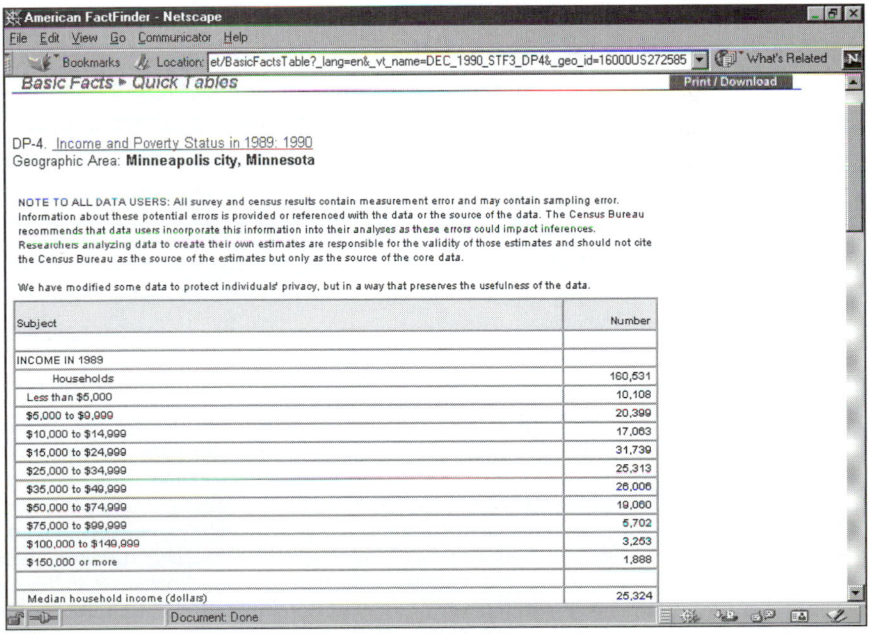
American FactFinder - Netscape
File Edit View Go Communicator Help
Bookmarks Location: et/BasicFactsTable?_lang=en&_vt_name=DEC_1990_STF3_DP4&_geo_id=16000US272585 What's Related
Basic Facts ▸ Quick Tables
Print / Download

DP-4. Income and Poverty Status in 1989: 1990
Geographic Area: **Minneapolis city, Minnesota**

NOTE TO ALL DATA USERS: All survey and census results contain measurement error and may contain sampling error. Information about these potential errors is provided or referenced with the data or the source of the data. The Census Bureau recommends that data users incorporate this information into their analyses as these errors could impact inferences. Researchers analyzing data to create their own estimates are responsible for the validity of those estimates and should not cite the Census Bureau as the source of the estimates but only as the source of the core data.

We have modified some data to protect individuals' privacy, but in a way that preserves the usefulness of the data.

Subject	Number
INCOME IN 1989	
Households	160,531
Less than $5,000	10,108
$5,000 to $9,999	20,399
$10,000 to $14,999	17,063
$15,000 to $24,999	31,739
$25,000 to $34,999	25,313
$35,000 to $49,999	26,006
$50,000 to $74,999	19,060
$75,000 to $99,999	5,702
$100,000 to $149,999	3,253
$150,000 or more	1,888
Median household income (dollars)	25,324

Document: Done

set is selected. The FactFinder site makes selecting long form data confusing because it calls this information "Census sample data" or the "STF-3" file. No matter which label is used, make sure long form data are selected before choosing any table or geographic area. Once long form data are selected, Quick Tables selections can show high-level information, such as average household income for the entire country, as easily as low-level information, such as total Social Security payments received in a particular neighborhood.

Practice Question

How many households in Houston, Texas, earn between $50,000 and $75,000 a year?

Practice Question

What percentage of families living in the Bronx have income of less than $10,000 per year? The Census Bureau classifies this New York City borough as Bronx County.

The primary drawback to using census data is that they are collected only once every 10 years. The Census Bureau is beginning in 2003 the new American Community Survey, which will begin providing income data more often for all parts of the country.[1] Until then, business managers who need income information should use data from the March Current Population Survey, or CPS.

Income Information from the March Current Population Survey

Each month the Census Bureau contacts about 50,000 households to calculate the United States unemployment rate. This survey, called the Current Population Survey (CPS), is described in Chapter 12, "Labor Market Information." Since interviewers are already doing a national face-to-face survey, it costs the government relatively little to add supplemental questions to the basic survey to cover other facets of American life. The extra questions in the March CPS supplement investigate people's annual earnings.[2]

While this survey interviews only a small portion of the households covered by the Census, it is fielded every year and data are available online quite quickly. In addition, this survey asks more detailed questions about income than does the census. While the census asks eight income questions,

[1] While the American Community Survey is slated to begin nationwide interviewing in 2003, data from a number of test cities is currently available on the FactFinder website.
[2] Yearly income data are also available for Canada. Until 1998 the government added a supplemental set of questions called the Survey of Consumer Finances (SCF) to the April labor force survey. Since then a more detailed supplement called the Survey of Labour and Income Dynamics (SLID) has tracked income. Unfortunately, there is no low-cost method of accessing this information. To read more about these surveys, go to Statistics Canada (**www.statcan.ca**) and search for publication 75F0002MIE, entitled *Income Trends in Canada (1980–1998)—User's Guide*.

TABLE 5.1
March CPS
Income Categories

1. Earnings, wages, salaries	10. Pension or retirement plans
2. UI compensation	11. Interest
3. Workers' compensation	12. Dividends
4. Social Security	13. Rents, royalties, trusts
5. SSI	14. Educational assistance
6. Public assistance	15. Alimony
7. Veterans' payments	16. Child support
8. Survivor benefits	17. Outside assistance
9. Disability benefits	18. Other income

Note: UI stands for Unemployment Insurance while SSI is Supplemental Security Income.

the March CPS asks 18 for each person in the household 15 years of age and older. Table 5.1 shows the 18 specific types of income included in the March CPS.

To ensure that the income of Hispanics is accurately measured, each March an additional 2,500 Hispanic households are added to the general CPS sample. Even though the March CPS contacts 52,500 households, there are only enough respondents to provide information at the state level, unlike the census, which breaks income down to individual neighborhoods.

Quick Income Information

The quickest way to find basic income information from the March CPS is to look in the *Statistical Abstract of the United States* (pick the "Statistical Abstract" link on the Census Bureau's homepage, **http://www.census.gov**). The section entitled Income, Expenditures, and Wealth, contains facts and figures on United States income. The first part of this chapter contains tables with footnotes that state the tables are based on the National Income and Product Accounts (NIPA). **Do not** use NIPA income figures for sales or marketing purposes. NIPA figures are based on how much industry produces and provide a very skewed picture of family and household income. Business and marketing managers should only use tables in the *Statistical Abstract* whose footnotes state they come from either the census or Current Population Survey reports.

Browsing through the tables in the Income, Expenditures, and Wealth chapter, you will see how the income data can help your business. For example, these tables can answer which general areas of the country are ripe for expanding your business. Since income is a key part of the answer, look at the table, shown in Figure 5.3, entitled Money Income of Households— Median Income, by State. This table contains typical family earnings by state for a number of years. Since all numbers are already adjusted for inflation,

FIGURE 5.3
Household
Income by State

Acrobat Reader - [StatAbstract2000_IncomeSpendingWealth_Sec14.pdf]

File Edit Document View Window Help

No. 742. Money Income of Households—Median Income by State in Constant (1998) Dollars: 1988 to 1998

[Constant dollars based on the CPI-U-X1 deflator. Data based on the Current Population Survey; see text, Sections 1 and 14, and Appendix III. The CPS is designed to collect reliable data on income primarily at the national level and secondarily at the regional level. When the income data are tabulated by state, the estimates are considered less reliable and, therefore, particular caution should be used when trying to interpret the results]

State	1988	1990	1995 [1]	1997	1998	State	1988	1990	1995 [1]	1997	1998
U.S. . . .	$37,512	$37,343	$36,446	$37,581	$38,885						
						MO	32,301	34,087	37,247	37,122	40,201
AL	27,485	29,129	27,799	32,436	36,266	MT	30,631	29,152	29,688	29,667	31,577
AK	45,611	49,010	51,289	48,742	50,692	NE	34,665	34,274	35,219	35,232	36,413
AZ	36,424	36,446	33,010	33,250	37,090	NV	38,556	39,937	38,594	39,459	39,756
AR	27,794	28,417	27,609	26,569	27,665	NH	47,708	50,889	41,895	41,637	44,958
CA	41,731	41,517	39,583	40,312	40,934						
						NJ	49,998	48,306	46,979	48,769	49,826
CO	36,119	38,328	43,537	43,906	46,599	NM	26,587	31,227	27,799	30,555	31,543
CT	49,896	48,476	43,042	44,670	46,508	NY	39,841	39,398	35,325	36,356	37,394
DE	42,031	38,417	37,357	43,703	41,458	NC	33,640	32,836	34,203	36,398	35,838
DC	36,845	34,161	32,887	32,356	33,433	ND	33,195	31,508	31,112	32,154	30,304
FL	35,006	33,280	31,814	32,961	34,909						
						OH	38,222	37,430	37,371	36,697	38,925
GA	36,604	34,372	36,471	37,234	38,665	OK	32,610	30,410	28,141	31,839	33,727
HI	45,502	48,540	45,831	41,572	40,827	OR	38,233	36,517	38,904	37,827	39,067
ID	32,311	31,559	34,949	33,924	36,680	PA	36,847	36,173	36,925	38,101	39,015
IL	40,680	40,584	40,719	41,926	43,178	RI	41,118	39,868	37,818	35,339	40,686
IN	36,228	33,583	35,707	39,495	39,731						
						SC	35,181	35,836	31,093	34,796	33,267
IA	33,489	34,032	37,989	34,309	37,019	SD	30,718	30,643	31,635	30,157	32,786
KS	35,226	37,310	32,451	37,039	36,711	TN	28,737	28,175	31,033	31,113	34,091
KY	27,429	30,904	31,883	33,973	36,252	TX	34,395	35,204	34,267	35,621	35,783
LA	28,242	27,942	29,893	33,778	31,735	UT	36,255	37,591	39,017	43,441	44,299
ME	36,378	34,251	36,213	33,282	35,640						
						VT	39,941	38,783	36,177	35,599	39,372
MD	50,363	48,460	43,896	47,412	50,016	VA	44,984	43,741	38,741	43,626	43,354
MA	45,763	45,205	41,257	42,678	42,345	WA	44,542	40,048	38,042	45,256	47,421
MI	40,608	37,335	38,960	39,345	41,821	WV	26,666	27,608	26,611	27,916	26,704
MN	40,078	39,241	40,571	43,227	47,926	WI	40,750	38,301	43,804	40,212	41,327
MS	25,030	25,165	28,384	28,943	29,120	WY	36,401	36,740	33,722	33,944	35,250

[1] Full implementation of the 1990 census-based sample design and metropolitan definitions, 7,000 household sample reduction and revised race edits

237%   23 of 36   5.76 x 9.18 in

multiyear comparisons are easy. While the exact rankings change over time, Alaska ($50,692 in 1998) and New Jersey ($49,826 in 1998) consistently hold the top rankings, while Arkansas ($27,665 in 1998) and West Virginia ($26,704 in 1998) consistently rank at the bottom.

Financial planners who need quick information showing how a client's total income compares to other families should turn to the table entitled Share of Aggregate Income Received by Each Fifth and Top 5 Percent of Families. This table, shown in Figure 5.4, breaks family income down into groups from poor to rich. To see how a family ranks, compare its income in a given year to the table.[3] For example, if a family's income in 1998 was $56,000 then they ranked at the top of the third percentile. Being the top of the third percentile means they earned more money than 60 percent and less money than 40 percent of all other families.

The *Statistical Abstract* provides a quick source of basic information, but you may need more details. For example, how much do Gen-X males or Baby Boomer females over age 50 earn? The answers to these more detailed questions are found in the next section, which discusses the Census Bureau's annual income reports.

---

[3]Since this table publishes numbers a few years out of date, use the formulas in Chapter 10, "Prices," to update the table.

FIGURE 5.4
Average Income for
Poor, Middle-Class,
and Rich Households
over Time

No. 745. Share of Aggregate Income Received by Each Fifth and Top 5 Percent of Families: 1970 to 1998

[Families as of March of the following year. Income in constant 1998 CPI-U adjusted dollars]

Year	Number of families (1,000)	Income at selected positions (dollars)					Percent distribution of aggregate income					
		Upper limit of each fifth				Top 5 percent	Lowest 5th	Second 5th	Third 5th	Fourth 5th	Highest 5th	Top 5 percent
		Lowest	Second	Third	Fourth							
1970	51,948	20,128	32,837	44,594	61,297	95,708	5.4	12.2	17.6	23.8	40.9	15.6
1980	60,309	20,598	34,680	49,118	68,923	108,931	5.3	11.6	17.6	24.4	41.1	14.6
1985	63,558	20,125	34,669	50,221	73,061	119,622	4.8	11.0	16.9	24.3	43.1	16.1
1990	66,322	21,009	36,222	52,429	76,686	127,654	4.6	10.8	16.6	23.8	44.3	17.4
1991 [1]	67,173	20,345	34,839	51,461	75,386	123,057	4.5	10.7	16.6	24.1	44.2	17.1
1992 [1]	68,216	19,417	34,475	51,119	74,413	123,164	4.3	10.5	16.5	24.0	44.7	17.6
1993 [2]	68,506	19,143	33,841	50,795	75,346	127,672	4.1	9.9	15.7	23.3	47.0	20.3
1994 [3]	69,313	19,732	34,426	51,694	76,988	132,031	4.2	10.0	15.7	23.3	46.9	20.1
1995	69,597	20,396	35,279	52,392	77,286	132,257	4.4	10.1	15.8	23.2	46.5	20.0
1996	70,241	20,445	35,649	53,072	78,244	132,976	4.2	10.0	15.8	23.1	46.8	20.3
1997	70,884	20,907	36,561	54,451	81,246	139,215	4.2	9.9	15.7	23.0	47.2	20.7
1998	71,551	21,600	37,692	56,020	83,693	145,199	4.2	9.9	15.7	23.0	47.3	20.7

[1] Based on 1990 census population controls. [2] See text, Section 14, for explanation of changes in data collection method. [3] Introduction of new 1990 census sample design. [4] Persons of Hispanic origin may be of any race.

Source: U.S. Census Bureau, *Current Population Reports*, P60-206; and <http://www.census.gov/hhes/income/histinc/f02.html> (accessed 26 October 1999).

Practice Question

Your company is beginning its Midwest expansion in either Kansas or Oklahoma. The planning committee asks you, "Which state has higher household income?"

Practice Question

You are marketing a new up scale apartment complex for families who earn more than $75,000. You suggest to the builder advertising not only on the local English-speaking stations but also the local Spanish-language television stations. Before committing to this plan, the builder asks how many Hispanics earn over $75,000 a year.

More Detailed Income Information

After running each March CPS supplemental survey, the Census Bureau produces a thick report on the income of United States residents. This report, published each year under the general title "Money Income in the United States," is part of a set of reports designated the P60 series. While earlier editions are found only in major libraries, the Census Bureau has put the latest editions on-line. To read these reports go to the Census Bureau homepage (**http://www.census.gov**) and select the Income link (found under the People category). This selection brings you to the Income homepage, shown in Figure 5.5.

The most detailed tables are found by picking the P60 "Money Income in the United States" link and downloading the PDF report. The level of detail is

FIGURE 5.5
Census Bureau's
Income Homepage

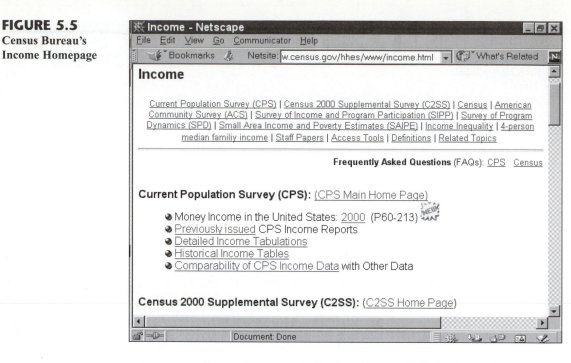

quite extraordinary; for example the 1998 report (P60-206) contains over 100 pages of tables completely filled with numbers. These reports break earnings down by many different demographic characteristics such as race, age, sex, residence, region, family size, and education. To reduce printing costs and increase the number of tables provided, starting with the year 2000 (P60-213). The Census Bureau's report contains only a summary of findings and the detailed tables exist solely in electronic form under the pick Detailed Income Tabulations.

In the chapter's first scenario, buyers filled in a product registration form with demographic information, but many left the income question blank. Using the tables from the Money Income report, it is easy to fill in missing figures with good estimates. Let's assume the product registration form asks the purchaser's sex, age, education, and whether he or she is working. For example, let's assume you receive a registration card from a 23-year-old working male with an associate's degree.

To find an estimate of this person's earnings choose Detailed Income Tabulations. For each year this brings up the following list:

- Household

- Family

- Person

FIGURE 5.6
Money Earnings of Males from the Report "Money Income in the United States"

	Total	Less Than 9th Grade	High School 9th to 12th Nongrad	Graduate Incl Ged	Some College No Degree	Associate Degree	Tot
Male							
All Races							
Total Work Experience							
Number with Earnings							
Total............	76,998	3,165	6,741	24,422	15,424	5,981	21,2
Under 65 years.......	73,751	2,004	6,418	23,462	14,929	5,823	20,2
18 to 24 years.....	10,813	321	2,068	3,618	3,518	528	7
25 to 34 years.....	17,222	634	1,348	5,551	3,294	1,401	4,9
25 to 29 years...	8,172	293	695	2,670	1,736	612	2,1
30 to 34 years...	9,050	341	653	2,881	1,558	788	2,8
35 to 44 years.....	20,746	798	1,405	7,100	3,572	1,776	6,0
35 to 39 years...	10,313	417	743	3,525	1,731	822	3,0
40 to 44 years...	10,433	381	662	3,575	1,841	955	3,0
45 to 54 years.....	16,690	627	931	4,713	3,150	1,583	5,6
45 to 49 years...	9,112	335	577	2,739	1,628	944	2,8
50 to 54 years...	7,578	292	353	1,974	1,522	639	2,7
55 to 64 years.....	8,280	504	665	2,480	1,395	535	2,7
55 to 59 years...	5,162	260	379	1,553	906	375	1,6
60 to 64 years...	3,118	245	286	927	489	160	1,0
65 years and over....	3,247	281	324	960	496	158	1,0
65 to 74 years...	2,576	221	251	771	375	136	8
65 to 69 years...	1,704	140	175	516	245	115	5
70 to 74 years...	873	81	77	256	130	21	3
75 years and over..	670	60	72	189	121	21	2
Male							
All Races							
Total Work Experience							
Mean earnings							
Total............	42,975	20,994	21,934	32,019	35,709	42,549	70,8
Under 65 years.......	43,421	21,572	22,112	32,295	36,026	42,990	71,7
18 to 24 years.....	15,055	14,858	9,979	17,384	12,091	20,248	27,9

- Selected Characteristics of Households and Families by Quintile

- Detailed Noncash Tables[4]

- Experimental Measures of Income and Poverty

Most business managers need to look at only the top three selections: households, families, and persons. What is the difference between these three selections? A person is a single individual. A family is two or more people related by birth, marriage, or adoption living together. A household consists of all people living together no matter what their relationship. For example, if three college students share an apartment, they are recorded as three individuals and one household.

Since we want information on an individual, select the link under March 2001 (2000 Income) labeled Person. Then select table PINC-04 which is entitled Educational Attainment—People 18 Years Old and Over, by Total Money Earnings in 2000, Work Experience in 2000, Age, Race, Hispanic Origin, and Sex. Then pick the link entitled Male, All Races since the registration card does not provide any racial data. The resulting table, shown in Figure 5.6, reveals in the bottom right corner that a good estimate in 2000 for this person's income is $20,248.

[4]Noncash means the value of government programs such as food stamps, school lunches, rental subsidies, and Medicaid.

FIGURE 5.7

Sources of Income from the Report "Money Income in the United States"

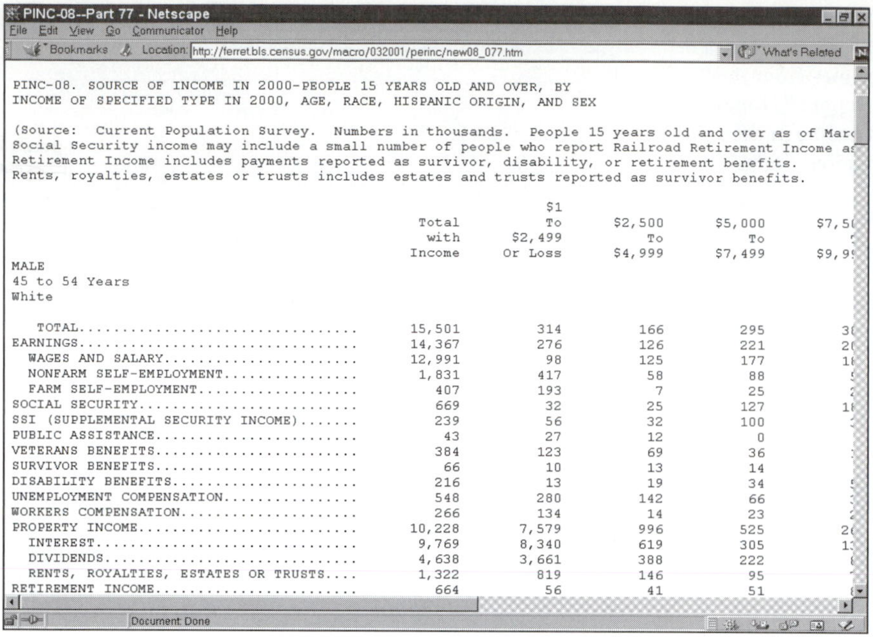

```
PINC-08--Part 77 - Netscape
File  Edit  View  Go  Communicator  Help
     Bookmarks    Location: http://ferret.bls.census.gov/macro/032001/perinc/new08_077.htm        What's Related

PINC-08.  SOURCE OF INCOME IN 2000-PEOPLE 15 YEARS OLD AND OVER, BY
INCOME OF SPECIFIED TYPE IN 2000, AGE, RACE, HISPANIC ORIGIN, AND SEX

(Source:  Current Population Survey.  Numbers in thousands.  People 15 years old and over as of Marc
Social Security income may include a small number of people who report Railroad Retirement Income as
Retirement Income includes payments reported as survivor, disability, or retirement benefits.
Rents, royalties, estates or trusts includes estates and trusts reported as survivor benefits.
```

	Total with Income	$1 To $2,499 Or Loss	$2,500 To $4,999	$5,000 To $7,499	$7,5($9,9!
MALE					
45 to 54 Years					
White					
TOTAL................................	15,501	314	166	295	3(
EARNINGS.............................	14,367	276	126	221	2(
WAGES AND SALARY....................	12,991	98	125	177	1(
NONFARM SELF-EMPLOYMENT.............	1,831	417	58	88	!
FARM SELF-EMPLOYMENT................	407	193	7	25	;
SOCIAL SECURITY.....................	669	32	25	127	1(
SSI (SUPPLEMENTAL SECURITY INCOME)......	239	56	32	100	:
PUBLIC ASSISTANCE...................	43	27	12	0	
VETERANS BENEFITS...................	384	123	69	36	
SURVIVOR BENEFITS...................	66	10	13	14	
DISABILITY BENEFITS.................	216	13	19	34	!
UNEMPLOYMENT COMPENSATION...........	548	280	142	66	;
WORKERS COMPENSATION................	266	134	14	23	;
PROPERTY INCOME.....................	10,228	7,579	996	525	2(
INTEREST..........................	9,769	8,340	619	305	1;
DIVIDENDS.........................	4,638	3,661	388	222	(
RENTS, ROYALTIES, ESTATES OR TRUSTS....	1,322	819	146	95	
RETIREMENT INCOME...................	664	56	41	51	

```
     Document: Done
```

When using these tables, beware of two potential problems. First, the top section of these tables reports the number of people, families, or households in each category, not the amount of money earned. Earning information is found in the middle section of the tables. Do not report the wrong figure. Second, be careful to select the correct line and column. Given the mass of statistics it is very easy to make a mistake. For example, in the table shown in Figure 5.6 there are broad age groupings, such as 25 to 34 years, that are inserted between the specific age ranges of 18 to 24 and 25 to 29. When searching for the correct line for a 27-year-old buyer, it is easy to select the more general age category and not notice that a more specific line is available.

Are you marketing or thinking about selling financial products? If you are, two sets of online tables in the "Money Income in the United States" report are particularly useful. Under the Person heading there are two Source of Income tables (PINC-08 and PINC-09 in the 2000 report), which contain details by age and race about where people earned their income. This table breaks down income into over 70 different categories, partially shown in Figure 5.7. For example, you can see exactly how much different types of individuals earn in interest, dividends, annuities, and trust payments. This information not only helps you gauge how your clients compare to national averages, but also is useful for roughly calculating the amount of financial assets various demographic groups own.[5]

[5]A rough estimate is calculated by dividing the amount paid by the yearly rate of return. For example, if someone reports $100 per year in savings interest and interest rates are around 5 percent, then they hold approximately $2,000 in savings ($100/0.05).

FIGURE 5.8
**FERRET Survey
Selection Page**

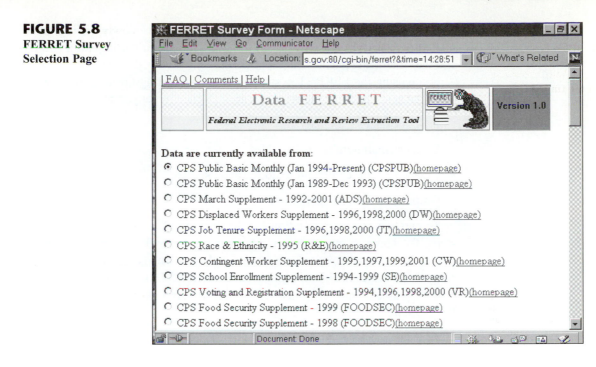

Practice
Question

You design custom vacations for the very wealthy and want to know roughly the size of your market. How many households earn more than $250,000 a year? How many families earn more than $250,000? Why is there a difference in the two numbers?

Practice
Question

You are the head of admissions for your local community college. A middle-aged white woman with a high school degree just came in the office and wants to know if getting an associate's degree will boost her income enough so that she can start saving for a new car. What can you tell her about her probable income after earning a degree?

Custom Income Tabulations

The problem with preprinted reports is that when you need precise information, they have almost, but not exactly, what you want. Customized income information is available online via the FERRET system. FERRET, which stands for Federal Electronic Research and Review Extraction Tool, is a joint project of the Bureau of Labor Statistics and the Census Bureau. This website allows you to create tables and extract very specific data from the March CPS income supplement.

FERRET contains not only the March CPS but also a number of other government surveys. Figure 5.8 shows part of the list of the surveys currently available under FERRET. While many of the surveys are supplements to the

CPS, run during months other than March, FERRET is slowly adding other non-CPS surveys like the Survey of Income & Program Participation (SIPP) and the American Housing Survey (AHS).

Since using the FERRET system involves navigating through many windows, keep in mind that the windows are designed to get you to:

• Pick one data set to analyze.

• Select a small number of variables.

• Create a SAS® command to do the analysis.[6]

• Output your custom tabulation.

To create a custom tabulation for the March CPS, there are nine simple steps. To show you exactly what is happening, we will answer the chapter's second scenario, where you are a financial planner who is constantly asked by clients "How does my income compare to others'?" To keep the problem specific, let's assume the person asking this question is a 38-year-old male with a PhD. The nine steps are:

Step 1. Go to the Internet URL **http://ferret.bls.census.gov**.

Step 2. Read the introduction and choose the Get FERRET Data link at the bottom of the page.

Step 3. Register by typing in your e-mail address and pick Continue.

Step 4. Select a survey (see the previous figure). To analyze income information select the CPS March Supplement from the list and pick Continue.

Step 5. Pick the general types of data you want to search. FERRET provides some introductory text about the survey you selected. After reading this text, pick Continue to advance to the primary control page, which is shown in Figure 5.9.

The top part of the March Supplement's control page asks you to pick the year(s) to analyze. Until you are comfortable using the system, just select one year at a time. For our example choose 2001.

The bottom part of the March Supplement control page allows you to pick the general categories of variables to search. There are three choices with check boxes, which are identical to the main choices discussed previously in the P60 reports "Money Income in the United States":

[6]SAS® is a statistical processing package sold by the SAS Institute in North Carolina. You do **not** need to own or understand this program because it is part of FERRET.

FIGURE 5.9
FERRET Main
Control Page

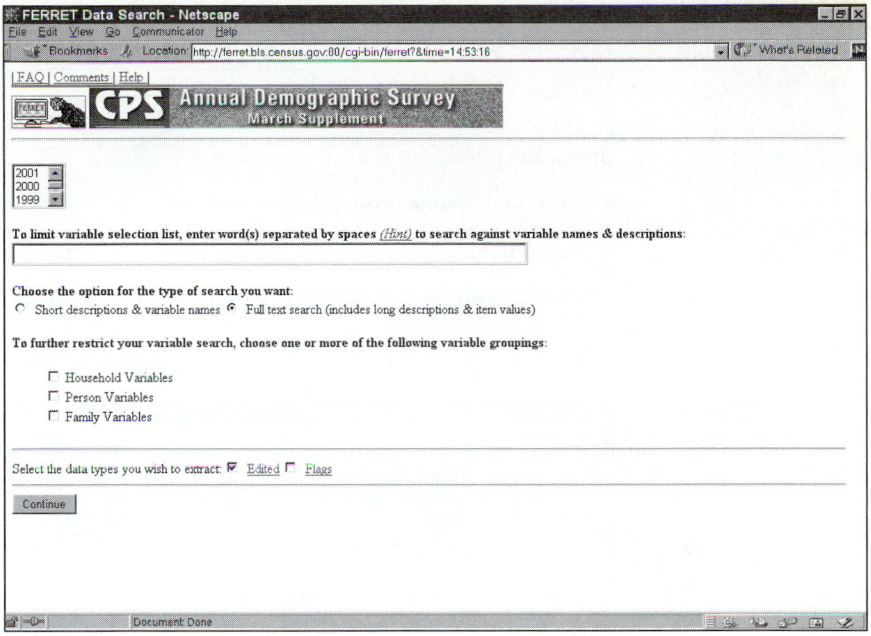

☑ Household Variables

☑ Person Variables

☑ Family Variables

For our example, select both person and family variables. The bottom of the page asks you to "Select the data types you wish to extract: ☐ Edited ☐ Flags." Until you become experienced with the March Supplement, just pick "Edited." When you are satisfied with your choices pick Continue to advance to the next page. The next page, shown in Figure 5.10, lists the variables found in the survey that meet the criteria specified on the previous control page.

Step 6. Select specific variables for tabulation.

• To select/deselect a single line just move the mouse and click. The line will either be highlighted or stop being highlighted.

• To select/deselect multiple lines hold down the Control (Ctrl) key while simultaneously selecting each line.

For our example the following four lines were picked: age, education, and sex from the person records and total income from the family records. Be careful when selecting lines; there are a number of lines that look quite

FIGURE 5.10
FERRET Variable
Selection Page

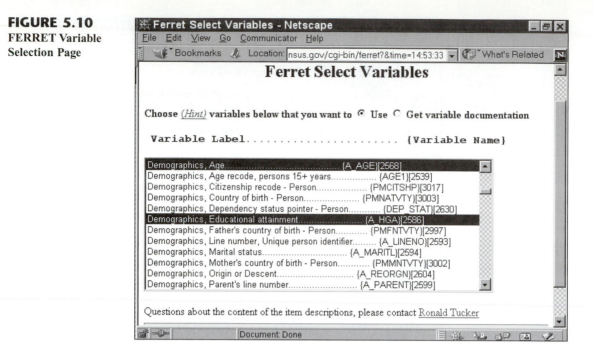

similar. For example, the "Total income amount recode" line is preceded by "Total income amount."[7]

Demographics, Age . . . . (A_AGE)

Demographics, Educational attainment. (A_HGA)

Demographics, Sex . . . . (A_SEX)

Total income amount recode—Family . . . . (FTOT_R)

Step 7. Pick the specific range to analyze for each variable. This page, shown in Figure 5.11, allows you to select the relevant part of each variable. If you do not want to limit a variable, either leave the box blank or use the default settings so that all possible values are returned. In our example we want to know how much 38-year-old men with PhD's earn. We can specify exactly this kind of information using this page.

In the first boxes, we limit the age range on the A_AGE variable to 35 for the starting and 41 for the ending value. We could ask for just 38-year-olds, but in the March 2001 survey there were only 11 people who were 38-year-old men with a PhD. By broadening the age category to cover 35- to 41-year-olds, we capture the same characteristics but have a sample of 93 people.[8] When

---

[7]Recoded variables have their values collapsed into a smaller number of categories. For example, the total income recode line divides money into 41 brackets.
[8]The number of observations is found at the very end when FERRET produces output.

FIGURE 5.11
FERRET Value
Setting Page

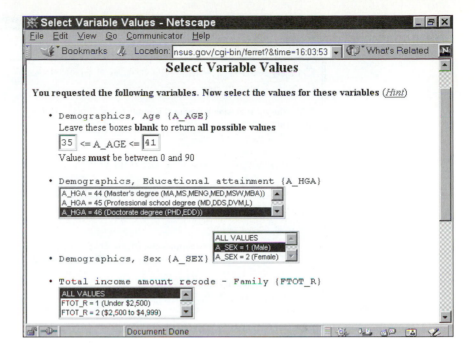

using FERRET the rough rule of thumb is **ensure your data set is based on answers from about 100 people.** Results based on smaller numbers of people are unreliable.

After setting the age range we select A_HGA = Doctorate Degree to capture only those individuals who have a PhD or EDD. Then set A_SEX = Male so that only males are tabulated. Finally, since we want all income values, we either leave FTOT_R alone or select All Values.

The bottom of the page determines how the output is returned. Most of the time you will want to "Create crosstabs, frequencies, or SAS dataset for downloading or printing," so leave the switch alone.

Step 8. Customize the output tabulation. This is the last page where you make selections. It displays what you previously picked and the survey months being analyzed so that you can verify your selections. If you do not like the choices use the BACK button on your browser to fix the problem.

This page, shown in Figure 5.12, allows you to customize both how the output is received and what it will look like. For our example, since we only care about the income variable, check Cross-tabulation and Freq and choose FTOT_R as the row variable. Since we do not care about seeing output based on the other variables, it is not necessary to select a column, page, or chapter. Experiment to see what fits best for your problem.

FIGURE 5.12
**FERRET Output
Control Page**

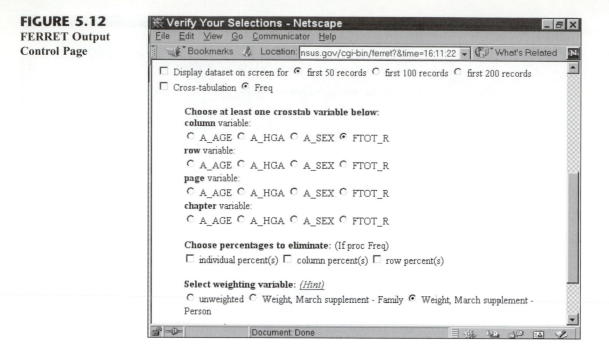

The bottom of the page asks you to "Select weighting variable." For this example, since we are extracting data on individuals, select the Weight, March supplement—Person, otherwise just leave the default value, which is set to Family, alone. The default value weights or corrects for the special sampling and clustering features that ensure the survey covers every state in the Union. Not weighting produces very skewed results, so make sure you **never select unweighted.**

Step 9. Look at your answers. This last page shows your custom tabulation. Figure 5.13 is part of the output from our example.

What does this output mean? The title says, "SAS Data Set with 93 obs (sic) was created for your query." This means that in March 2001 the CPS survey recorded income information from 93 individuals who met our age, sex, and educational criteria. Because you asked for weighted results, the experiences of this group are transformed so that the table accurately represents the experiences of over 211,630 individuals (bottom number in Cumulative Frequency column). The Frequency column states the number of men in the entire country with the specific income shown in each row. The Percent column states the percentage of men in the country with our selected characteristics. The Cumulative Frequency and Percent columns just total up all the numbers from the beginning to the line at which you are looking.

FIGURE 5.13
FERRET Output

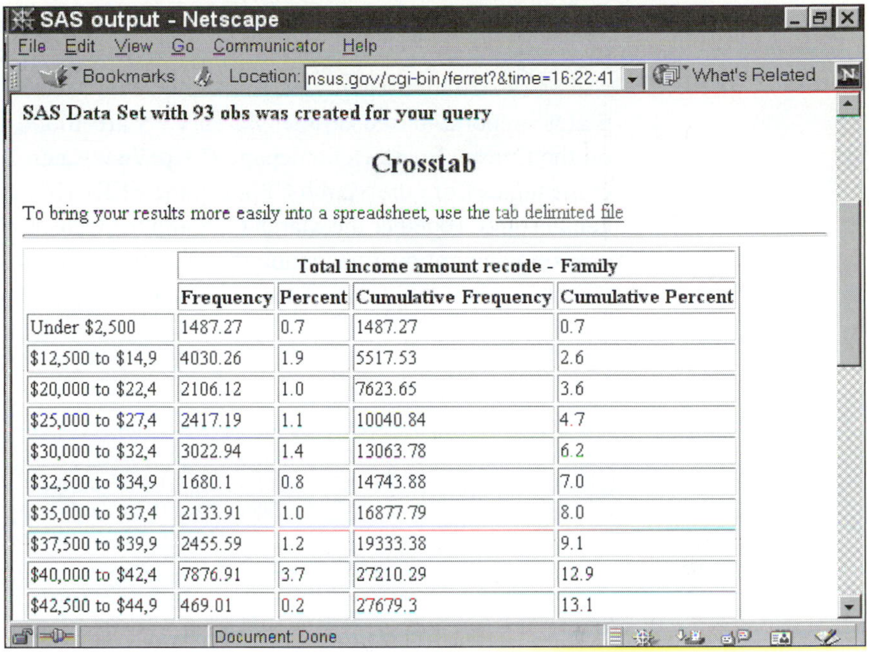

SAS Data Set with 93 obs was created for your query

Crosstab

To bring your results more easily into a spreadsheet, use the tab delimited file

	Total income amount recode - Family			
	Frequency	Percent	Cumulative Frequency	Cumulative Percent
Under $2,500	1487.27	0.7	1487.27	0.7
$12,500 to $14,9	4030.26	1.9	5517.53	2.6
$20,000 to $22,4	2106.12	1.0	7623.65	3.6
$25,000 to $27,4	2417.19	1.1	10040.84	4.7
$30,000 to $32,4	3022.94	1.4	13063.78	6.2
$32,500 to $34,9	1680.1	0.8	14743.88	7.0
$35,000 to $37,4	2133.91	1.0	16877.79	8.0
$37,500 to $39,9	2455.59	1.2	19333.38	9.1
$40,000 to $42,4	7876.91	3.7	27210.29	12.9
$42,500 to $44,9	469.01	0.2	27679.3	13.1

What does the table show? Looking at the Cumulative Percent column shows that if the client's family earns around $25,000, they are in the bottom 5 percent of the income distribution. Let's assume your client's total family income is $95,000. The bottom part of the results (not shown) reveals they are doing better than less than half (47.2%) of all middle-age-males with a PhD. Clearly the client needs professional financial advice on boosting his income.

Practice Question

Does it make any difference if your 38-year-old client with a PhD is a female, instead of a male?

Practice Question

You are a financial planner and another client just walked in. This client is a divorced 45-year-old male with a bachelor's degree who earns $65,000 a year. Before hearing the latest stock pitch, he wants to know how his income compares with others'.

Summary

How much money do people earn? To answer this question there are two major sources of data, the census long form and the CPS's March Demographic Supplement. The census long form (**http://factfinder.census.gov**) is your source of income information if you need a specific geographic area. While the census is done only every 10 years, it provides income data for areas ranging from the entire country down to a few city blocks.

While the March CPS does not have the geographic detail of the census, it provides income information broken down by age, sex, race, education, and work status for each year. Preprinted P60 "Money Income in the United States" reports, based on the March CPS are found under the Income link on the Census Bureau's homepage (**http://www.census.gov**). For custom income tables from the March CPS, use the FERRET system (**http://ferret.bls. census.gov**). Together the March CPS and the Census of Population present an amazing amount of information that can answer almost every business question about an individual's income.

Chapter 6

Consumer Spending

How much do consumers buy? This simple question about purchasing habits is the focus of many retail business discussions. Information on how much families spend on particular products is needed to calculate your market share; determine how responsive consumers are to price changes; and show whether advertising, promotions, or product changes increase purchases for all brands in a given category or just shift sales between brands. Given the importance of tracking spending, this chapter gives you the tools to determine exactly how much money consumers spend in particular product categories ranging from air travel to zoo trips. Combining this precise national data on family spending with your internal sales data creates a powerful source of information for making business decisions.

In this chapter's first scenario, you work for a national retail chain of children's clothing. Sales in your stores that are open more than 12 months are increasing much slower than the average growth rate for all retail stores. Your next quarterly report to shareholders needs to explain if the sales shortfall is unique to your chain or a general problem for all children's clothing retailers.

In the second scenario, imagine you work for an oil company with a giant network of gas stations. Upper management is discussing a frequent buyer program to increase brand loyalty. To ensure the program's reward structure is neither too generous nor too stingy, you must estimate how much gasoline different types of families purchase.

The Consumer Expenditure Survey

The answers to these and other spending questions are found in the Consumer Expenditure Survey. This Federal government survey is the best publicly available source of consumer spending information, and it is a hidden gold mine

TABLE 6.1
Typical Family
Spending from the
Consumer
Expenditure Survey

Type	2000 Spending	Type	2000 Spending
Food	$ 5,158	Personal care	$ 564
Alcoholic beverages	372	Reading	146
Housing	12,319	Education	632
Apparel	1,856	Tobacco and smoking	319
Transportation	7,417	Miscellaneous	776
Health care	2,066	Cash contributions	1,192
Entertainment	1,863	Insurance	399

for marketing and sales professionals. This survey is not new. The United States government first began tracking consumer purchases back in 1888. While information prior to World War II provides a fascinating view of historical spending habits, most managers should use data only from the mid-1980s, when the survey's questions and format were standardized and the data began to be collected annually.[1]

While the survey greatly helps marketing departments, the United States government's primary reason for running the survey is to ensure that the goods and services selected to calculate inflation rates match the buying patterns of households. Nevertheless, no matter how the government uses this survey, it contains an amazing amount of marketing and sales information that is all **free.** To provide a rough idea of what the survey covers, Table 6.1 shows the 14 broadest categories and the typical United States family's spending in each group.

The Consumer Expenditure Survey actually produces these broad spending categories and more detailed breakdowns from two different surveys. The first survey is called the *Diary Survey*. Just like the name implies, the government periodically asks 5,000 families to write down in a special diary all items purchased while shopping over a two-week period. The second survey is called the *Interview Survey*. Respondents in this survey engage in a lengthy face-to-face interview in which they are asked about all major purchases and large recurring bills, like rent and mortgage payments, that the household made over the last quarter (3 months). All Consumer Expenditure Survey tables provided either in print or on the Internet automatically combine the information from these two surveys so no complicated calculations are needed.[2]

[1]Prior to 1980 the survey was fielded roughly every 15 years.
[2]Only users of the micro data, discussed at the end of this chapter, can see responses for either part alone.

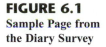

FIGURE 6.1

Sample Page from the Diary Survey

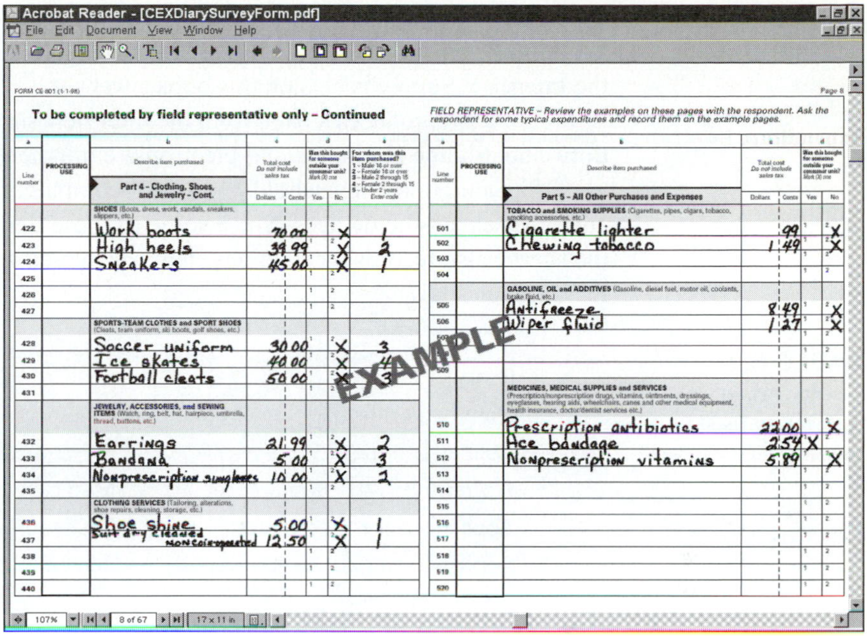

The simplest way to understand the Diary Survey is to look at it. A copy of the survey is on the book's website and a sample page is shown in Figure 6.1. Each Diary Survey household is given a booklet in which they are asked to record all purchases. Each day of the diary is divided into five sections: food for home consumption; food and beverages purchased as gifts; food bought and eaten away from home; clothing, shoes, and jewelry; and all other purchases and expenses. Each of these broad categories is further broken down so that more specific information is recorded. Interviewers drop off these diaries in each household and explain what items to include and how to mark down purchases in the diary. Then, before leaving the house, interviewers record the families' demographic characteristics.

Over the next two weeks, everyone in the household records details about all items purchased each day. The diary is very specific and asks respondents not only to write down the general item they purchased, like bread, but also to record the exact type, like a two-pound loaf of pumpernickel. The respondents also mark whether each item was purchased for usage by a household member or bought as a gift for nonmembers. When the two-week period is finished, the interviewer returns and goes over the diary to fill in missing or partially completed items.

The Interview Survey, which randomly selects a different group of respondents, is a more complex questionnaire than the Diary Survey. Instead of giving each household a simple booklet in which to write down their purchases, the interviewer asks detailed questions about the amount of money spent over the last three months for the 20 broad categories shown in Table 6.2. A copy of the Interview Survey is also on this book's website.

Figure 6.2 reproduces a page from the interview survey that contains questions about home appliance and electronic equipment purchases. This page asks if anyone in the household purchased computers, software, telephones, and other electronic devices. Since some of these items are quite expensive, the survey also records whether any item was rented and if the price reported includes sales tax.

TABLE 6.2
Twenty Broad Categories Used in the Interview Survey

Rent	Vehicle expenses
Home and mortgage payments	Health insurance
Utilities and fuel	Other insurance
Property construction and repairs	Medical expenses
Appliances and electronics	Educational expenses
Appliance and equipment repairs	Recreational expenses
Home furnishings	Trips and vacations
Clothing	Miscellaneous expenses
Rented and leased vehicles	Food, alcohol, and tobacco
Owned vehicles	Credit card and other debt

FIGURE 6.2
Sample Page from the Interview Survey

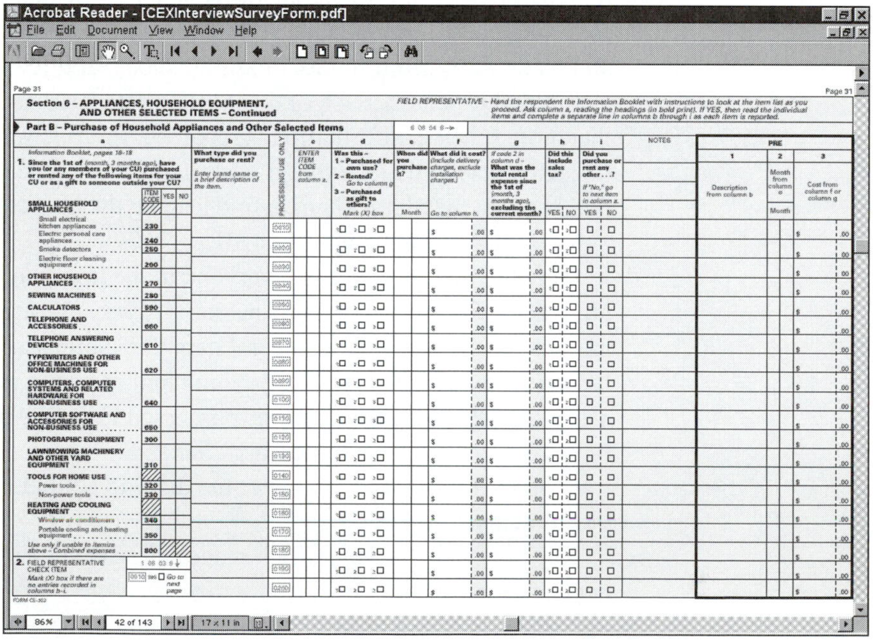

Before looking at spending information produced from the Consumer Expenditure Survey, you need to understand the survey's small but important drawbacks. The biggest drawback is that spending data are for entire households and not for individuals within the household. The survey does not ask who in the family actually made the purchase. This means that it is difficult to estimate how much particular individuals spend. For example, it is very easy to use the Consumer Expenditure Survey to calculate how much households containing teenagers spend overall (see the next section for the actual numbers). It is impossible, however, to tell from the survey how much of that spending is done by teenagers and how much of the spending is done by their parents. Additionally, the questionnaire does not ask who in the family bought a particular item, so this survey cannot be used to understand who makes purchasing decisions for a particular product or service.

The second problem with the survey is that the averages are for all families, not just families purchasing the product. For many food, housing, and transportation categories, this distinction is meaningless since almost all families buy items, like milk. However, the distinction is important for a few select categories where families either make infrequent purchases, like new cars, or potentially never purchase the product, like tobacco.

For example, Table 6.1 showed that the typical United States family spent over $300 on tobacco and smoking products. Given that a majority of families in the United States spend nothing on tobacco, this figure grossly underestimates tobacco spending by families who smoke. If you need information only for families who purchase the product, not the national average, read the end of this chapter, which discusses the Consumer Expenditure Survey's underlying micro data.[3]

Quick Spending Information

The quickest way to find basic spending information from the Consumer Expenditure Survey is to look in the *Statistical Abstract of the United States* (pick the "Statistical Abstract" link on the Census Bureau's homepage **http://www.census.gov**). The section entitled Income, Expenditures and Wealth, contains spending facts and figures. Spending information starts with the table Annual Expenditure per Child by Husband-Wife Families, which tracks expenditures

---

[3]Canada also runs a yearly expenditure survey called the Survey of Household Spending. This survey collects less detail on specific spending than the Consumer Expenditure Survey. However, by sampling over 20,000 households, Canada is able to produce estimates of spending by province per year. High level tables are available at the Statistics Canada website (**www.statcan.ca**) by making the following selections "Canadian Statistics / The People / Families / Expenditures."

FIGURE 6.3

Annual Spending on
Children by Parents

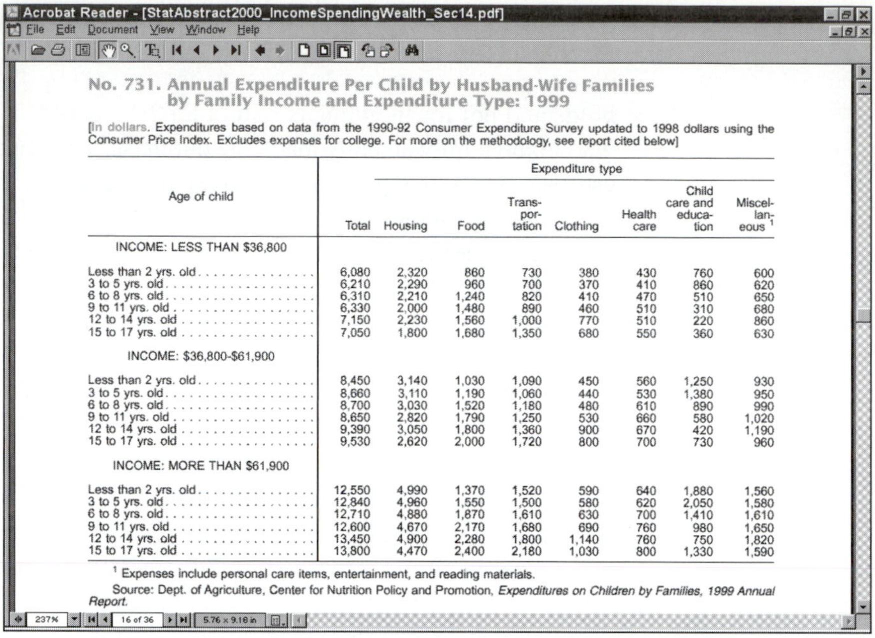

```
Acrobat Reader - [StatAbstract2000_IncomeSpendingWealth_Sec14.pdf]        _ 8 x
File  Edit  Document  View  Window  Help                                   _ 8 x
```

No. 731. Annual Expenditure Per Child by Husband-Wife Families by Family Income and Expenditure Type: 1999

[In dollars. Expenditures based on data from the 1990-92 Consumer Expenditure Survey updated to 1998 dollars using the Consumer Price Index. Excludes expenses for college. For more on the methodology, see report cited below]

Age of child		Expenditure type						
	Total	Housing	Food	Trans-por-tation	Clothing	Health care	Child care and educa-tion	Miscel-lan-eous [1]
INCOME: LESS THAN $36,800								
Less than 2 yrs. old	6,080	2,320	860	730	380	430	760	600
3 to 5 yrs. old	6,210	2,290	960	700	370	410	860	620
6 to 8 yrs. old	6,310	2,210	1,240	820	410	470	510	650
9 to 11 yrs. old	6,330	2,000	1,480	890	460	510	310	680
12 to 14 yrs. old	7,150	2,230	1,560	1,000	770	510	220	860
15 to 17 yrs. old	7,050	1,800	1,680	1,350	680	550	360	630
INCOME: $36,800-$61,900								
Less than 2 yrs. old	8,450	3,140	1,030	1,090	450	560	1,250	930
3 to 5 yrs. old	8,660	3,110	1,190	1,060	440	530	1,380	950
6 to 8 yrs. old	8,700	3,030	1,520	1,180	480	610	890	990
9 to 11 yrs. old	8,650	2,820	1,790	1,250	530	660	580	1,020
12 to 14 yrs. old	9,390	3,050	1,800	1,360	900	670	420	1,190
15 to 17 yrs. old	9,530	2,620	2,000	1,720	800	700	730	960
INCOME: MORE THAN $61,900								
Less than 2 yrs. old	12,550	4,990	1,370	1,520	590	640	1,880	1,560
3 to 5 yrs. old	12,840	4,960	1,550	1,500	580	620	2,050	1,580
6 to 8 yrs. old	12,710	4,880	1,870	1,610	630	700	1,410	1,610
9 to 11 yrs. old	12,600	4,670	2,170	1,680	690	760	980	1,650
12 to 14 yrs. old	13,450	4,900	2,280	1,800	1,140	760	750	1,820
15 to 17 yrs. old	13,800	4,470	2,400	2,180	1,030	800	1,330	1,590

[1] Expenses include personal care items, entertainment, and reading materials.

Source: Dept. of Agriculture, Center for Nutrition Policy and Promotion, *Expenditures on Children by Families, 1999 Annual Report.*

```
237%   |◄ ◄  16 of 36  ► ►|   5.76 x 9.18 in
```

by two-parent families, and ends with Average Annual Expenditures of All Consumer Units, by either Metropolitan Area or region.

If you ever need to know how expensive it is to raise children, just look at the table Annual Expenditure per Child by Husband-Wife Families, shown in Figure 6.3. The table, from the 2000 edition, tracks how much poor, middle-class, and well-to-do families spend on children of different ages. For example, the figure shows that in 1999 poor families (<$36,800 income per year) spent over $7,000 per year per child on teens age 15 to 17 years old. Middle-class families ($36,800 to $61,900) spent over $9,500 on each teen, while well-to-do families ($61,900+) spent $13,800 per year, or almost double what poor families spent. Given there are usually two children (the mean is 1.85) in a typical two-parent family with offspring, the amount of money spent on children adds up very quickly.[4]

Managers needing to negotiate relocation packages should examine Average Annual Expenditures of All Consumer Units, by Metropolitan Area, which lists spending patterns for major United States cities. Moving an employee from one area to another often involves a salary readjustment since the cost of living varies dramatically from city to city. How much is a reasonable

[4]By this point you should be able to find the answer to "how many children do married couples have?" in the *Statistical Abstract*. If you have difficulty, look in the *Abstract*'s Population chapter.

FIGURE 6.4

Typical Amount Spent by a Household in Various Major Cities

```
Acrobat Reader - [StatAbstract2000_IncomeSpendingWealth_Sec14.pdf]          _ □ ×
File  Edit  Document  View  Window  Help                                     _ 8 ×
```

No. 735. Average Annual Expenditures of All Consumer Units by Metropolitan Area: 1997-98

[In dollars. Metropolitan areas defined June 30, 1983. CMSA=Consolidated Metropolitan Statistical Area; MSA=Metropolitan Statistical Area; PMSA=Primary Metropolitan Statistical Area. See text, Section 1, Population, and Appendix II. See headnote, Table 738]

Metropolitan area	Total expendi-tures [1]	Food	Housing				Transportation				Health care
			Total [1]	Shel-ter	Utility, fuels [2]		Total [1]	Vehicle pur-chases	Gaso-line and motor oil		
Anchorage, AK MSA	$49,510	6,469	16,306	9,805	2,557		9,617	4,152	1,284		2,030
Atlanta, GA MSA	$39,315	4,010	13,481	7,716	3,040		8,787	4,287	1,158		1,872
Baltimore, MD MSA	$35,552	4,793	11,949	7,304	2,361		5,493	2,236	952		1,600
Boston-Lawrence-Salem, MA-NH CMSA	$38,029	4,542	14,799	9,370	2,536		6,145	2,274	1,020		1,693
Chicago-Gary-Lake County, IL-IN-WI CMSA	$36,497	4,978	13,071	7,695	2,598		5,859	2,557	982		1,976
Cincinnati-Hamilton, OH-KY-IN CMSA	$36,772	5,055	12,091	6,784	2,389		6,481	2,704	1,109		2,312
Cleveland-Akron-Lorain, OH CMSA	$36,450	5,027	11,721	6,345	2,604		6,658	3,030	939		1,518
Dallas-Fort Worth, TX CMSA	$44,182	5,994	13,315	7,200	2,907		8,985	4,701	1,290		2,102
Denver-Boulder-Greeley, CO CMSA	$42,862	5,119	14,997	8,733	2,128		7,846	2,781	1,099		1,713
Detroit-Ann Arbor, MI CMSA	$35,658	5,057	11,789	6,809	2,505		7,069	2,629	1,055		1,604
Honolulu, HI MSA	$42,636	6,206	14,775	10,233	2,011		6,845	2,394	1,111		1,905
Houston-Galveston-Brazoria, TX CMSA	$40,017	4,906	12,231	6,536	2,802		9,118	4,657	1,254		1,935
Kansas City, MO-Kansas City, KS CMSA	$35,890	5,490	11,334	6,036	2,667		6,686	3,005	1,144		2,056
Los Angeles-Long Beach, CA PMSA	$41,597	5,060	15,562	10,078	2,321		7,696	2,870	1,185		1,590
Miami-Fort Lauderdale, FL CMSA	$35,131	4,317	12,911	7,815	2,662		6,973	2,819	952		1,418
Milwaukee, WI PMSA	$36,310	4,537	13,333	8,114	2,224		6,176	2,599	1,036		1,806
Minneapolis-St. Paul, MN-WI MSA	$47,198	5,607	14,766	8,135	2,292		9,129	4,117	1,258		2,184
New York-Northern New Jersey-Long Island, NY-NJ-CT CMSA	$41,103	6,090	15,153	9,711	2,501		6,293	2,030	870		1,873
Philadelphia-Wilmington-Trenton, PA-NJ-DE-MD CMSA	$38,131	4,134	14,713	9,428	2,821		7,159	2,978	1,015		1,682
Phoenix-Mesa, AZ MSA	$37,504	4,744	12,956	7,477	2,577		7,236	3,277	1,025		1,736
Pittsburgh-Beaver Valley, PA CMSA	$36,239	5,029	11,170	5,329	2,609		6,572	2,909	946		1,798
Portland-Vancouver, OR-WA CMSA	$40,685	5,648	13,315	8,074	2,044		7,266	3,559	993		1,845
San Diego, CA MSA	$39,917	4,979	15,388	10,037	1,990		6,713	2,394	1,091		1,791
San Francisco-Oakland-San Jose, CA CMSA	$47,458	6,377	16,052	10,467	2,276		7,754	2,799	1,179		1,781
Seattle-Tacoma, WA CMSA	$43,251	5,461	15,310	9,637	2,272		7,880	3,306	1,221		1,644

```
237%    19 of 36    5.76 x 9.19 in
```

increase?[5] The numbers in this table provide one method for calculating an employee's financial needs. For example, the version of this table in the 2000 edition, shown in Figure 6.4, reveals that in 1998 consumers in the Miami-Fort Lauderdale area spent $7,815 on shelter, while those in San Francisco spent $10,467. Hence, housing costs will be one-third more for employees being moved from southern Florida to the Bay Area.

When calculating salary readjustments from Consumer Expenditure Survey information, you should use percentage changes, **not** absolute amounts. Relocations often involve senior-level employees whose expenditures exceed the average consumer values shown in this table. Another key point to understand is that the metropolitan areas shown in the tables cover very wide geographic areas. For example, the boundaries of the New York City CMSA extend deep into Connecticut, New Jersey, and Long Island. This table is not designed to provide accurate cost-of-living adjustments for moving in or out of high-cost center-city areas, like Manhattan.

Practice Question

In which region (Northeast, Midwest, South, or West) do families spend the most on reading materials, like books, magazines, and newspapers?

---

[5]Few workers will agree to a salary reduction just because they are being relocated to a lower cost area.

FIGURE 6.5
Consumer
Expenditure
Survey Homepage

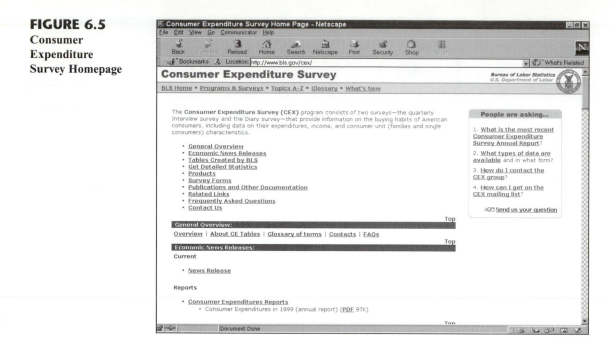

<table>
<tr><td>

**Practice
Question**

You need to move an employee from the New York City metropolitan area to the Pittsburgh area. What type of salary adjustment is needed?

Detailed Spending Information

The Bureau of Labor Statistics periodically publishes more detailed spending information in thick bulletins with titles like Consumer Expenditure Survey, 1996–97.[6] While these bulletins are excellent, they are hard to find even in many research libraries. Fortunately, the tables from these bulletins are also available online. To get detailed printed information go to the Consumer Expenditure Survey's homepage (**http://www.bls.gov/cex**), shown in Figure 6.5.

Once at the homepage, select the link labeled Tables Created by BLS. This presents spending data using the following types of tables: standard, expenditure shares, aggregate expenditure shares, cross-tabulated, metropolitan statistical areas, regions, high income, and multiyear. For business use, the most helpful information is found by selecting the Multiyear entry at the bottom of the list. Multiyear provides the data to answer the chapter's first scenario in which you work for a children's clothing retailer with lagging sales. Currently, there are two sets of multiyear tables, one until 1992 and the other for years

---

[6]The 1996–97 edition is BLS Report 935.

FIGURE 6.6
Consumer
Expenditure Survey's
Multiyear Table

Netscape — http://www.bls.gov/cex/2000/standard/multiyr.pdf

Average annual expenditures and characteristics of all consumer units, Consumer Expenditure Survey, 1993-00 - Continued

Item	1993	1994	1995	1996	1997	1998	1999	2000
Furniture	317	318	327	321	387	377	365	391
Floor coverings	87	120	177	101	78	144	44	44
Major appliances	143	149	155	162	169	164	183	189
Small appliances, miscellaneous housewares	87	81	85	84	92	80	102	87
Miscellaneous household equipment	493	581	557	607	707	729	692	731
Apparel and services	1,676	1,644	1,704	1,752	1,729	1,674	1,743	1,856
Men and boys	426	395	425	423	407	399	421	440
Men, 16 and over	335	305	329	330	323	314	328	344
Boys, 2 to 15	90	90	96	93	84	85	93	96
Women and girls	658	652	660	718	680	651	655	725
Women, 16 and over	566	552	559	607	574	548	548	607
Girls, 2 to 15	93	100	101	111	106	103	107	118
Children under 2	79	80	81	82	77	73	67	82
Footwear	249	254	278	298	315	281	303	343
Other apparel products and services	264	264	259	230	250	270	297	266
Transportation	5,453	6,044	6,014	6,382	6,457	6,616	7,011	7,417

beyond 1992. Scroll down halfway through either table until you see the heading "Apparel and services." Under this heading are the entries "Boys, 2 to 15" and "Girls, 2 to 15." The version of this table for 1993 to 2000, part of which is shown in Figure 6.6, is easy to understand, with the numbers in the first column representing spending in 1993, the next column 1994 and so forth. For example, beside "Boys, 2 to 15" is 90 followed by a 90. These numbers mean that in 1993 and 1994 the typical family spent $90 a year on boys clothing and alterations.

Do not use the multiyear table's values directly. Prices and income in the United States have changed dramatically since the 1980s. For example, the tables show that income before taxes rose from $23,464 in 1984 up to $44,649 in 2000 (not shown), a gain of 90%. To adjust for these changes, you can either remove inflation's effects by using the Consumer Price Index, discussed in Chapter 10, or work in percentage terms. Since both methods in this case produce similar answers, let's use the percentage adjustment to understand how it works.

To use the percentage adjustment, you need to answer the question, "What fraction of total spending does children's clothing constitute?" To put clothing in percentage terms, simply divide the amount spent on children's clothing by that year's total expenditures. The graph in Figure 6.7 shows quite clearly that the typical family is spending slightly less over time on boys' clothing and

FIGURE 6.7

Percent of Total Expenditures Devoted to Children's Clothing

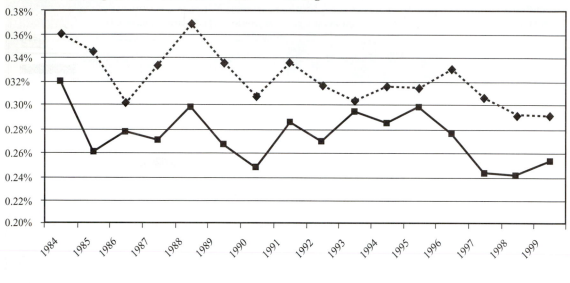

- - ◆ - - Girls' Clothing   ━━■━━ Boys' Clothing

TABLE 6.3

Standard Consumer Expenditure Survey Tables Provided Online

Age of reference person	Occupation of reference person
Composition of consumer unit	Origin of reference person
Education of reference person	Quintiles of income before taxes
Housing tenure	Region of residence
Income before taxes	Size of consumer unit
Number of earners in consumer unit	Selected age of reference person

dramatically less since 1988 on girls'. Since the total number of children in the United States has been growing by only 1 percent a year since 1984,[7] your company's positive sales growth is a major accomplishment.

Another very useful set of precreated tables is found under the "Standard" heading. Under Standard are 12 predefined tables for every survey year, shown in Table 6.3. For example, selecting the Age of Reference Person table breaks down spending into eight different categories based on the household head's age.

---

[7]See tables in the *Statistical Abstract* labeled "Resident Population by Age and Sex."

FIGURE 6.8
Custom Table
Generator for
Consumer
Expenditure Survey

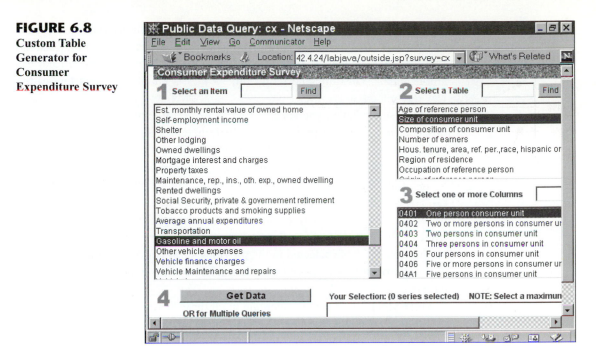

Practice
Question

The United States Poultry Council hired you to research consumer spending. It is concerned that the Pork Council's ad campaign, "Pork the Other White Meat," is luring consumers away. It wants to know if consumers are spending relatively more or less on poultry as compared to pork.

**Practice
Question**

Many business commentators have expressed concern over the growing indebtedness of United States families. What percentage of the typical family's after-tax income was spent on mortgage interest and charges in 1985, 1990, 1995, and presently?

Custom Spending Tabulations

When the *Statistical Abstract* and predefined tables do not have exactly what you need, try creating your own tables. To create custom tables from the Consumer Expenditure Survey, go to the survey's homepage (**http://www.bls. gov/cex**) and select the choice Get Detailed Statistics followed by Create Customized Tables (one screen). The main data query screen, shown in Figure 6.8, lets you design a custom table using a simple four-step process. Using this custom table generator, let's answer the chapter's second scenario and estimate how much various types of households spend on gasoline.

In the first step, from a list of almost 140 different items you must choose the specific category, such as the amounts spent on reading matter, personal care products, and floor coverings, that you need information on. For our example select "Gasoline and motor oil," which is about three-quarters of the way down the list.

In the second step, you specify 1 of 11 different demographic characteristics, such as region of the country, occupation, education, age of the household head, and household size. For our example, select "Size of consumer unit," which breaks spending data down by the number of people in the family.

The third step provides a method for selecting subcharacteristics of interest. For example, if you picked age in the second step, the system presents the following choices for the reference person; under age 25, 10-year age intervals from 25 to 74, and age 75 and over. Items on this third list change depending on the specific table selected in the previous step. For our example, highlight the "One-person consumer unit" to track gasoline expenditures by single people.

Once you have selected something in all three boxes, the Get Data button at the bottom of the screen becomes available. Pressing this button causes the custom table generator to display the output seen in Figure 6.9, which shows that single people spend around $500 per year on gasoline and motor oil.

FIGURE 6.9
**Results for
Custom Consumer
Expenditure Survey
Query**

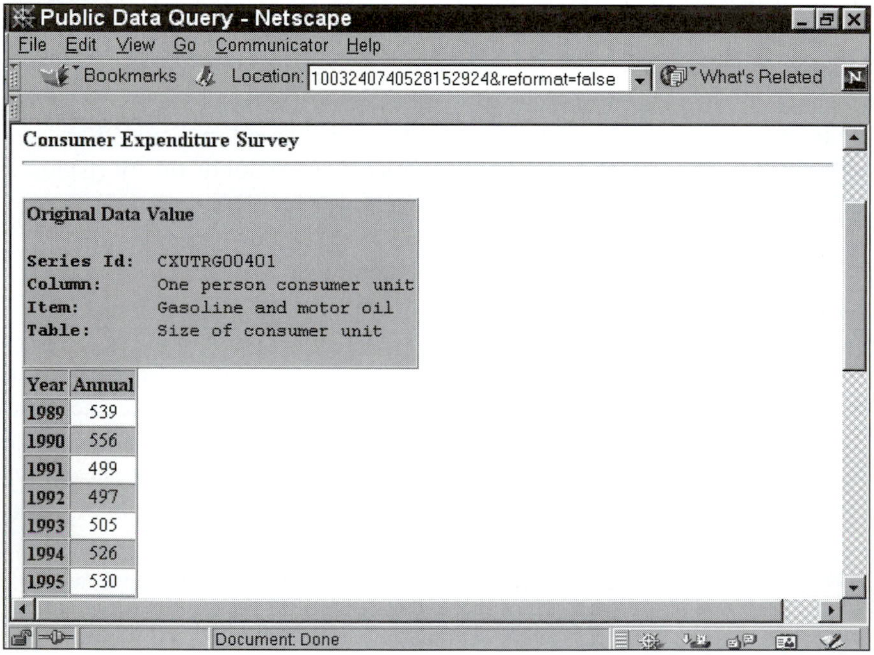

Public Data Query - Netscape

File   Edit   View   Go   Communicator   Help

Bookmarks   Location: 10032407405281529924&reformat=false   What's Related

Consumer Expenditure Survey

Original Data Value

Series Id:	CXUTRG00401
Column:	One person consumer unit
Item:	Gasoline and motor oil
Table:	Size of consumer unit

Year	Annual
1989	539
1990	556
1991	499
1992	497
1993	505
1994	526
1995	530

Document: Done

If you need information for earlier years or want to change other methods of viewing the data, select the reformat button at the output page's top. Pressing this button, shown in Figure 6.10, also provides a simple way of obtaining information back to 1984.

There is one very important idea to remember when examining custom tables; the **data are not adjusted for inflation.** If you create a table that contains spending amounts for multiple years, remember that the prices of most products have changed over time. Remove inflation's effects either by using the Consumer Price Index (CPI) discussed in Chapter 10 or by using percentages as we did earlier in the children's clothing example.

Practice Question

As a financial planner and advisor, you are constantly asked about parents' ability to save money for their children's college education. How much money does a single person earn, spend, and save? How much does a married couple with children earn, spend, and save?

Micro Data

The custom table generator and the preformatted online tables have one drawback—reported spending is the average of *all* households, not just households making purchases. For example, using the custom table generator you

FIGURE 6.10
Consumer Expenditure Survey Reformatting Screen

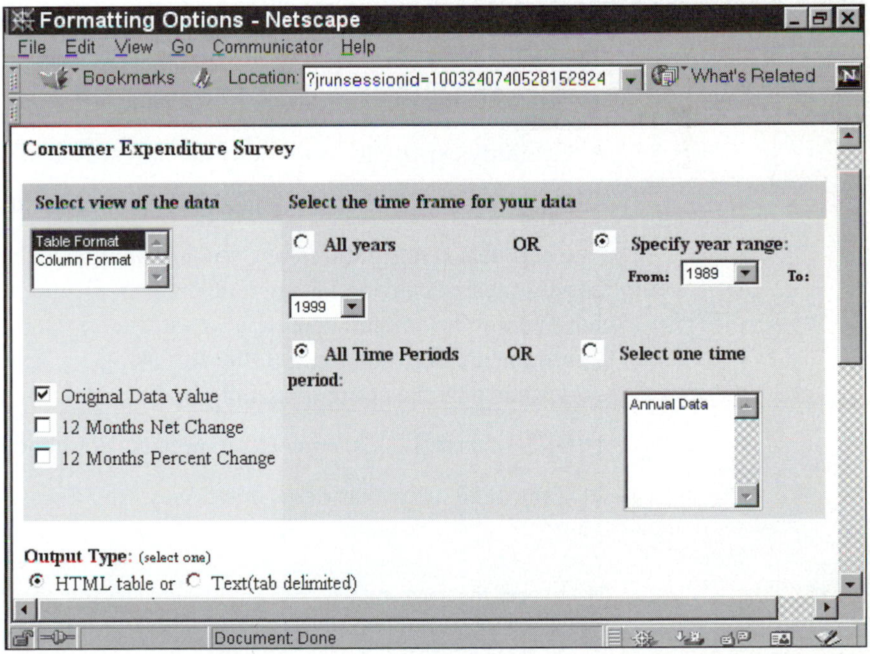

can find that in 1998 the average United States household spent $1,383 on new car and truck purchases. Since many United States households did not buy a new car or truck in 1998, their expenditure of zero is combined with families spending tens of thousands of dollars. Many marketing managers do not want the all-family average but instead want the average amount spent by consumers who actually purchased a new car or truck. To get this kind of information from the survey you must analyze the micro data.

Analyzing micro data is not something most managers have the time or skill to handle on their own. However, knowing what is available is important since it is easy to hire people to process the data. Current Consumer Expenditure Survey micro data are only available on CD-ROM and are not available online.[8] Additionally, analyzing micro data takes time and a working knowledge of a statistical package like SAS, SPSS, or RATS.

If you need very precise details about United States families' spending habits, however, the micro data provide a wealth of information. First, since the micro data contain records for each individual household, it is simple to examine only those households that purchased the item of interest, such as a new car or truck. This ensures you produce figures based only on actual buyers, instead of all families.

Micro data also provide spending information broken down into finer categories. Let's assume you are interested in spending on alcohol. The custom and previously prepared tables only provide data on total yearly alcohol spending. Extracting micro data, however, enables you to split total alcohol spending along the following time and purchase dimensions.

• Quarterly expenditures for beer and wine served at home.

• Quarterly expenditures for other alcohol served at home.

• Quarterly expenditures for alcohol drunk outside the home.

Charitable contribution data provide another example of the finer categories that are available in the micro data. While the prepared tables provide a summary of the amount households contribute each year, the micro data break this summary information into the following six specific contribution categories made by the entire household in the past 12 months.

1. Gifts of cash, bonds, or stocks to persons not in household.

2. Contributions to charities (United Way, Red Cross, etc.).

---

[8]If you need the micro data, each CD-ROM currently costs about $145 and contains one year of data. To order this CD-ROM call the Consumer Expenditure Survey office at (202) 691-6900, or e-mail it at cexinfo@bls.gov.

3. Contributions to church or other religious organizations.

4. Contributions to educational organizations.

5. Political contributions.

6. Contributions to other organizations.

Hence, using the micro data you can understand not only the types of families that make donations but also to whom the money is donated.

Finally, by analyzing the micro data, managers can examine answers from the Interview and Diary Surveys separately. Managers interested in big-ticket purchases like automobiles should analyze just the Interview Survey, while those interested in only small purchases like specific food, personal care products, and nonprescription drugs should use the Diary Survey.[9] For managers interested in spending between these two extremes, comparing answers in the Interview and Diary Surveys provide a simple method of tracking how much the typical family thought they were spending over time versus how much families actually recorded spending.

Summary

How much money do people spend on various products? The Consumer Expenditure Survey provides answers to this question. This yearly survey gives marketing, sales, and product development managers a wealth of free information on the United States consumers' spending habits for both small items, via the Diary Survey, and big-ticket purchases, via the Interview Survey. The simplest way to access this spending information is at the Consumer Expenditure Survey's homepage (**http://www.bls.gov/cex**). Managers should first try the Standard option under the Tables heading, which breaks down spending based on predefined demographic categories. They can also use the Create Customized Tables link to create personalized answers. Whatever way the data are accessed, using this survey is a fast and cheap method for tracking how much consumers spend on various products.

[9]Since there is a lot of information in both surveys, each CD-ROM is broken into major sets of variables. The first set, which lists the characteristics of each family answering the survey, is named FMLY. The second set, which lists the characteristics of each family member, is called MEMB. The families' income variables are called either DTAB (for annual income) or ITAB (for monthly income). The last set of files lists the specific expenditures. Files that begin with EXPN list weekly expenditures while MTAB variables detail monthly expenditures.

Chapter 7

People Details

The previous three chapters described the demographic, income, and spending information available from cross-sectional or single snapshot sources. Where do you go if even more detail is needed on people's lives? Detailed long-term information can be found in longitudinal surveys. Longitudinal surveys follow the same individual or family over long periods of time and show how people change.

When is longitudinal information useful? Let's assume you work for a large family-oriented restaurant chain. Using the Consumer Expenditure Survey (see Chapter 6), it is easy to track the amount of money families spend eating out in any given year. But how will restaurant spending change if another baby boom or bust occurs? There is no way to answer these questions using Consumer Expenditure Survey data. However, a longitudinal survey easily provides the answers since these kinds of surveys track how a family's habits change when children are born, grow up, and finally leave home.

There are numerous longitudinal surveys. One of the largest and most well-known is the Framingham Heart Study,[1] which by following over 5,000 people since 1948, showed that smoking, obesity, and physical inactivity cause heart disease. While heeding the Heart Study's suggestions such as do not smoke, eat in moderation, and get regular exercise helps business managers live longer, the Heart Study is not useful for many other business purposes.

This chapter provides details on four longitudinal studies that are useful for general business purposes: the Panel Study of Income Dynamics (PSID), the Health and Retirement Survey—Asset and Health Dynamics among the Oldest Old (HRS-AHEAD), the Survey of Income and Program Participation (SIPP), and the National Longitudinal Surveys (NLS). Since the name of each

[1]Details on this survey are available online at **http://www.nhlbi.nih.gov/about/framingham**.

FIGURE 7.1
Panel Study of
Income Dynamics
(PSID) Homepage

Copyright the University of
Michigan Board of Regents.
Used with permission.

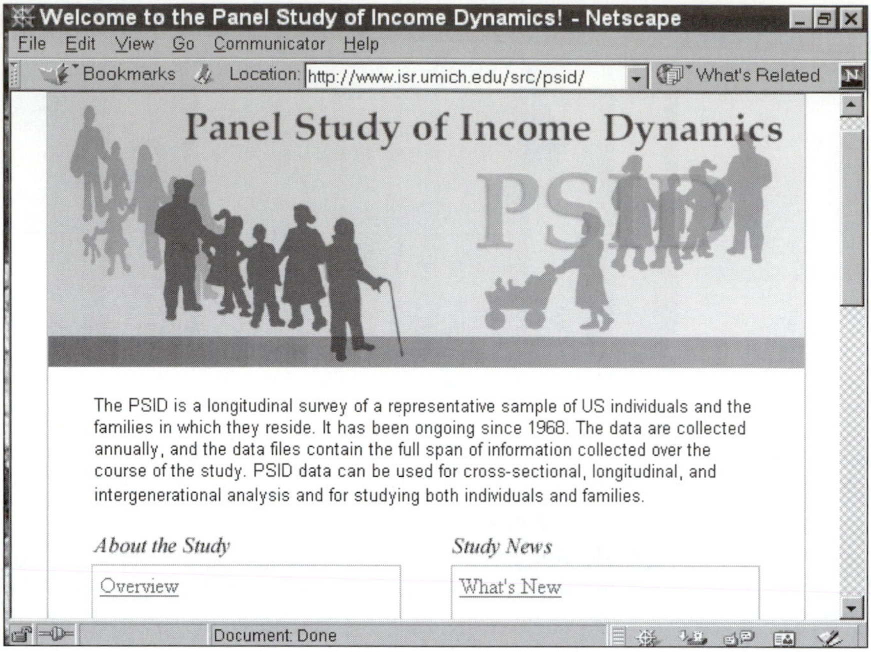

survey is a mouthful, all are commonly called just by their abbreviations. Each study provides a different kind of information about the demographic, income, and spending patterns of United States residents. The chapter ends by showing you where to find longitudinal information for other countries.

Before reading the rest of this chapter, it is important to understand that all longitudinal surveys have one common drawback. Because longitudinal surveys consist of multiple interviews, processing the data that follows an individual or family over time is much more complicated than processing data from a single cross-sectional survey. While longitudinal surveys provide information that goes well beyond the sources discussed so far, managers extracting and analyzing data from these surveys need some advanced technical skills. To give you an idea of what is involved, the end of the chapter shows how to process data from the NLS.

Since longitudinal surveys are complex, most managers needing information from these sources should familiarize themselves with this chapter's contents but let specialists do the actual data processing and statistical analysis.

PSID

The Panel Study of Income Dynamics (PSID) is designed to examine how families change over time.[2] This survey began in 1968 with interviews of

[2] The PSID is conducted by the University of Michigan's Institute for Social Research.

5,000 randomly selected United States households. Managers using the survey get a very detailed picture of how families change since the chosen households were interviewed yearly from 1968 to 1996 and every other year since. The PSID homepage, shown in Figure 7.1, contains general information, data, and documentation. The homepage is located at **http://www.isr.umich.edu/ src/psid**.

Since families are not static, the number of families followed in the PSID both grows and shrinks in each interview. In households where divorce occurs or children leave, the survey grows by tracking these new families. The survey shrinks when all family members in a household die. Because of these changes, by 2001 the PSID's sample had grown to more than 7,000 households.

The survey offers business managers the ability to track income, housing, food expenditures, health status, working habits, and demographic changes over very long periods of time. In the introduction scenario you imagined working for a large restaurant chain. The PSID has summary variables that track family size, composition, income, and restaurant spending year after year. This means that the PSID provides a free source of information for tracking how a family's restaurant habits change when children are born, grow up, and finally leave home.[3]

Health care managers will also find that the PSID is a wonderful resource. Since the mid-1980s, the study has asked individuals about their health status, out-of-pocket medical expenditures, and insurance coverage. In addition, the PSID data set has a new Medicare claims file. For each respondent over age 55 who gives permission, the PSID extracts all Medicare claim forms from the federal government's administrative records. Looking at the data from these forms enables health care managers to track not only usage but also total health care costs.

A third example of the unique data found in the PSID is the questions it asked the household head about military combat experience.[4] Business school lore states that the great leadership of combat-hardened veterans dramatically improved American industrial performance after World War II. Using the PSID questions, you can personally check whether combat experience really alters work traits.

These three examples are only a small portion of the topics covered by the PSID surveys. To see the complete list go to the PSID homepage

---

[3]By using PSID data instead of other data sources on income and restaurant expenditures, you are implicitly removing the effects of foreign travelers and business meals on the restaurant industry. If your chain caters primarily to families, eliminating these effects is exactly what you want. Conversely, if your restaurant caters primarily to visitors and individuals on expense accounts, using the PSID is the wrong choice.

[4]These questions were asked in the 1994 survey but cover the household head's entire life.

(**http://www.isr.umich.edu/src/psid**) and pick the link labeled Overview. This link not only shows the topics that have been included but also explains who participates and how the survey has changed over time.

HRS and AHEAD

The Health and Retirement Survey (HRS) and Asset and Health Dynamics Among the Oldest Old (AHEAD) are a pair of surveys designed to provide information about the elderly population. These surveys are important to business because the elderly are currently the fastest growing demographic group in the country. The HRS began in 1992 with a random group of individuals born during the Great Depression (1931 to 1941) who were approaching retirement age. The AHEAD survey began a year later and selected people at least 70 years old in order to provide details on the country's oldest citizens. The HRS-AHEAD homepage (**http://www.umich.edu/~hrswww**), shown in Figure 7.2, contains general information about the survey, data, and documentation.

Respondents answer these surveys roughly every two years. Since the two surveys initially interviewed over 20,000 individuals, managers using these

FIGURE 7.2

Health and Retirement Study (HRS) and Asset and Health Dynamics among the Oldest Old (AHEAD) Homepage

Copyright the University of Michigan Board of Regents. Used with permission.

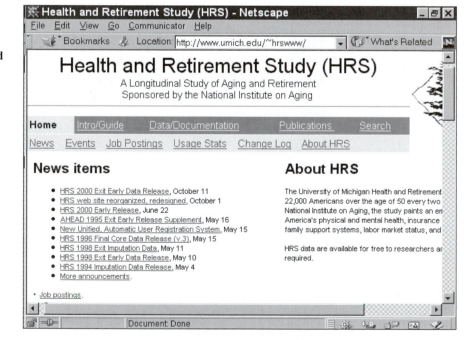

data have a tremendous amount of information about the elderly. To save money, the two surveys were combined into one beginning in 1998. Additionally, since a number of the original elderly respondents are now deceased, the program began surveying two additional groups of elderly respondents in 1998. These new groups provide information about the retirement experiences of children who grew up during the Great Depression (born before 1924) and babies born during World War II.

Business managers care about the elderly not only because they are the fastest growing demographic group, but also because they are the richest. Families headed by someone between 65 and 74 had a median net worth of $146,500 in 1998.[5] Compared to all other age ranges, the just retired are on average the wealthiest individuals in the country.

HRS-AHEAD data provide financial services managers with detailed information on the amount of, composition of, and changes in asset holdings among the elderly. Each survey asks a lengthy set of questions about the amount of financial holdings like stocks, bonds, and treasury bills as well as nonfinancial holdings, such as real estate. In addition to these questions, the HRS collects detailed data on annuities, which are a rapidly growing financial market product. Combining these wealth questions with the extensive demographic data provides managers with a complete picture of what assets and liabilities are held by different groups of elderly individuals. Since the HRS-AHEAD is a longitudinal survey, managers using these data also have the ability to track how the elderly change their wealth holdings over time.

Other information in HRS-AHEAD is useful for financial planners and lawyers who specialize in estate planning. For example, a number of survey questions ask whether the respondent has written a will or created a trust agreement. Using these questions and demographic answers, estate planners can determine exactly which types of elderly individuals prepare these documents. Moreover, questions in the survey that ask about the will's beneficiaries and provisions provide estimates of how much the elderly expect to bequeath to family members and charity.

These examples are only a small portion of topics covered by the HRS-AHEAD surveys. To see the complete list go to the survey's homepage (**http://www.umich.edu/~hrswww**) and pick the questionnaires link under the heading labeled Data/Documentation.

---

[5]Wealth information from table 3 of Arthur Kennickell, Martha Starr-McCluer, and Brian J. Surette, "Recent Changes in United States Family Finances: Results from the 1998 Survey of Consumer Finances," *Federal Reserve Bulletin,* January 2000.

FIGURE 7.3
Survey of Income
and Program
Participation (SIPP)
Homepage

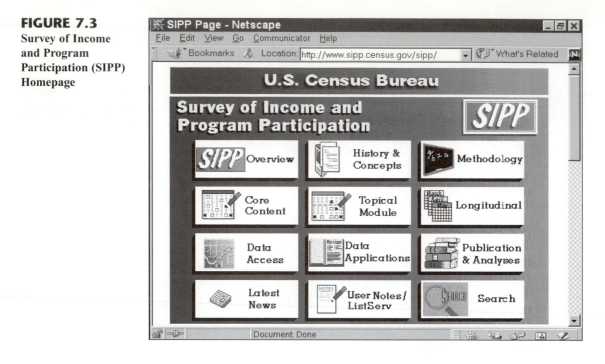

SIPP

Does your business need very accurate income data? The Survey of Income and Program Participation (SIPP) provides extremely accurate data down to the month. While all the other longitudinal surveys discussed in this chapter follow an individual or family until death, participation in the SIPP is limited to a range of between two and four years because families are surveyed so many times. Details about the SIPP are found on its homepage (**http://www. sipp.census.gov/sipp**), shown in Figure 7.3.

The SIPP began in October of 1983 by interviewing almost 20,000 households every four months over a three-year period. Since then the SIPP has created 11 groups, or panels, of households who participate every four months for between two and four years.[6] The survey asks a set of core questions, which determine the family's income, tax payments, wealth, and participation in any government aid program such as food stamps or unemployment insurance. Additional questions provide information on work status, child care problems, child support payments and schooling so that businesses have a very detailed short run picture of the family.

[6]A 12th panel is planned for 2001.

TABLE 7.1
Percentage of Families Owning Various Types of Assets by Household Head's Age

Source: SIPP wealth analysis for 1995 (**http://www.census.gov/hhes/www/wealth.html**).

	<35 years	35 to 44	45 to 54	55 to 64	65 to 69	70 to 74	75+ years
Checking account	46.8%	48.9%	53.2%	47.6%	41.2%	39.3%	36.2%
Stocks—mutual funds	13.3%	19.3%	25.8%	24.1%	27.2%	26.1%	22.0%
Own a business	7.8%	13.3%	16.1%	12.2%	7.0%	4.7%	1.5%
Own vehicles	88.2%	92.2%	93.2%	91.5%	89.4%	87.2%	75.4%
Own home	38.2%	64.9%	73.2%	78.6%	81.0%	80.8%	72.5%
Rental property	2.1%	5.6%	10.0%	12.3%	10.3%	9.1%	8.5%
U.S. savings bonds	15.3%	22.0%	22.5%	20.6%	21.8%	16.4%	10.0%

Managers in financial services can use the very detailed income and wealth questions of the SIPP to determine the profiles of typical clients. For example, Table 7.1 uses SIPP data to show the type of assets owned at various stages in life.

SIPP data are also useful to managers thinking about opening on-site day care or managers already in the day care industry. SIPP information on child care patterns, income, and work status can help you to accurately estimate the amount parents can pay and their expected day care usage.

Homebuilders are a third example of businesses who will find the SIPP useful. Using SIPP data, builders can precisely compute the home price people can afford. Matching construction costs to affordability prevents completed homes from sitting vacant for months or even years waiting for a qualified buyer. The Census Bureau shows how to calculate housing affordability in the report "Who Can Afford to Buy a House?" The report's Table 3 uses SIPP data to determine what boosts the ability of renters to buy a home. The table shows a large drop in mortgage rates of 3 percentage points only slightly increases the number of renters able to purchase a home. However, giving renters $5,000 toward a down payment more than doubles the number of renters able to purchase a home.[7] Hence, the best way for builders to move unsold moderately priced homes is to provide buyers with down payment "gifts."

The SIPP's original purpose was to improve the accuracy of the income measures provided by the March CPS Supplement, previously discussed in the Chapter 5. The March CPS, which annually asks respondents about their

[7] The numbers are from Census Bureau Current Housing Report H121/971 (July 1997) by Howard Savage. The report is under "Publications" at the SIPP's website. The mortgage rate drop increases the percentage able to buy from 11.4% to 12.3%. The extra down payment increases the percentage able to buy from 11.4% to 25.8%.

income over the previous calendar year, has three problems. First, small or irregular payments are often forgotten since the survey asks respondents to remember money they received up to 15 months earlier. Because respondents answer the SIPP multiple times each year, they are less likely to forget small or irregular payments.

Second, many households change composition during the year as individuals die, move in, or move out. If the composition of the household changes, the March CPS does not accurately determine the family's income. It makes an incorrect calculation because it simply totals the amount received in the previous year by all individuals living in the home during March. For families who have lost members over the past year, this procedure understates the total amount of money earned by the household, while families who gained members have their income overstated. For example, if a working female marries a working male in October, the March CPS would record the family as if two income-producing adults lived in the residence for the entire 12 months, even though this was true for only three months. Since the SIPP carefully tracks both income and household changes, its income calculations are neither over- nor underinflated.

The last problem is that the March CPS does not collect wealth information. Knowing about wealth is important because assets are used to supplement income during retirement, layoffs, and periods of sickness. For business managers working in companies or industries that extend credit to individuals, such as credit card companies, banks, and mortgage companies, the SIPP's detailed income and wealth data provide a great source of information.

These examples are only a small portion of topics covered by the SIPP. More details are found on the survey's homepage (**http://www.sipp.census. gov/sipp**) under the headings SIPP Overview and Core Content.

NLS

The National Longitudinal Surveys (NLS) primarily track the lives of individuals from childhood into adulthood. Unlike the HRS-AHEAD, which follows people at the end of their lives, the NLS starts near the beginning. The NLS program includes groups of respondents who were teenagers in the 1960s, the late 1970s, and the mid-1990s. Business managers can track detailed information on employment, rate of pay, job search, training, and education. The surveys also contain background data on family structure, income, wealth, health, and demographics, as well as more unique information on topics like hair color, height, weight, drug and alcohol usage, to name only a few items. The NLS homepage (**http://www.bls.gov/nls**) is pictured in Figure 7.4.

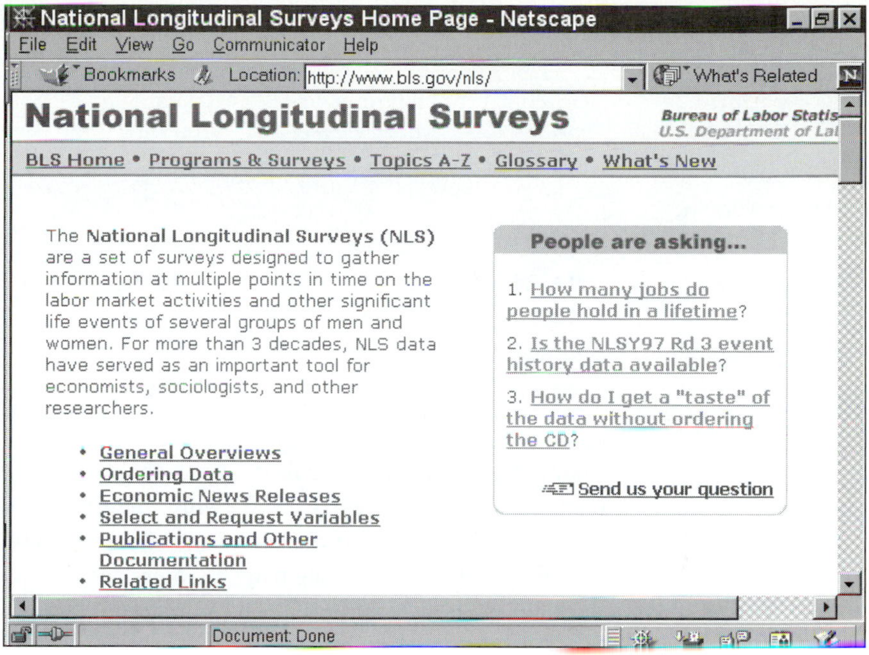

FIGURE 7.4
National
Longitudinal Surveys
(NLS) Homepage

The NLS did not begin as a method for tracking how teens age. Instead the surveys began during the mid-1960s because the United States Department of Labor noticed that the labor force participation rates of African-American males were declining over time. Existing data sets, such as the Current Population Survey (CPS), did not collect enough historical data to explain the downward trend. Ohio State University submitted a proposal for a longitudinal survey designed to answer this question and to explore the variety of factors responsible for the labor market behavior of men about ready to retire.[8] One by-product of selecting a random sample of men approaching retirement was a list of households containing teenage children. Using this list, it was relatively inexpensive to begin surveying teenagers. The success of the 1960s surveys led to the formation of additional surveys covering teenagers from other generations.

The NLS is not one survey but instead is a collection of seven different surveys, each tracking the experiences of a different cohort. Table 7.2 lists the seven cohorts' names and details about their ages and interview status. The

[8]It took a while to collect enough data, but by using NLS data, Donald Parsons showed that the progressive structure of Social Security benefits made not working increasingly attractive to all men but especially to black males ("Racial Trends in Male Labor Force Participation," *American Economic Review,* 1980, and "The Decline in Male Labor Force Participation," *Journal of Political Economy,* 1980).

TABLE 7.2
The NLS Cohorts as of 2002

Cohort	Original Age	Number of Interviews	First Interview	Latest Interview	Original Size
Older men	45–59	13	1966	1990	5,020
Mature women	30–44	20	1967	2001	5,083
Young men	14–24	12	1966	1981	5,225
Young women	14–24	21	1968	2001	5,159
NLSY79	14–21	20	1979	2002	12,686
NLSY79 children	Birth–22	9	1986	2002	≈9,000
NLSY97	12–16	5	1997	2002	8,984

Young Men and Women cohorts track the experiences of people who were teenagers during the early 1960s while the Older Men and Mature Women track the experiences of these teenagers' parents and others of similar ages. The NLSY79 follows young baby boomers, individuals who were teenagers in the late 1970s, while the NLSY79 Children follows the children of young baby boomer mothers. The latest NLS survey is the NLSY97, which tracks people who were teens during the late 1990s. To see the types of questions asked in an NLS survey, go to this book's website and examine the NLSY79 1998 questionnaire.

Creating Custom NLS Tables

As an example of using longitudinal data, let's use the NLS to see how many young baby boomers had ever drunk alcohol by their late teens to early 20s. To answer this question you need to access NLSY79 data.

While currently no NLS data are released online, work is being done during the production of this book to enable Internet access. Presently, all data are released on CD-ROMs, which are distributed by the NLS User Services office at Ohio State University (Telephone: 614 442-7300 or email: usersvc@post office.chrr.ohio-state.edu) for a cost of around $20 for each cohort.

Both the CD-ROM and the planned web interface use a program called NLS Investigator to extract data and documentation.[9] If using a CD-ROM, first install the extraction program and then do the following steps to answer the question.

[9]Some older CD-ROMs were manufactured with a DOS version of this program. If your CD-ROM does not contain the Windows version of the software, download it from **http://www.chrr.ohio-state.edu/manuals/gator**.

FIGURE 7.5

NLS Investigator Top Level Screen

Copyright The Ohio State University. Used with permission.

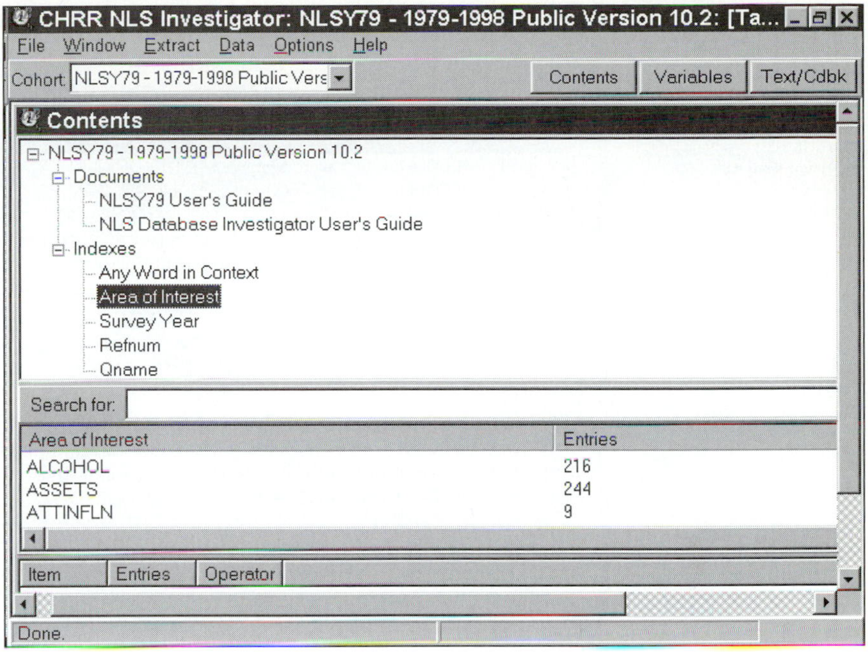

Step 1. Run the extraction program by inserting the CD-ROM into the computer and launching the NLS Investigator. A screen like Figure 7.5 will then appear.

Step 2. Pick the variables of interest. There are five ways to select variables: Any Word in Context, Area of Interest, Survey Year, Reference Number, and Question Name. Unless you have the survey questionnaire in front of you searching by Question Name is not useful. Given the huge number of questions in a single survey, searching by Survey Year or Reference Number is also not useful for a beginner.

Beginners should start by selecting Area of Interest. This will bring up a list of broad categories shown in the bottom of Figure 7.5 such as Alcohol, Assets, Child Care, Health, and Income. Selecting one of these categories picks all questions that relate to this topic from all surveys.

Another popular approach is to pick the Any Word in Context selection. This provides a list of questions, which contains the word or words of your choice. For example, selecting Color on the NLSY79 CD-ROM brings up two questions that asked respondents, "What is your natural hair color?" and "What is your natural eye color?"

Double clicking on the results of either search reveals the list of all associated questions. Figure 7.6 shows the results of double clicking on the Alcohol—Area of Interest. Each survey question is listed by date asked. The

FIGURE 7.6

NLS Investigator List of Variables in the Alcohol Group

Copyright The Ohio State University. Used with permission.

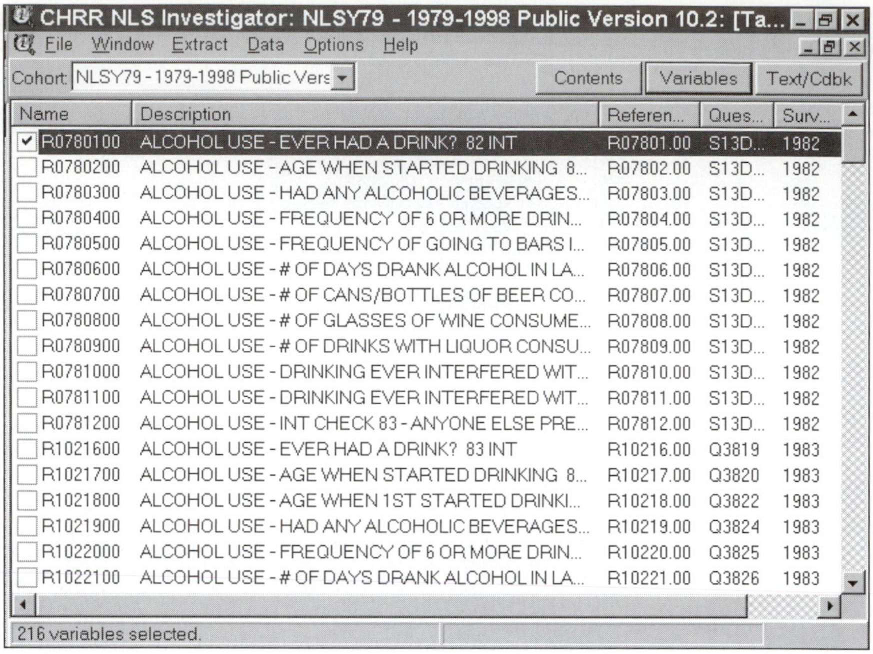

top question in the list is reference number R0780100. This question appeared in the 1982 survey and asked young baby boomers if they had every drunk alcohol. To choose this variable, click on the left-hand side check box, as shown.

Step 3. Make sure you have the correct variable by reading the codebook page. After finding a variable or question that looks interesting, read the question's text by double clicking on the variable's name. Figure 7.7 shows the result of double clicking on our alcohol question, R0780100, which asked young baby boomers if they had ever had a drink. The codebook page shows that the specific question was "Next I'd like to ask you some questions about drinking alcoholic beverages, including beer, wine, and liquor. Have you ever had a drink of an alcoholic beverage?" Additionally, the codebook shows that 11,131 respondents stated Yes they had tried alcohol, 991 stated No they had not tried alcohol, and the remainder either refused to answer the question or were not interviewed.

What does this tell you about the proportion of young baby boomers that have drunk alcohol? If everyone in the country were equally likely to be selected for the sample, then using the ratio of these raw numbers would be fine. However, in almost all major surveys, including the NLS, it is important **not** to base decisions on raw numbers. Using the raw numbers is problematic because everyone in the country did not have the same chance of being selected for the survey. Almost all large-scale national surveys are done

FIGURE 7.7

NLS Investigator
Code Book Page for
Alcohol Use Question

Copyright The Ohio State
University. Used with
permission.

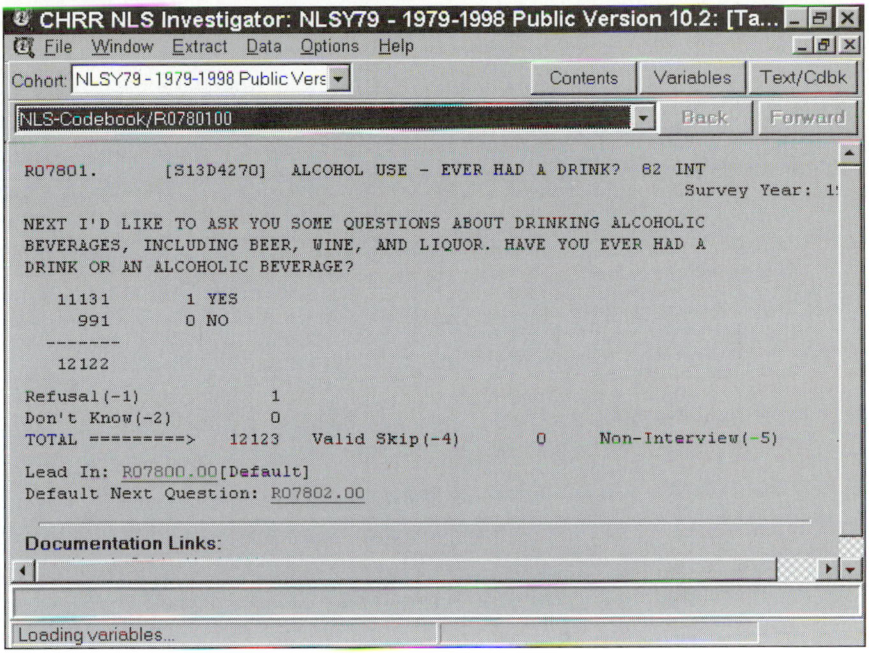

using multistage cluster sampling. These fancy words mean that some groups, geographic areas, or businesses are more likely to be selected than others.[10]

These special sampling methods mean you must adjust raw answers to account for the unequal chances people or businesses had to be selected. Adjusting is not hard. There are two ways to adjust for this special sampling. If you use a statistical package like SAS, SPPS, TSP, RATS, or another commercial software program, save the sampling weight[11] or sample adjustment variable found in every survey. These variables tell the statistical package how to correct for the different probability that people or businesses had of being selected.

---

[10]Survey designers do this both to gain statistical precision and to reduce the cost of fielding the survey. For example, all NLS surveys oversample blacks. This means that any African-American is more likely to be selected for an NLS survey than a white person. Using the raw data, without adjusting, means your results will overrepresent black experiences and underrepresent whites. In the March Demographic Supplement of the CPS (see Chapter 4) Hispanics are oversampled. In annual business surveys, like the Annual Survey of Manufactures (ASM), discussed in Chapter 8, the government automatically includes the largest companies in each industrial sector.

[11]To find the NLS sampling weights quickly, pick "any word in context" and search for "sampling." Beginning users should use just the sampling weight from the first NLS survey.

If you do not use a statistical package, read the survey documentation and determine how many different groups were sampled. For example, in the NLSY79, blacks, whites, and Hispanics each have a different probability of being selected. To bypass the weighting step, just look at answers from these three groups separately. Separating the groups corrects for most sample selection issues. To select this variable for the NLSY79, search using the any word in context function for the string "racial." Then select the variable entitled "R's Racial/Ethnic Cohort from Screener 79 Int."

Step 4. After picking the variables of interest, extract the data. On the pulldown Extract menu choose the option to Run the Extract, which is the window shown in Figure 7.8. If you are using a statistical package, check off the boxes you need under Extract Data File Type and Optional Output Files.

If you are not using a statistical processing package, then pick the Edit Boolean Expression button. The Boolean pick screen, shown below, filters out unwanted answers so the results make sense. The first filter most people use is to eliminate invalid responses. For our example, we want to keep only respondents who either stated Yes (a 1 value) they had a drink or No (a 0 value) they did not. All the extra codes for people who refused (a -1 value) or did not participate in the survey (a -5 value) are irrelevant. The simplest way to get rid of these extraneous cases is to put "R0780100 > = 0" into the Boolean expression. This statement tells the program to ignore all the extra codes for this reference number.

FIGURE 7.8
NLS Investigator Extraction Screen

Copyright The Ohio State University. Used with permission.

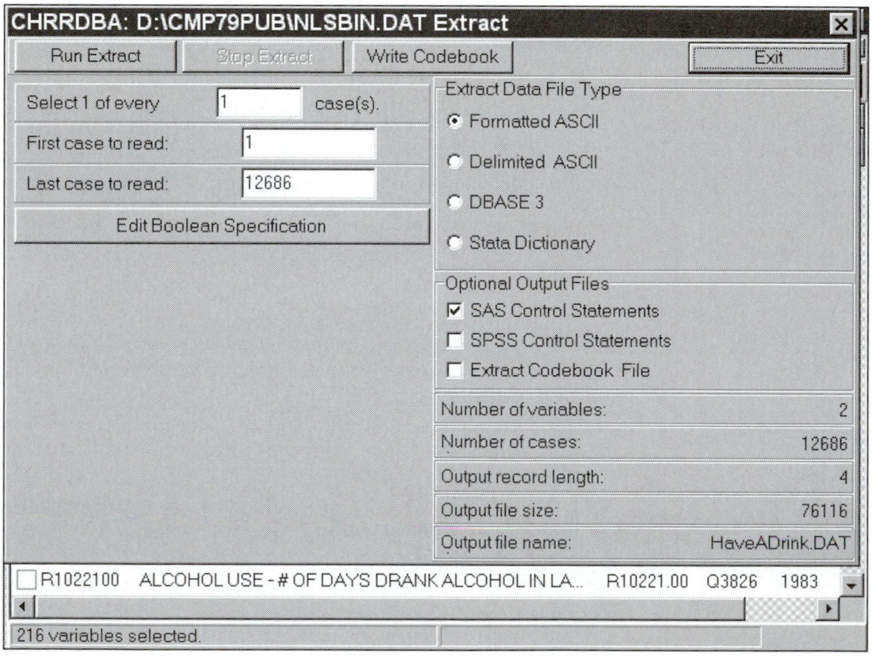

The second filter needed is to separate respondents into Hispanic, black, and white groups to correct for the special oversampling discussed earlier. To separate these three groups, find and check off reference number R0214700, which contains the key racial/ethnic variable. Bringing up R0214700's code book page shows that this variable is set to 1 for Hispanic respondents, 2 for blacks, and 3 for all others. To capture whites, set the Boolean filter as R0214700 = 3.

Putting the ampersand sign (&) between these two filters, as shown in Figure 7.9, tells the program to extract the data for respondents who are white AND who answered either Yes or No to the alcohol question. When the Boolean expression is correct pick Exit to return to the previous screen and then push the Run Extract button.

Step 5. The last step is to exit the program and analyze the data. If you used the Boolean Specification button, open the file the extraction program created that ends with a *.doc extension. This file, shown in Figure 7.10, contains the question name and the average for each variable extracted. The 0.957 value to the right of the Ever Had a Drink label means that 95.7% of all white young baby boomers had tried alcohol by 1982.

The other analysis method is to load the variables into a commercial statistical package like SAS or SPSS. While you are doing your analysis, do not forget to use the sampling weights when producing summary statistics like means, medians, and standard deviations.

Another example using NLS data investigates a common hiring problem. After interviewing, many managers come up with two candidates who have

FIGURE 7.9
NLS Investigator
Boolean Specification
Function

Copyright The Ohio State
University. Used with
permission.

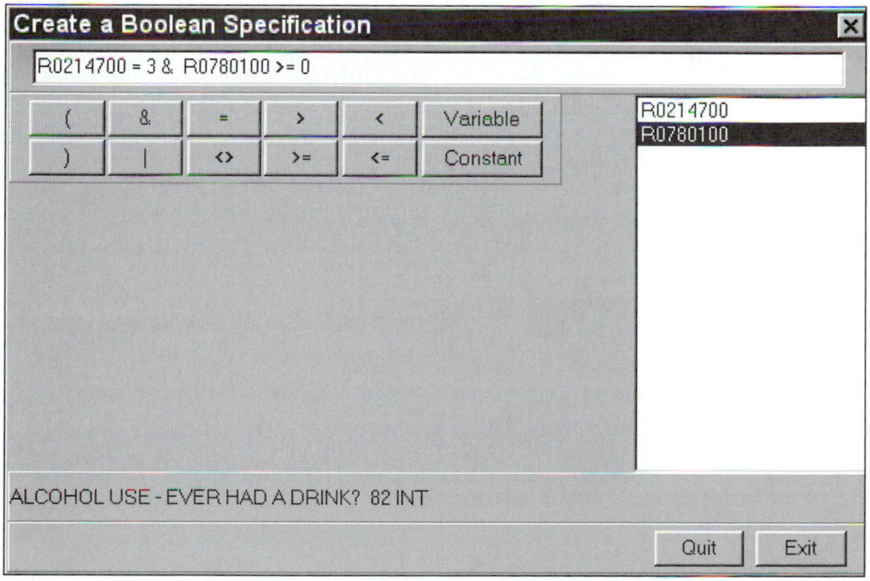

Create a Boolean Specification

R0214700 = 3 & R0780100 >= 0

(& = > < Variable
) | <> >= <= Constant

R0214700
R0780100

ALCOHOL USE - EVER HAD A DRINK? 82 INT

Quit   Exit

FIGURE 7.10
Results from NLS Investigator

Copyright The Ohio State University. Used with permission.

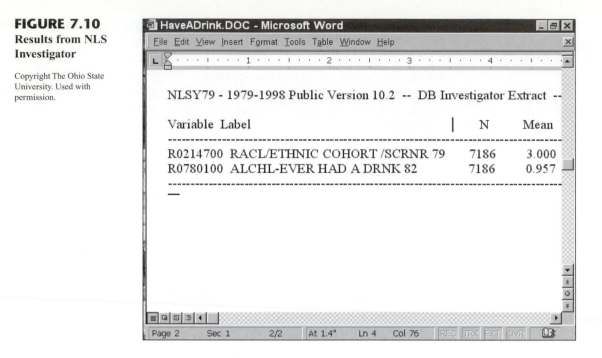

similar backgrounds. Which person should you hire? Human resource folklore holds that smarter people are more productive but more likely to quit when better opportunities arise. Based on this folklore, managers who value productivity should pick the smartest candidate, while managers valuing loyalty should not. Since the NLSY79 contains detailed information on the IQ,[12] sex,[13] and number of jobs ever held[14] by a nationally representative sample, it is easy to see if this bit of H.R. folklore is true. Running a weighted correlation of I.Q. and number of jobs by sex reveals a negative or inverse correlation (−0.07) for men but a positive correlation (0.10) for women. In English this means that smarter young baby boomer men quit more often but the reverse is true for women. Given that both numbers are close to zero, the relationship is not very strong.

[12] The IQ variable is R0618300, which has the oblique title "PROFILES, AFQT PERCENTILE 1989 (REV) 81."
[13] The sex variable is R0214800, labeled "SEX OF R."
[14] The number of jobs variable used is R5168800, labeled "NUMBER OF DIFFERENT JOBS EVER REPORTED."

TABLE 7.3
Partial List of Other Countries' Longitudinal Surveys

Country	Survey Name	Topics
Australia	Living in Australia Survey (HILDA) **http://www.melbourneinstitute.com/hilda**	Income, labor, and family transitions
Britain	British Household Panel Survey **http://www.iser.essex.ac.uk/bhps**	Health, education, income, consumption
Canada	Survey of Labour and Income Dynamics **http://www.statcan.ca/english/SLID/diction.htm**	Income and labor force changes
Germany	German Socio-Economic Panel **http://www.diw.de/english/sop**	Reunification, health, earnings, time use
Japan	Japanese Panel Survey on Consumers **http://www.kakeiken.or.jp/english**	Consumption, savings, wealth, time use
Korea	Korean Labor and Income Panel Study **http://www.kli.re.kr/klips/klips_eng.htm**	Labor, working conditions, income
Russia	Russian Socio-Economic Transition Panel **http://home.pscw.uva.nl/saris**	Employment, health, political participation
Switzerland	Swiss Household Panel **http://www.unine.ch/psm/**	Education, employment status, opinions

Information for Other Countries

The United States is not the only nation to run longitudinal surveys. Many other countries also gather data this way. When properly designed, a longitudinal survey not only provides time series information but also eliminates the need for many cross-sectional surveys. For example, Canada until the late 1990s collected income data each April by running a cross-sectional survey called the Survey of Consumer Finances (SCF). The longitudinal Survey of Labour and Income Dynamics (SLID) replaced this cross-sectional survey in 1998. The SLID is cleverly designed so that it produces annual income data, similar to the SCF information, as it also gathers longitudinal information.

A partial list of longitudinal surveys being run in countries outside the United States is shown in Table 7.3. The first column contains the name of the country, the second the survey name and the key Internet URL, and the third some key topics. It is important to understand that the cost and ease of access to these data vary greatly from country to country.

Summary   If you need more details on individuals or families than provided by the cross-sectional surveys discussed in Chapters 4, 5, and 6, turn to longitudinal surveys. This chapter provides details on four longitudinal studies that are useful for general business purposes: the PSID, which tracks how families change (**http://www.isr.umich.edu/src/psid**); the HRS-AHEAD, which tracks the elderly (**http://www.umich.edu/~hrswww**); the SIPP, which provides very detailed income and wealth information (**http://www.sipp.census.gov/sipp**); and the NLS, which shows how teenagers grow into adults (**http://www.bls.gov/nls**). While each study focuses on different groups, together they provide an unsurpassed level of detail about the demographic, income, and spending patterns of United States residents. Many other countries track similar types of longitudinal information. The key URLs for these other surveys are provided in Table 7.3.

Chapter  8

Industry Data

Overall, how profitable are companies in your industry? Do a lot of competitors exist for your new product line, or are there just a few? How many people work in this trade? Answering these kinds of questions lets you compare a specific business with industry averages, map out new strategies, and write effective new business plans. This chapter helps you answer these questions by explaining how to find trade association data and how the industrial classification coding systems work. The chapter then explains how to use the Census of Business and annual business surveys.

In the chapter's first scenario, your new business plan is almost complete. To finish the plan you need figures on worldwide sales of semiconductor chips. Where do you find the information to complete the plan? In the second scenario, you are a Midwest manufacturer of antique sink and tub replicas. You sell your fixtures to plumbing wholesalers. Business is good but you are interested in expanding into East Coast markets. You need to find out how many plumbing wholesalers there are in a major East Coast city, like Boston, in order to determine the number of sales representatives to hire.

Trade Associations

Trade associations are often an excellent source of information about a product or industry. Trade associations range from the very specific, such as IAEKM, which stands for the International Association of Electronic Keyboard Manufacturers (**http://www.iaekm.org**), a group promoting just electronic pianos and organs, to the very general like the National Retail Federation (**http://www.nrf.com**), which promotes all kinds of retail stores. While many associations collect data as a service to their members, nonmembers are often allowed access both as a public service and as a method of expanding the industry.

Annually, two competing guides each publish a list of all trade associations and their addresses. Unfortunately, both guides are outside the nominal cost criteria used by this book. The *Gale Encyclopedia of Business and Professional Associations,* published by Gale Research (**http://www.gale.com**), not only lists contact information for over 8,000 organizations but also has extensive details about the budget, membership, and publications of each association. *National Trade and Professional Associations of the United States* by Columbia Books (**http://www.columbiabooks.com**) is much cheaper than the Gale publication but does not contain nearly as much detail about each organization. Since the reference departments of most large libraries have at least one of these books, few managers need to buy their own copy.

For business managers who cannot conveniently go to a library, or who are looking for a free source of information, much of the same information is available from the American Society of Association Executives (**http://www. asaenet.org/main**). This group is the trade association for all United States associations and maintains a free database listing the Internet URLs of over 6,500 organizations. To see this online list, go to the association's homepage and pick the link labeled "Find Associations, people, businesses." Then use the pull-down list until you reach "Gateway to associations." This link will bring you to the online search page, pictured in Figure 8.1.

FIGURE 8.1
Online List of United States Trade Associations

Copyright American Society of Association Executives. Used with permission.

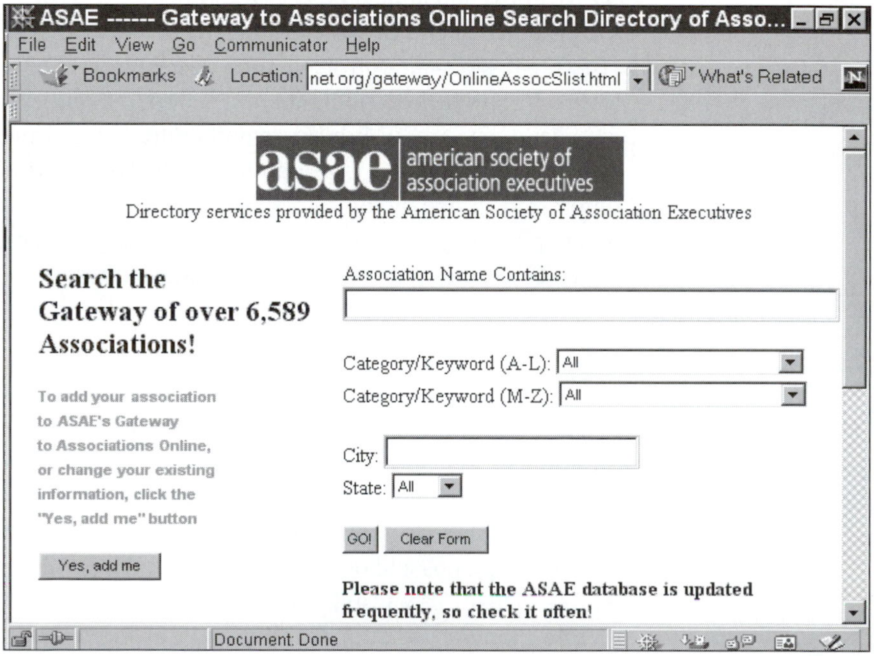

Using this page, it is easy to find an association by typing the keyword of interest in the box "Association Name Contains." For example, to answer the first scenario where you need information on the semiconductor industry, type the word "semiconductor" in that search box and press Go. The site currently returns the names of two semiconductor associations:

1. Semiconductor Equipment and Materials International (**http://www.semi.org**).

2. Semiconductor Industry Association (**http://www.semichips.org**).

Picking the second "semichips.org" entry brings up the chip industry association's homepage. The chip industry website has an Industry Statistics selection, under which are worldwide sales figures, market share, and forecasts for computer processors.

Since many managers do not know the exact name of the industry association, the search page has two selections: *Category/Keyword (A–L)* and *(M–Z)*. These windows bring up predefined groups like marketing, motor vehicles, or music where all industry associations related to the category are listed no matter what the group's exact name. City, state, and country searches are also available, but these methods primarily bring up groups focused on businesses located in a particular geographic area, not groups related to a specific industry.

There are also lists of trade associations located in countries outside the United States. For example, in Great Britain the Trade Association Forum provides a website (**http://www.taforum.org.uk**), which has a free directory that is searchable by both name and industry of most British associations. Industry Canada also provides a free list of Canadian associations at **http://strategis.ic. gc.ca**. To find the list, type "professional associations" in the search box. The list of associations is currently under the Canadian Business Map.

The primary drawback to using trade association data is that the quality, quantity, and availability vary widely. Some sites provide information only to members, others rarely update their information, while a third group contains high-quality information found nowhere else in the world. Enough trade associations fall into this third category of providing high-quality data that you should check the relevant association's website before trying other research options.

Practice Question

Your best friend whispers in your ear that pork bellies are the next hot investment trend. What are the names and URLs of the pork industry's trade associations?

Industrial Classifications

If trade associations do not provide the needed information, the next step is to use government sources. To access these data you must understand industrial classification systems, because all government data are released using one of these systems. In order to find information on a particular industry, you need to know its classification code. Additionally, the code provides an accurate and detailed definition of what the industrial data are tracking.

From the 1930s until the late 1990s, the United States industrial classification system was called the Standard Industrial Classification (SIC) codes. Since their inception, SIC codes have been periodically reviewed and updated. During the mid-1990s the periodic review resulted not in a minor update like previous reviews, but in an overhaul so dramatic the entire classification system was renamed. This new classification, finalized in 1997, is called the North American Industry Classification System, or NAICS. It is important to understand both the SIC and NAICS sets of codes because, while some government agencies and businesses have quickly adopted NAICS, others have no plans to switch from the SIC system.

The new NAICS definitions were created in conjunction with Canadian and Mexican officials. This cooperation means that since 1997 some of the business data from United States, Canadian and Mexican sources have been gathered and released using common definitions. This enables business managers to easily make cross-country comparisons in North America. The NAICS revision not only ensured that data from the three countries are compatible but also created a number of major new industrial classifications such as Information and Education Services, that did not exist under the SIC system.

Beyond cross-country compatibility and major new classifications, NAICS introduced two more major changes. First, industries are now classified by what they produce, not by an ad hoc decision that was sometimes based on what they produce and sometimes on how the industry sold its goods. Second, the older SIC system was designed to provide very fine detail on manufacturing industries but relatively little detail on services. With the decline of manufacturing and growth of services, the newer NAICS system now reverses the focus and provides a much greater emphasis on the service sector.

The SIC codes, last published in the *Standard Industrial Classification Manual, 1987,* break businesses into 10 high-level groups.[1] These 10 high-level groups are shown in Table 8.1.

---

[1]The United States Government Printing Office publishes the SIC manual for the Office of Management and Budget.

TABLE 8.1
SIC High-level
Sector Names and
Associated Two-Digit
Codes

Note: Companies that are not classified are given an SIC code of 99.

SIC Sector	SIC Codes	SIC Sector	SIC Codes
Agriculture and forestry	1–9	Wholesale trade	50–51
Mining	10–14	Retail trade	52–59
Construction	15–17	Finance, insurance, & R.E.	60–67
Manufacturing	20–39	Services	70–89
Transportation/commun.	40–49	Public administration	91–97

TABLE 8.2
NAICS High-Level
Sector Names and
Associated Two-Digit
Codes

NAICS Sector	NAICS Code	NAICS Sector	NAICS Code
Agriculture and forestry	11	Real estate	53
Mining	21	Professional services	54
Utilities	22	Management of companies	55
Construction	23	Administrative support	56
Manufacturing	31–33	Educational services	61
Wholesale trade	42	Health care	62
Retail trade	44–45	Arts, entertainment	71
Transportation	48–49	Accommodation and food	72
Information	51	Other services	81
Finance and insurance	52	Public administration	92

NAICS doubles the list of high-level entries to 20 as shown in Table 8.2. The entire list of all 1,172 NAICS industries names, codes and descriptions is published in the book *North American Industry Classification System—United States.*[2]

Both NAICS and SIC arrange industrial data in a hierarchy. Each industry is given a numeric code. Fewer digits indicate a more aggregated or higher industry level; a larger number of digits means a finer level of disaggregation. For example, the highest-level NAICS codes are two digits long while the lowest-level are six digits. Below is the NAICS hierarchy of codes for one part of the trucking industry.

- NAICS Code 48   Transportation

- NAICS Code 484   Truck transportation

- NAICS Code 4841   General freight trucking

[2] The book is available in print and CD-ROM from the NTIS (**http://www.ntis.gov**).

- NAICS Code 48412   General freight trucking, long-distance

- NAICS Code 484122   General freight trucking, long-distance, less than truckload

In this example, the two-digit NAICS code 48 covers all industries in the transportation sector. Transportation is then broken down into subgroups represented by three-digit codes, like 484 for truck transportation. The lowest-level six-digit NAICS code, in this case 484122, captures just trucking companies involved in general long-distance freight deliveries of partial truckloads.

The corresponding SIC hierarchy, shown below, contains much less information about this portion of the trucking industry than its NAICS counterpart.

- SIC Code 42   Motor freight transportation and warehousing

- SIC Code 421   Trucking and courier services, except air

- SIC Code 4213   Trucking, except local

If you do not need the detailed descriptions and just want the SIC or NAICS code to match a particular industry name, go online and use the NAICS homepage. This page, pictured in Figure 8.2, is found at **http://www. census.gov/naics**.

FIGURE 8.2
North American Industry Classification System (NAICS)

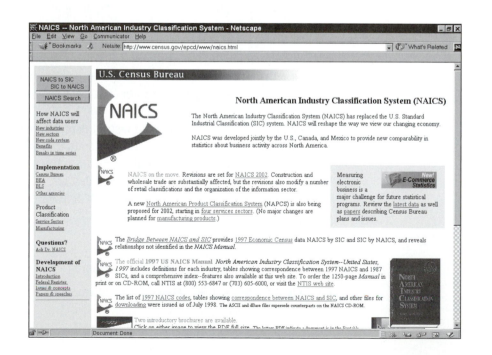

In the top left corner of the NAICS homepage are two big buttons labeled NAICS to SIC/SIC to NAICS and NAICS Search. The first button is useful for converting codes from one system to the other. The second button is used when you do not know the industrial classification code in either system. Let's assume you are in the computer software business and want to look up your industry's NAICS code. Press the second button, labeled NAICS Search, and type "software" in the search box. The NAICS system returns a number of entries, some of which are shown in Figure 8.3, like 5112 for software publishers.

To find the matching SIC code, go back to the top-level page and select NAICS to SIC. On the left side of the page is a table that lets you convert from NAICS to SIC codes, while the right side converts the other way. For example, to find software publishing's SIC code, start by selecting Information 51 on the left side. Then look at the next page until you find the NAICS code 5112, Software Publishers. Selecting this entry brings up the older SIC classification that is 7372.

Practice Questions

What are the SIC and NAICS codes for greeting cards?

What are the SIC and NAICS codes for book stores?

FIGURE 8.3
NAICS Codes for Software Programming and Publishing

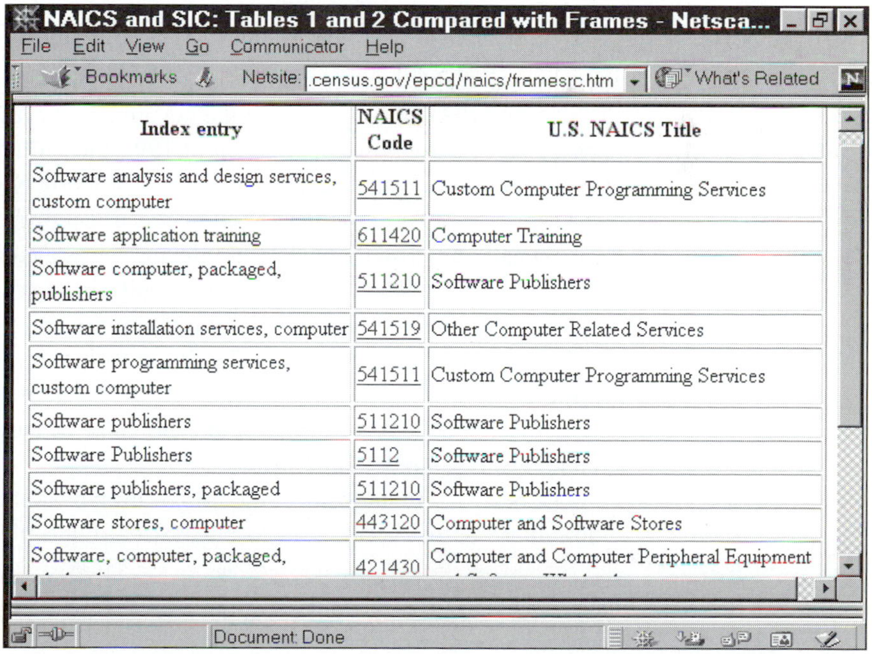

Index entry	NAICS Code	U.S. NAICS Title
Software analysis and design services, custom computer	541511	Custom Computer Programming Services
Software application training	611420	Computer Training
Software computer, packaged, publishers	511210	Software Publishers
Software installation services, computer	541519	Other Computer Related Services
Software programming services, custom computer	541511	Custom Computer Programming Services
Software publishers	511210	Software Publishers
Software Publishers	5112	Software Publishers
Software publishers, packaged	511210	Software Publishers
Software stores, computer	443120	Computer and Software Stores
Software, computer, packaged,	421430	Computer and Computer Peripheral Equipment

Industrial Census

The United States government not only periodically tracks and publishes detailed information about the country's population but also about the country's businesses. The first countrywide enumeration of businesses was done in 1810, and named the *Census of Manufactures*. During the 1800s, industrial and agricultural data were collected every 10 years in conjunction with the Census of Population. By the end of the 1800s it was clear that United States industry was changing rapidly. In response to these rapid changes, the Census Bureau began running industrial censuses roughly every five years and also expanded the scope beyond manufacturing to include four more business censuses: Service Industries; Wholesale Trade, Retail Trade, and Transportation; Communications; and Utilities Industries.

The primary problem with using these old data collections was that each census was run during a different year to distribute the government's workload evenly. This means that while all individual businesses provided information every five years, there was no single year in which information was available showing how all businesses in the entire country were doing. To fix this problem, the various industrial censuses were consolidated into one set in 1954 and run at the same time. To reduce the costs of running this consolidated census, the 1954 program no longer sent a census taker to the doorstep of every business; instead, each business was required to report its information by filling in forms and mailing them back.

After the 1954 changes, the next major innovation was ensuring that the census was fielded every five years, in years ending in a 2 or 7, (i.e. 1987, 1992, and 1997). This means that the next major survey of United States businesses will be done in 2002.[3] Then in 1997 the industrial census underwent three more transformations. First, instead of using SIC codes, all industries were classified using the new NAICS codes. Second, the questions and data were standardized so that identical information is available for each industrial sector. Finally, instead of publishing results in lengthy reports, the Census Bureau began publishing a few summary reports and put the rest of the industrial information on the Internet. To find information for the 1997 census, go to the Economic Census homepage (**http://www.census.gov/econ97.html**), shown in Figure 8.4. Information on the 2002 census is available at **http://www.census.gov/econ2002.html**.

The best way to understand the information available from the census is to look at the actual forms sent to businesses. Examples of these surveys are

---

[3]Since there is a lag between collection and release of the 2002 Census information, most public documents will be released beginning in 2004.

FIGURE 8.4

1997 Economic
Census Homepage

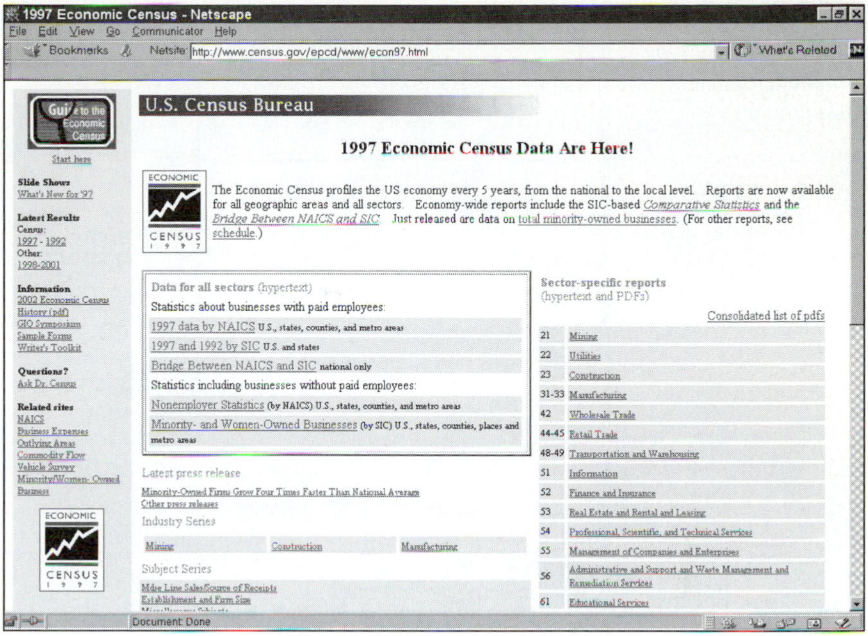

found on this book's website and under the Sample Forms link located on the top left-hand side of the Economic Census homepage. Each company is required by law to fill in four pages of information. The next two pictures show the key pieces of the 1997 census form sent to computer service companies.

Part of the form, shown in Figure 8.5, asks each company to report its physical location and number of months it actively operated in 1997. The form also asks how the company is legally organized (incorporated, partnership, sole proprietorship, etc.), if it was owned or controlled by another company, and the names of other companies that it owns and controls. These answers provide the ability not only to break industries down by geographic area, but also to track trends in the number of sole proprietorships, partnerships, and incorporated businesses and to examine the extent of interlocking ownership.

Other pages on the form ask for total receipts and the amount of receipts from various subcategories. For example, the third page of the computer services form, shown in Figure 8.6, asks how much money the company earned from categories like software publishing, computer programming, software maintenance, and system design work. Each business is also asked to break receipts down by customer class so that the amount purchased by individuals, other businesses, and the government is identifiable. Additionally, receipts are broken down by the amount of money earned from exported goods and services. Finally, the right-hand side of the figure shows that the census

FIGURE 8.5
First Page of the 1997
Economic Census
Questionnaire

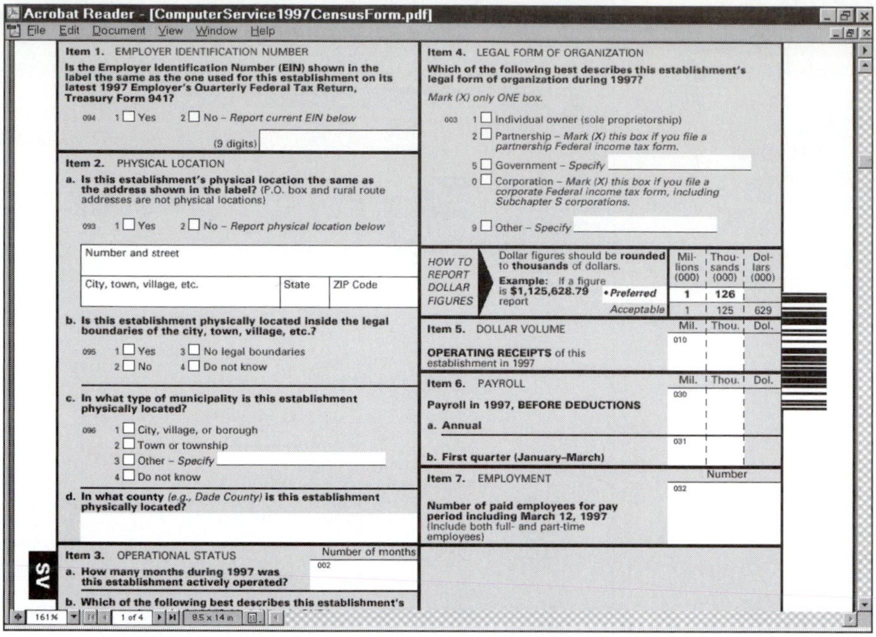

Acrobat Reader - [ComputerService1997CensusForm.pdf]
File　Edit　Document　View　Window　Help

Item 1.　EMPLOYER IDENTIFICATION NUMBER

Is the Employer Identification Number (EIN) shown in the label the same as the one used for this establishment on its latest 1997 Employer's Quarterly Federal Tax Return, Treasury Form 941?

094　　1 ☐ Yes　　2 ☐ No – *Report current EIN below*

(9 digits)

Item 2.　PHYSICAL LOCATION

a. Is this establishment's physical location the same as the address shown in the label? (P.O. box and rural route addresses are not physical locations)

093　　1 ☐ Yes　　2 ☐ No – *Report physical location below*

Number and street

City, town, village, etc.　　State　　ZIP Code

b. Is this establishment physically located inside the legal boundaries of the city, town, village, etc.?

095　　1 ☐ Yes　　3 ☐ No legal boundaries
　　　　2 ☐ No　　　4 ☐ Do not know

c. In what type of municipality is this establishment physically located?

096　　1 ☐ City, village, or borough
　　　　2 ☐ Town or township
　　　　3 ☐ Other – *Specify*
　　　　4 ☐ Do not know

d. In what county *(e.g., Dade County)* **is this establishment physically located?**

Item 3.　OPERATIONAL STATUS　　Number of months

a. How many months during 1997 was this establishment actively operated?　002

b. Which of the following best describes this establishment's

Item 4.　LEGAL FORM OF ORGANIZATION

Which of the following best describes this establishment's legal form of organization during 1997?

Mark (X) only ONE box.

003　　1 ☐ Individual owner (sole proprietorship)
　　　　2 ☐ Partnership – *Mark (X) this box if you file a partnership Federal income tax form.*
　　　　5 ☐ Government – *Specify*
　　　　0 ☐ Corporation – *Mark (X) this box if you file a corporate Federal income tax form, including Subchapter S corporations.*
　　　　9 ☐ Other – *Specify*

HOW TO REPORT DOLLAR FIGURES	Dollar figures should be **rounded** to **thousands** of dollars. Example: If a figure is **$1,125,628.79**	Mil-lions (000)	Thou-sands (000)	Dol-lars (000)
	• *Preferred* report	1	126	
	Acceptable	1	125	629

Item 5.　DOLLAR VOLUME　　Mil.　Thou.　Dol.
010
OPERATING RECEIPTS of this establishment in 1997

Item 6.　PAYROLL　　Mil.　Thou.　Dol.
030
Payroll in 1997, BEFORE DEDUCTIONS

a. Annual
031
b. First quarter (January–March)

Item 7.　EMPLOYMENT　　Number
032
Number of paid employees for pay period including March 12, 1997 (Include both full- and part-time employees)

161%　1 of 4　8.5 x 14 in

FIGURE 8.6
Third Page of the
1997 Economic
Census

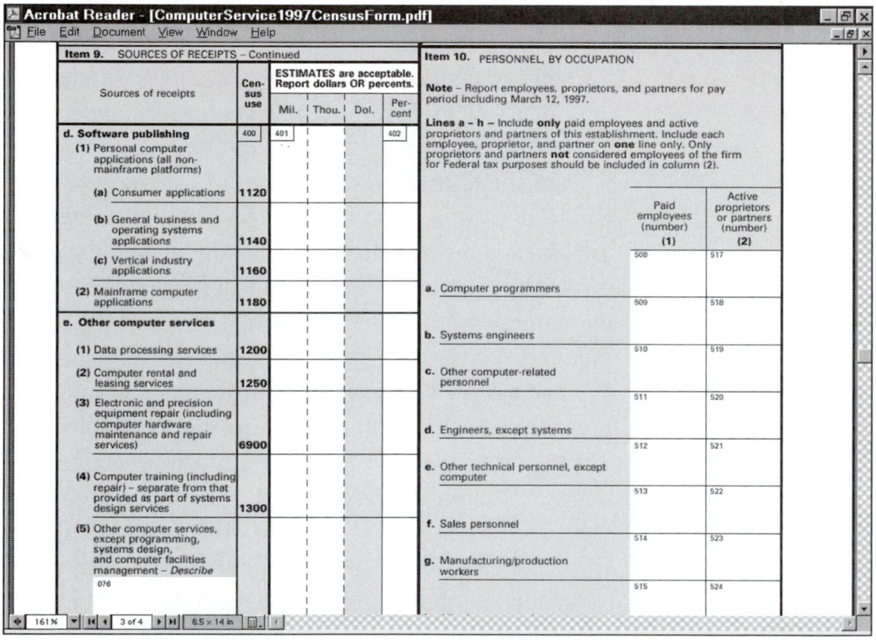

Acrobat Reader - [ComputerService1997CensusForm.pdf]
File　Edit　Document　View　Window　Help

Item 9.　SOURCES OF RECEIPTS – Continued

Sources of receipts	Census use	ESTIMATES are acceptable. Report dollars OR percents.			
		Mil.	Thou.	Dol.	Per-cent
d. Software publishing	400	401			402
(1) Personal computer applications (all non-mainframe platforms)					
(a) Consumer applications	1120				
(b) General business and operating systems applications	1140				
(c) Vertical industry applications	1160				
(2) Mainframe computer applications	1180				
e. Other computer services					
(1) Data processing services	1200				
(2) Computer rental and leasing services	1250				
(3) Electronic and precision equipment repair (including computer hardware maintenance and repair services)	6900				
(4) Computer training (including repair) – separate from that provided as part of systems design services	1300				
(5) Other computer services, except programming, systems design, and computer facilities management – *Describe*	076				

Item 10.　PERSONNEL, BY OCCUPATION

Note – Report employees, proprietors, and partners for pay period including March 12, 1997.

Lines a – h – Include **only** paid employees and active proprietors and partners of this establishment. Include each employee, proprietor, and partner on **one** line only. Only proprietors and partners **not** considered employees of the firm for Federal tax purposes should be included in column (2).

	Paid employees (number) (1)	Active proprietors or partners (number) (2)
	508	517
a. Computer programmers	509	518
b. Systems engineers	510	519
c. Other computer-related personnel	511	520
d. Engineers, except systems	512	521
e. Other technical personnel, except computer	513	522
f. Sales personnel	514	523
g. Manufacturing/production workers	515	524

161%　3 of 4　8.5 x 14 in

form asks for the total number of employees and the number of workers by occupation.

By combining all information from every company in the United States, the Census Bureau creates a rich picture of the country's industrial structure.

FIGURE 8.7
American FactFinder
Homepage

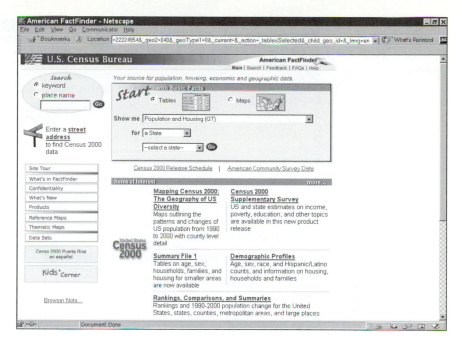

To see this information you can either read preprinted reports or create custom tables. All preprinted reports are published online as Adobe PDF files and are located at the Economic Census homepage (**http://www.census.gov/econ97.html**) under one of three major topics: geographic, industry, and subject.

The geographic area series contains one report for each state in the United States, plus a national summary. These geographic reports provide information such as the number of businesses operating in a particular area. The industry reports break down census information from high-level NAICS categories into more specific types of businesses. For example, the construction industry has separate industry reports for companies in 1997 doing highway and street construction (report EC97C-2341A); bridge and tunnel construction (report EC97C-2341B); and water, sewer, and pipeline construction (report EC97C-2349A). The subject area set of reports consolidates specific NAICS categories into topics. For example, there is a report on the health care sector and another on arts and entertainment.

The problem with these preprinted reports is that they may not have exactly what you want. Additionally, some of the reports are quite long, with tables covering multiple pages. Since finding the exact piece of information you want in the preprinted reports is difficult, the Census Bureau designed a new website that creates custom tables. The site, called American FactFinder, is located at **http://factfinder.census.gov** and the top-level screen is shown in Figure 8.7.

FIGURE 8.8
Quick Industry Data
from American
FactFinder

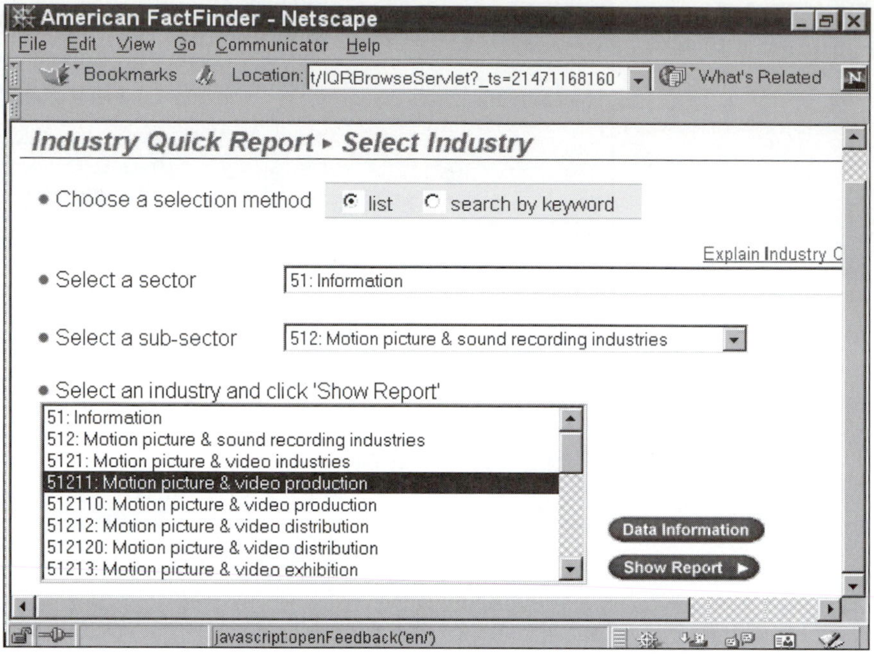

Economic census data are found under FactFinder Data Sources. Data are available under the two links labeled Industry Quick Reports and Geography Quick Reports. Industry Quick Reports use a simple format to provide detail from the broadest two-digit to the narrowest six-digit NAICS industry. Geography Quick Reports provide industrial information for regions, states, counties, PMSAs, MSAs, and cities.

Let's assume you need to know the number of movie and video production companies. To find out how many are operating in the United States pick Industry Quick Reports. To find movie and video production, you need to know the following NAICS hierarchy:

51: Information
512: Motion picture & sound recording industries
5121: Motion picture & video industries
51211: Motion picture & video production

Use this tree to fill in the economic sector, subsector, and industry on the Industry Quick Reports form. When done, your screen should look similar to Figure 8.8.

To see census data for the motion picture industry pick Show Report after filling in all the relevant boxes. This creates a table, shown in Figure 8.9, where the top line reveals that in 1997 there were 8,777 movie and video production companies in the United States. These companies employed 83,558 people with total sales of over $20 billion. Not surprisingly, the state totals

FIGURE 8.9
Industry Data for Motion Picture and Video Production

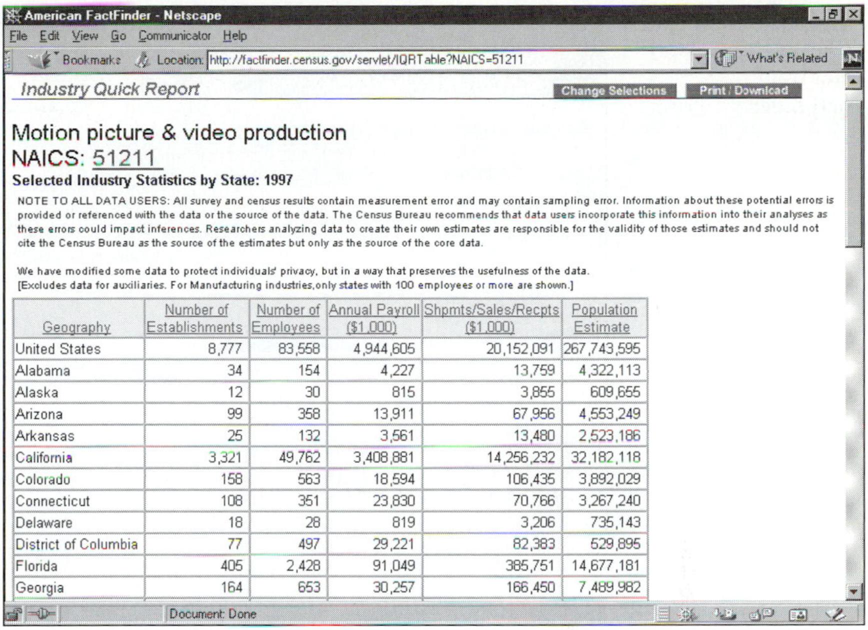

Motion picture & video production
NAICS: 51211
Selected Industry Statistics by State: 1997

NOTE TO ALL DATA USERS: All survey and census results contain measurement error and may contain sampling error. Information about these potential errors is provided or referenced with the data or the source of the data. The Census Bureau recommends that data users incorporate this information into their analyses as these errors could impact inferences. Researchers analyzing data to create their own estimates are responsible for the validity of those estimates and should not cite the Census Bureau as the source of the estimates but only as the source of the core data.

We have modified some data to protect individuals' privacy, but in a way that preserves the usefulness of the data.
[Excludes data for auxiliaries. For Manufacturing industries, only states with 100 employees or more are shown.]

Geography	Number of Establishments	Number of Employees	Annual Payroll ($1,000)	Shpmts/Sales/Recpts ($1,000)	Population Estimate
United States	8,777	83,558	4,944,605	20,152,091	267,743,595
Alabama	34	154	4,227	13,759	4,322,113
Alaska	12	30	815	3,855	609,655
Arizona	99	358	13,911	67,956	4,553,249
Arkansas	25	132	3,561	13,480	2,523,186
California	3,321	49,762	3,408,881	14,256,232	32,182,118
Colorado	158	563	18,594	106,435	3,892,029
Connecticut	108	351	23,830	70,766	3,267,240
Delaware	18	28	819	3,206	735,143
District of Columbia	77	497	29,221	82,383	529,895
Florida	405	2,428	91,049	385,751	14,677,181
Georgia	164	653	30,257	166,450	7,489,982

show that the vast majority of companies, workers, and sales were in California, followed by New York at a distant second.

Practice Question

You are thinking about broadening your Connecticut insurance brokerage business by creating a claims adjustment subsidiary. How many claims adjustment companies are currently competing for business in the Nutmeg State?

Practice Question

You are in living in the Pacific Northwest and searching for a little-known book about the Cascades. How many bookstores exist in Oregon and Washington?

The second way to access the census through the FactFinder website is by using Geography Quick Reports, which provides data for all industries in a selected geographic area. Let's now answer our second scenario, in which you manufacture antique sink and tub replicas and you are interested in expanding into the greater Boston area. You know that one key to a successful expansion is accurately estimating the number of account representatives needed. Hiring too few representatives results in little product momentum, but hiring too many results in a demoralized sales force that focuses more on turf battles than selling. The number of account representatives needed is easy to determine if you know how many plumbing wholesalers exist in Boston. Using Geographic Quick Reports you can find the number of plumbing wholesalers or the number of businesses operating in any other industry for a specific area of the country.

FIGURE 8.10
Geographic Industry
Data from
FactFinder

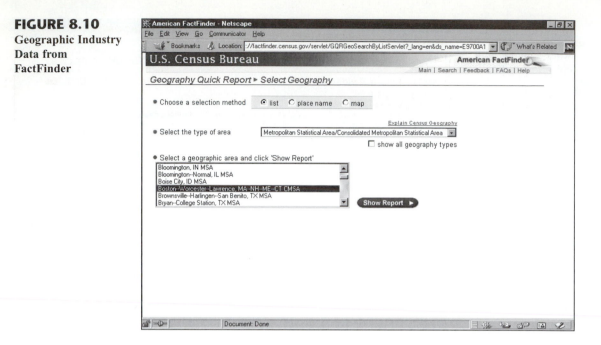

To find the number of plumbing wholesalers in greater Boston, first choose Geography Quick Reports on the FactFinder main page. Under the "Select the type of area" pick are options that range from the entire United States to Primary Metropolitan Statistical Area (PMSA). To select the greater Boston area, pick the Boston-Worcester-Lawrence CMSA, like in Figure 8.10.

Once you have a particular place selected, pick the Show Report button. Picking this button generates a summary table of *all* two-digit NAICS industries in the greater Boston area and also enables a new function entitled Change Selections at the top of the screen. The Other Reports button under this pick enables you to expand the summary report from the two-digit level of detail up to the six-digit level. Since plumbing and heating supply wholesalers is the five-digit NAICS code 42172, select Other Reports and increase the precision so that six-digit industries are shown. Then picking the OK button produces the detailed table of businesses in the greater Boston area shown in Figure 8.11. Scrolling down the list reveals that there are 123 plumbing wholesalers in business in the greater Boston area. Using this information, you decide to hire three sales representatives for the new territory.

**Practice
Question**

After successfully expanding your antique sink and tub replicas into the greater Boston area, you now set your sights on New York City. How many plumbing wholesalers do your account representatives need to service in the five boroughs of New York City?

FIGURE 8.11
Industrial Data for Greater Boston

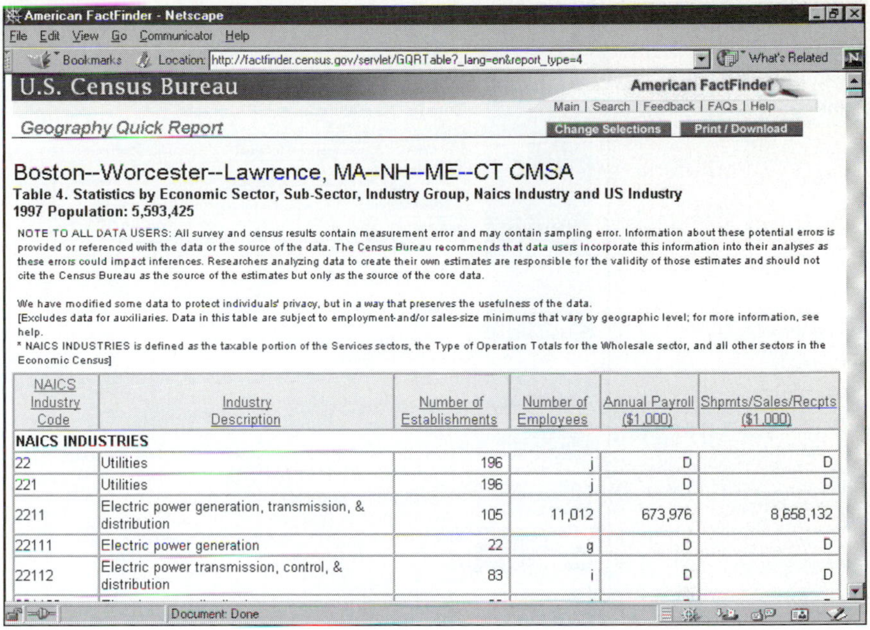

American FactFinder - Netscape

File Edit View Go Communicator Help

Bookmarks Location: http://factfinder.census.gov/servlet/GQRTable?_lang=en&report_type=4 What's Related

U.S. Census Bureau

American FactFinder

Main | Search | Feedback | FAQs | Help

Geography Quick Report

Change Selections Print / Download

Boston--Worcester--Lawrence, MA--NH--ME--CT CMSA

Table 4. Statistics by Economic Sector, Sub-Sector, Industry Group, Naics Industry and US Industry
1997 Population: 5,593,425

NOTE TO ALL DATA USERS: All survey and census results contain measurement error and may contain sampling error. Information about these potential errors is provided or referenced with the data or the source of the data. The Census Bureau recommends that data users incorporate this information into their analyses as these errors could impact inferences. Researchers analyzing data to create their own estimates are responsible for the validity of those estimates and should not cite the Census Bureau as the source of the estimates but only as the source of the core data.

We have modified some data to protect individuals' privacy, but in a way that preserves the usefulness of the data.
[Excludes data for auxiliaries. Data in this table are subject to employment-and/or sales-size minimums that vary by geographic level; for more information, see help.
* NAICS INDUSTRIES is defined as the taxable portion of the Services sectors, the Type of Operation Totals for the Wholesale sector, and all other sectors in the Economic Census]

NAICS Industry Code	Industry Description	Number of Establishments	Number of Employees	Annual Payroll ($1,000)	Shpmts/Sales/Recpts ($1,000)
NAICS INDUSTRIES					
22	Utilities	196	j	D	D
221	Utilities	196	j	D	D
2211	Electric power generation, transmission, & distribution	105	11,012	673,976	8,658,132
22111	Electric power generation	22	g	D	D
22112	Electric power transmission, control, & distribution	83	i	D	D

Document: Done

Practice Question

Searching every bookstore in Oregon and Washington for that special book about the Cascades is too large a task. How many bookstores are located in greater Portland?

Industrial Surveys

The United States government not only runs a business census every five years but also conducts many annual surveys of significant industries between each census. This surveying provides business managers with key industry information more frequently than just twice a decade. The homepage (**http://www.census.gov/business**) for these other business surveys is shown in Figure 8.12. The key area is the links just above the words "More Economic Data." By picking items like Service, Transportation, or Retail, you can access annual and quarterly surveys that provide additional information not found in the census.

There are a number of important differences between the census and these more frequent surveys. First, the census covers all businesses while the industrial surveys do not. Since the Census Bureau does not run industrial surveys for all businesses, industries like mining or utilities are only tracked systematically every five years. Even though only some industries are covered by annual surveys, the surveys do cover important sectors like manufacturing,

FIGURE 8.12
Census Bureau
Economic Programs
Homepage

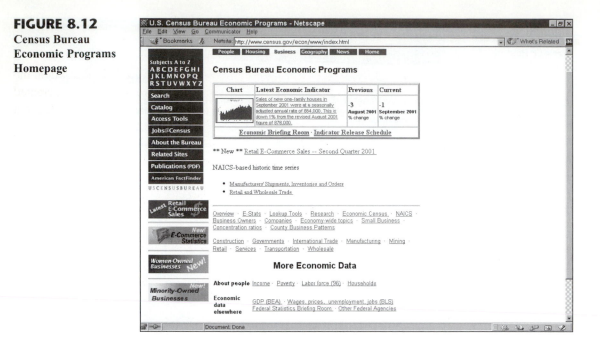

transportation, services, and communications. Second, because the surveys sample only a portion of the entire industry, survey data are not available at the detailed geographic level. This means the exact count of firms by city or zip code is available only at five-year intervals.

The annual and quarterly surveys make up for these drawbacks by producing a richer and more detailed set of industry data than the census. Unlike the census, each survey is not standardized. Since the annual surveys are not required to follow a uniform set of questions, they capture information that is missing from census questionnaires. For example, the *Annual Survey of Manufactures,* found under the Manufacturing link, provides estimates for employment, hours worked by plant employees, payroll, value added by manufacturing processes, capital expenditures, cost of materials, inventories, value of industry shipments, and energy costs, to name only a few topics.

It is impossible to summarize all the different surveys in only a few words. The best suggestion is to start following the links on the Census Bureau's Economic Program's homepage. Once you start exploring, you will quickly see that the government collects and releases an enormous amount of industry information.

Information for Canada

While all other major industrialized countries collect and publish industry information, much of it is either still in paper format or not consolidated on the Internet. Canada, however, has an extremely well-developed website, created by Industry Canada, which provides a great deal of industry knowledge in a simple-to-use format. To get to this website, go to Industry Canada's homepage (**http://strategis.ic.gc.ca**) and then select Economic Analysis, Statistics followed by Canadian Industry Statistics midway down the page. Canadian Industry Statistics provides information on over 20 high-level SIC categories. Selecting any category brings up a page that contains simple-to-read reports that overview the most important subcomponents of each industry. Additionally, each page contains over 20 tables that show trends over time for key data such as the industry's shipments, employment, salaries, value added, capital stock, investment, and exports.

Summary

If you need information on United States industries, there are three places to look. First, explore information available from trade associations. A free online list of trade associations is available from the American Society of Association Executives (**http://www.asaenet.org/main**) under the link labeled "Gateway to associations" found under the "find associations, people, businesses" pick.

The second place to find information about specific businesses is the United States industrial census. This census, run every five years, captures information from companies of every size. If all you need are preprinted census reports, look at the links listed under the Economic Census homepages (**http://www.census.gov/econ97.html** and **http://www.census.gov/econ2002. html**); if you need to create custom tables, use the FactFinder website (**http:// factfinder.census.gov**).

Finally, annual and quarterly survey data on United States industries is found at the Census Bureau's Economic Programs homepage (**http://www. census.gov/business**). Similar information is available for Canada at **http:// strategis.ic.gc.ca** under the Canadian Industry Statistics portion of this website. No matter which source you use, there is a wealth of high-quality free data available for tracking industries.

Chapter

Company Information

Who are my competitors? What are their annual sales? How do my financial ratios compare with these competitors? Long-time managers have learned the answers to these questions through experience. However, many people who are entering the business world, changing industries, or switching careers do not know the answers to these questions.

This chapter provides details on where to find company information. The first part shows you how to find basic information on individual companies. The second part details financial data available from the Securities and Exchange Commission (SEC).

The key problem when investigating individual companies is determining whether the firm is public, private, or owned as a public subsidiary. Public companies must provide extensive details about their business. Most private companies, however, provide almost no information to the general public. Subsidiaries of public companies fall somewhere in between, because most public companies do not break out specific details for subsidiaries. Nevertheless, if the subsidiary provides a large percentage of total company sales or profits, some information is usually provided.

Publicly traded corporations have extensive amounts of free information. Unfortunately, free information does not exist for private companies. If you need data on a private company, it will cost money.

In this chapter's first scenario, assume you were just hired as president of a kitchen stove maker. You were picked because of a stellar track record of turning around failing companies but know almost nothing about the appliance industry. Who are your biggest competitors? In the second scenario, the giant computer chip maker, Intel, has made an overture to buy your privately held company. Instead of receiving Intel stock, however, you are interested in cashing out quickly. How much cash does Intel currently have available to purchase your company?

Basic Company Information

Where do you find the name, address, and officers of a company? How can you find out the company's total annual sales? There are a large number of directories that contain all this basic information. Each book is slightly different, so it is often worthwhile to look up a company in more than one directory. Since purchasing any one of these directories is an expensive proposition, you should know that copies of these directories are located in most large libraries.

One of the leading directories is Standard & Poor's *Register,*[1] which lists the United States' and Canada's largest public and private companies. This directory, published annually, is available in almost every major library. Each company listing in this directory contains the name, stock exchange and ticker symbol if a public company, parent company name, address, primary bank, law and accounting firms, SIC code, business description, yearly sales, number of employees, and a list of officers and directors.

Dun & Bradstreet's (D&B) *Million Dollar Directory* lists similar details about leading public and private companies, but the print version focuses solely on the United States. This directory, however, covers a much wider range of companies since it includes smaller firms that do not meet Standard & Poor's listing criteria. Additionally, beside the name in each D & B listing is a symbol that tells if the company is publicly held (a ▲ symbol), a subsidiary of a publicly held business (a △ symbol), or private (no symbol).[2] Beyond the public-private information, a D & B listing also includes the state of incorporation, the date the company was founded, and the D-U-N-S number (Data Universal Numbering System), which is the linking identifier to detailed financial information in all D & B databases.

For people without easy access to these printed volumes, all of their information and more is available online. D & B's online database is very easy to use, relatively inexpensive, and provides detailed information on individual companies both in the United States and around the world. The D & B database is located at **http://dbreports.telebase.com** and is shown in Figure 9.1.

---

[1] The full title is *Standard & Poor's Register of Corporations, Directors and Executives.*
[2] The *Million Dollar Directory* is also available online at **http://www.dnbmdd.com/mddi**. The online version has separate directories for United States and Canadian companies but is not free.

FIGURE 9.1
Dun & Bradstreet's
Online Credit Report

Copyright Dun & Bradstreet.
Used with permission.

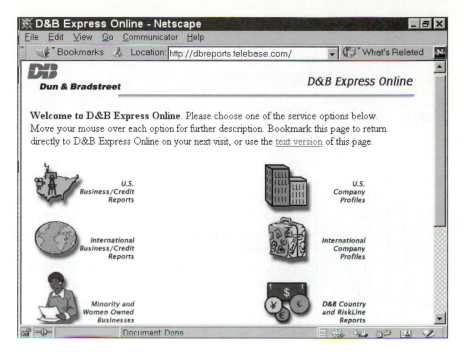

Going to this D & B URL gives you a number of ways to quickly find key information about the company. First pick either U.S. Company Profiles or International Company Profiles, depending on the situation, and then type in a company name, address, or D-U-N-S number. The D-U-N-S number is a nine-digit code assigned by D & B to uniquely identify more than 57 million companies worldwide and their branches. As a quick example, pick U.S. Company Profiles and type in 068718253 in the D-U-N-S field located in the bottom left corner. This brings up the name, address, and phone number for Butler Memorial Hospital in Butler, PA.

Most times you will not have the D-U-N-S number. It is just as easy to find a company by typing in its name. Let's say you need the address of Sony Corporation's headquarters. To find the address, this time pick International Company Profiles, and type Sony in the Name field. Then type Japan in the Country field and check the Limit to Headquarters box. Pressing the Find! button results in 31 companies. The top one, entitled Sony Corp is the parent company since pressing the More Information button lists not only the address, phone number, and line of business but also states this is the parent company.

If you need a little more beyond this basic information, D & B sells a company profile for $3.50.[3] Pressing the Info button allows you to see a sample of

---

[3]Dun & Bradstreet can and will change the prices of the profile and business reports.

what is contained in a company profile. D & B also sell a variety of reports containing much more information. The *Business Information Report* contains the most comprehensive amount of financial information on the company, while the *Business Background Report* contains the least. When this book was written, the *Business Information Report* for many United States companies cost around $100 and the *Business Background Report* cost $25. While both figures are outside of this book's free or nominal cost philosophy, it is virtually impossible to get accurate financial information on companies and organizations that are not publicly held without paying. Costs for reports on companies outside the United States are typically higher.

There are two other places to go for detailed information about your competition. First is the *Thomas Register* that is a directory of all manufacturing companies. As of beginning of 2002 there were about 173,000 United States and Canadian companies listed in the *Thomas Register*. The Internet version (**http://www.thomasregister.com**), shown in Figure 9.2, offers company profiles, which often include address, telephone number, asset ratings, company size, number of employees, and description of the company's business.

In the chapter's first scenario you need to understand who competes against your company in kitchen stove manufacturing. Using the online version of the *Thomas Register,* you can easily compile a list. Before searching you need a user id and password. These are provided for free, under the Membership link,

FIGURE 9.2
Thomas Register of American Manufacturers

in exchange for your name and address. After registering, use the search tools on the homepage and search for Products that are named Stove. Currently, the *Thomas Register* has 40 different stove categories ranging from the general, like gas and electric stoves and ranges, to the very specific, like enamels or hinges for stoves. Picking the entry Stoves & Ranges: Electric brings up a list of 17 different manufacturers who are your competitors. Clicking on any name provides that company's address.

While the *Thomas Register* is excellent for manufacturing, it does not list the competitors for nonmanufacturing industries or provide a measure of each competitor's size. *Ward's Business Directory of United States Private and Public Companies,* another book found primarily in libraries, provides this information.[4] This directory lists the United States' biggest companies broken down into four-digit SIC code groups. For example, under SIC code 3631, which tracks household cooking equipment; the 1999 directory lists the biggest company as GE Appliance, with $6.3 billion in sales. These sales figures swamp the second and third place companies, W.C. Bradley and Jenn-Air Corporations, which each have only $200 million in sales.

Unfortunately, sales rankings in *Ward's Directory* do not match research needs because Ward's assigns all of a company's sales to its most important SIC code. GE Appliance, for example, manufactures not only stoves but also refrigerators, washers, and dryers. However, sales of refrigerators and laundry machines are not broken into separate categories, but instead are all lumped with the company's biggest product line, kitchen stoves.

Practice Question	You are interested in contacting Polycom Inc., a company that makes video conferencing equipment. Unfortunately, you do not know where they are located. Use the D & B online database to find the address of Polycom's headquarters.
Practice Question	You are interested in building custom bicycles for serious triathletes but want to outsource making parts like bicycle wheels. Use *Thomas Register* to find how many bicycle wheel manufacturers exist in the United States and Canada.

SEC Information

The Securities and Exchange Commission (SEC) is the government agency charged with regulating financial markets. Since publicly traded companies must periodically file information with the SEC, its website, (**http://www.sec. gov**), which is pictured in Figure 9.3, contains a treasure trove of information

---

[4]The Gale Group (**http://www.gale.com**) publishes *Ward's.*

FIGURE 9.3
Securities
and Exchange
Commission (SEC)
Home Page

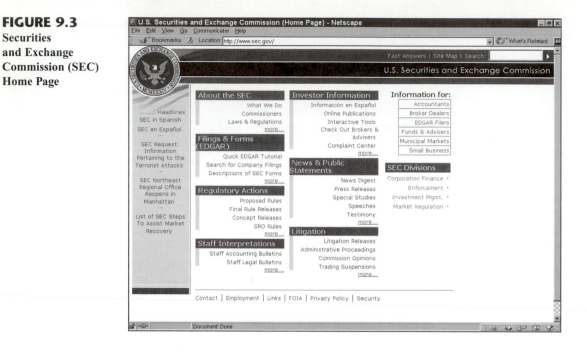

about individual firms. This treasure trove extends back to 1993 when United States companies began filing SEC forms electronically. The entire financial database is called EDGAR (Electronic Data Gathering, Analysis and Retrieval) and is designed to simplify the process of finding key financial documents about public companies.

Before jumping into EDGAR, you must understand the list of forms and acronyms. Each SEC form is given an oblique code, like SC-13D or 10Q. The most important forms are listed in Table 9.1. These forms sometimes have suffixes, of which the most common are /SB and /A. If you see a form that ends in the letters SB, like 10-KSB, this means the form is a simpler Small Business version of the 10-K form. If the form ends in /A, this means the form is an Amended version of something previously filed.

If you are just interested in an overall picture of a company, the key form to read is the 10-K; the rest are superfluous. The 10-K form contains two key parts: the past year's financial statement and a letter from upper management describing the past year's results and future directions for the company.

For a more detailed picture of a company, you should also read the DEF-14A form, which contains the annual proxy statement. Proxy statements describe the company's directors; list upper management's compensation amounts in cash, stock, and options; and show how the company's stock price has fared compared to the market and publicly traded competitors over time.

TABLE 9.1
List of the Most
Common EDGAR
Forms

Form	Short Description
8-K	Important news regarding a company's finances
10-K	Annual report
10-Q	Quarterly earnings report
10-C	Change in amount of shares outstanding
11-K	Employee stock ownership or purchase report
S-8	Employee benefit plan registration statement
SC-13D	Individual or business now owns 5% or more of shares
SC-13G	Bank or mutual fund now owns 5% or more of shares
SC-13E	Tender offer to take own company private
SC-14D	Tender offer to take another company private
DEF-14A	Proxy and executive compensation statement

Another form that helps fill in a detailed picture is the 10-Q report, which provides the company's quarterly unaudited financial results. This form provides a quick method of checking whether the company is on track for meeting its yearly financial goals. The 8-K forms provide news about important financial events affecting the company. The last set of important forms are those beginning with SC. These forms mean that a significant change in the company's ownership either happened or is proposed.

Using the EDGAR database is not difficult. Go to the SEC homepage (**http://www.sec.gov**) and pick the box labeled Search for Company Filings. This will bring you to the main EDGAR menu, which is pictured in Figure 9.4.

To find information about a publicly traded company, choose the link that reads Search EDGAR and then pick Quick Forms Lookup. This brings you to the EDGAR database search page, shown in Figure 9.5, which asks you to select an SEC form and a particular company's name. EDGAR provides both a pull-down list of forms and the ability to type in a form name. Then type in a company name in the box that states "Enter a company." It is important to note that EDGAR does **not** accept ticker symbols or more than the first 20 characters in the company name.

Let's answer the chapter's second scenario where Intel wants to buy your privately held company. Since you are interested in money, not stock, you want to know how much cash Intel has available to purchase your company. To answer this question, pick the 10-K annual report on the pull-down forms, type Intel in the company name box, and then pick Submit.

FIGURE 9.4
EDGAR Database
of Corporate
Financial Data

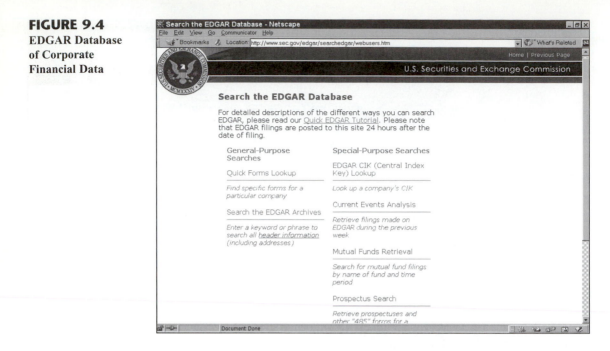

FIGURE 9.5
EDGAR Form
Selection Page

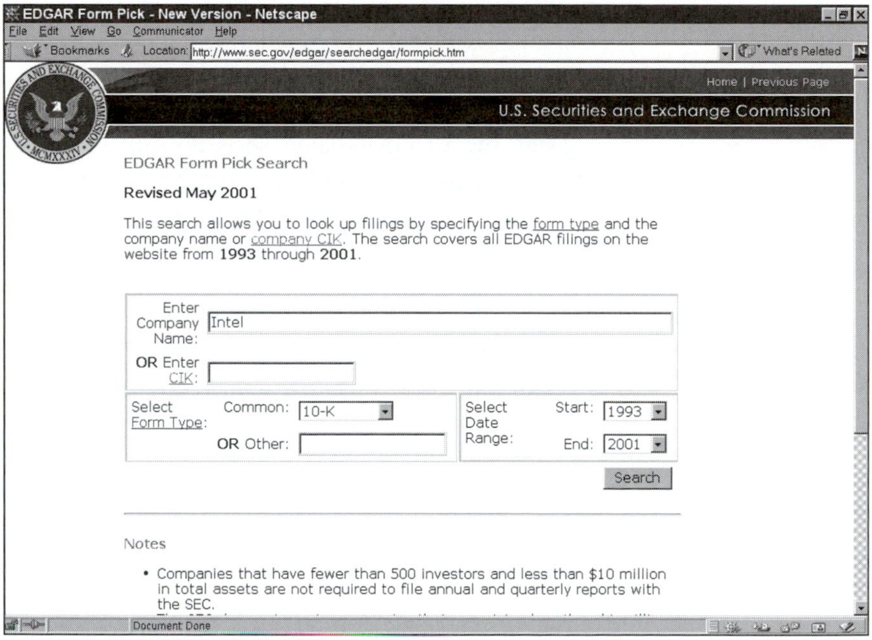

As Figure 9.6 shows, EDGAR returns links to Intel's 10-K forms since 1994. Another way to find Intel Corporation information uses the SEC company identifier, called the CIK code (Central Index Key), instead of typing in

FIGURE 9.6
EDGAR Search
Results for Intel

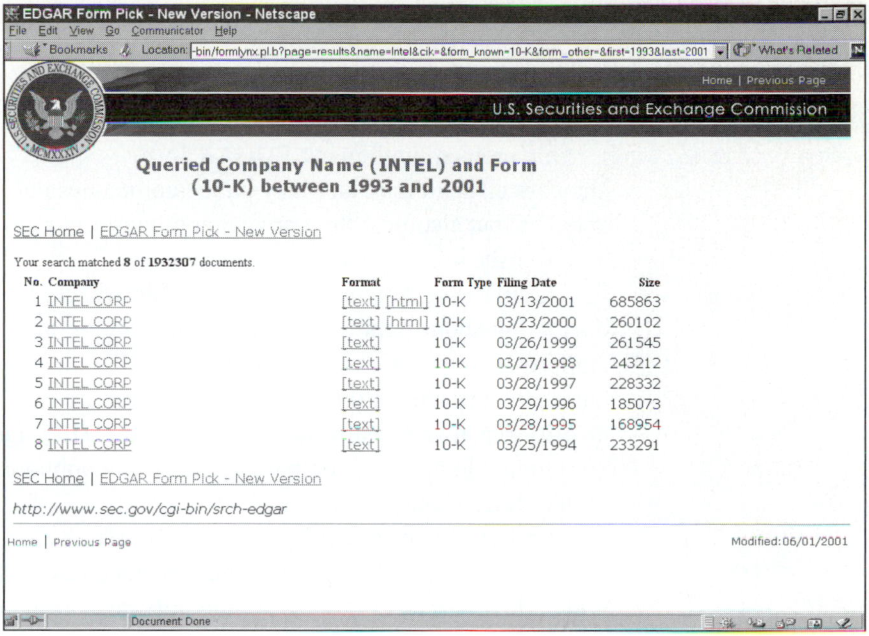

```
EDGAR Form Pick - New Version - Netscape                                    _ [8] X
File  Edit  View  Go  Communicator  Help
  Bookmarks    Location: -bin/formlynx.pl.b?page=results&name=Intel&cik=&form_known=10-K&form_other=&first=1993&last=2001 ▼  What's Related
                                                                    Home | Previous Page

                                               U.S. Securities and Exchange Commission

            Queried Company Name (INTEL) and Form
            (10-K) between 1993 and 2001

  SEC Home | EDGAR Form Pick - New Version

  Your search matched 8 of 1932307 documents.
  No. Company                     Format        Form Type  Filing Date    Size
   1  INTEL CORP            [text] [html]  10-K       03/13/2001     685863
   2  INTEL CORP            [text] [html]  10-K       03/23/2000     260102
   3  INTEL CORP            [text]         10-K       03/26/1999     261545
   4  INTEL CORP            [text]         10-K       03/27/1998     243212
   5  INTEL CORP            [text]         10-K       03/28/1997     228332
   6  INTEL CORP            [text]         10-K       03/29/1996     185073
   7  INTEL CORP            [text]         10-K       03/28/1995     168954
   8  INTEL CORP            [text]         10-K       03/25/1994     233291

  SEC Home | EDGAR Form Pick - New Version

  http://www.sec.gov/cgi-bin/srch-edgar

  Home | Previous Page                                        Modified: 06/01/2001

              Document: Done
```

the company name. The CIK code for Intel is 50863. However, learning the CIK codes is not an efficient use of time, unless you are a frequent EDGAR user. Picking the link at the bottom of the page entitled "a more flexible search is available" (not shown) not only links to Intel's 10-K forms but to all other forms that refer to Intel.

To see Intel's 10-K report, click on the html link at the right of a line. For example, clicking on the line for the 10-K report filed March 13, 2001, brings up Intel's annual report for 2000. Since the report is quite long, the fastest way to find out how much cash Intel has on hand is to search the document for the string *Cash and cash equivalents* in each html file. The corporate balance sheet entries, found in the subsidiary file a2040883zex-13.htm, show that at the end of 2000 Intel had almost $3.0 billion of cash on hand, which is more than enough to buy your company.

Given that the amount of cash corporations keep on hand fluctuates dramatically from month to month, always check the most recent 10-Q. The 10-Q report provides quarterly financial information for each company. Charting 10-Q values over time provides a better understanding of almost any company's finances than examining these measures at a single point in time.[5] To see Intel's most recent cash position go back to the Quick Forms Lookup page, shown in Figure 9.5, and change the form to 10-Q. November 11, 2001, is the

---

[5]Don't forget to adjust for inflation using the tools discussed in Chapter 10.

most recent form available when this book was written. This report shows that Intel's cash position strengthened since by September 29, 2001, six months beyond the annual report numbers, the company had increased its cash position to over $4.8 billion.

One problem with many EDGAR forms, especially the older ones, is that they are difficult to read. Many public companies not only send their forms to the SEC but also post their annual and quarterly reports on their own corporate website in an easier-to-read format.

The EDGAR system suffers another drawback. EDGAR contains only information about public companies and nothing about private companies or nonprofit organizations. Additionally, small companies, those that have fewer than 500 investors and less than $10 million in total assets, are not required to file annual and quarterly reports with the SEC. This means that, in addition to missing private companies, many tiny public companies are not in the EDGAR database.

The last drawback of the SEC's EDGAR site is that information is not posted for at least 24 hours after the SEC receives the forms. Instant access to EDGAR filings costs money, but this service is available on the Internet. Sites such as *EDGAR Online* (**http://www.edgar-online.com**) or *Free EDGAR* (**http://www.freeedgar.com**) provide easier-to-read forms, better searching capabilities, and no 24-hour delay, but they clutter your screen with ads or charge for services not provided by the SEC.

In addition to EDGAR information, the SEC website has other useful features under the Enforcement button (**http://www.sec.gov/divisions/enforce. shtml**). First, the SEC maintains a list of investor alerts that notify the public about financial frauds and fraudulent financial advisors. Second, the SEC has information on insider trading bounties. Insider trading occurs when people trade a stock based only on special information known only to insiders, like an impending acquisition. If you tip off the SEC about insider trading, it will pay up to 10% of any penalty it collects. Since fines for insider trading are up to triple the profit gained, bounties are potentially quite large. Third, the page contains general contact information for the SEC's enforcement division under the Complaint Center link. If someone breaks United States security laws by manipulating security market prices, sells worthless stock, or acts as an investment adviser and defrauds you of money, contact the enforcement division.

Practice Questions

How much cash did McDonald's hold last quarter?

How much did Michael Eisner, Chairman and CEO of Walt Disney, get paid last year?

Information for Canada

Canada has replicated and improved the United States' concept of a free on-line database of public company financial documents. The Canadian system is called SEDAR, an abbreviation for System for Electronic Document Analysis and Retrieval, and is located at **http://www.sedar.com**. This system, run by the Canadian securities regulatory authorities, is even better than EDGAR. All documents are available in PDF (Adobe's portable document format) so that you see an exact color replica of the information mailed to shareholders.[6] Additionally, there is no need to memorize obtuse report acronyms since SEDAR spells out all key items with labels like Annual Report instead of abbreviations like 10-K.

Let's assume you need more information about Molson, one of the world's major brewers. To find this company's annual report go to **http://www.sedar.com** and pick either the English or Francais (French) button. Then on the English site, select the Search Database button followed by Search For Public Company Documents. Type "Molson" in the box labeled Company Name and select Annual Report from the document type pull-down window. Pressing the "search" button brings up annual reports in both English and French for any period from 1997 to present.

Summary

The first step in finding basic information about companies is to search one of the many business directories like Standard & Poor's *Register* or D & B's *Million Dollar Directory*. Since each book is slightly different, it is often worthwhile to look up a company in more than one directory. If you need more than total sales, the company's address and the names of key company managers, try using the D & B's business report database located at **http://dbreports.telebase.com**. These reports, while expensive, provide extensive details about the financial characteristics of most public and private companies. If the company you are tracking is publicly traded in the United States, then search the Security and Exchange Commission's EDGAR database (**http://www.sec.gov**) for a free treasure trove of all major financial documents filed by the company from 1994 to present. Information on publicly traded Canadian companies is found on a similar system called SEDAR, located at **http://www.sedar.com**.

[6]Some documents prior to 1999 are available in other formats like Microsoft Word.

Chapter 10

Price Information

How much are other companies charging? Should our price change? How much are competitors raising their prices? These simple but common business questions arise constantly. Knowing how much competitors are changing their prices is a key piece of information for maximizing profits. Additionally, tracking other companies' pricing reduces the chances that you will increase prices on one day and then be forced the next day to roll them back.

Beyond determining the optimal price at which to sell your product or service, tracking price changes helps you control purchasing costs. When the price of a key or costly component changes, it is important to know if all vendors are making similar price changes, or just your vendor. If only your supplier is raising prices, it is either time to look for an alternate source or tell the vendor that this unmatched price increase means they will lose your business.

This chapter shows you how to track price movements using two giant databases maintained by the federal government. The federal government tracks prices via two closely related programs: the Consumer Price Index (CPI) and the Producer Price Index (PPI). Most managers listen carefully to the monthly CPI and PPI news reports to understand the country's inflation rate. Few realize, however, that to calculate the overall inflation rate the government needs to know the exact price on everything from consumer products like chocolate chip cookies and video rentals to industrial products like the price of steel plate and liability insurance. Since the government publicly releases massive amounts of highly specific information in addition to the general price indexes, the CPI and PPI databases provide managers with a high-quality, free method of tracking prices on just about every product and service.

In this chapter's first scenario let's assume you produce fishing gear for trout anglers and are thinking about raising prices by 5 percent. Before making the change you want to know how much competitors are raising fishing

TABLE 10.1 Major Restaurant Systemwide Sales (in billions of dollars)

Year	1990	1991	1992	1993	1994	1995	1996	1997	1998	1999	2000	Avg.
Sales	$18.8	$19.9	$21.9	$23.6	$26.0	$29.9	$31.8	$33.6	$36.0	$38.5	$40.2	
Change		5.9%	10.1%	7.8%	10.2%	15.0%	6.4%	5.7%	7.1%	6.9%	4.4%	**7.94%**

tackle and gear prices. In the second scenario, you need to create and justify a budget for purchasing computer software. You know how much was spent last year in your division. How do you estimate your spending needs for next year?

Understanding the Producer and Consumer Price Indexes

The federal government tracks prices via two closely related programs: the Consumer Price Index (CPI) and the Producer Price Index (PPI). So, what is the difference between the two indexes? First, the CPI covers only products purchased by consumers, like frozen chicken dinners, while the PPI covers products purchased by businesses, such as steel beams.

Second, the PPI measures how much money the first seller is paid for a product while the CPI measures how money the last buyer actually paid. The automotive industry shows just how important this difference is. Let's say Ford just sold a new Mustang convertible to a car dealer for $18,000. That price is used in the PPI calculation. The dealer then marks up the price to cover taxes, preparation, delivery, and his profit margin and then sells the car to an individual for $22,000. The $22,000 price is what goes into the CPI. While not every product has a large absolute markup, many products have a large percentage markup between the producer's selling price and the ultimate consumer's purchase price.

Which index should a manager use? If you are trying to track the price of a very specific product, you rarely have a choice because the two indexes are designed to avoid overlaps. While some categories, like chicken, sound similar, the Producer Price Index is always tracking bulk purchases while the Consumer Price Index records quantities a typical family would purchase.

Sometimes, you do not care about a specific product but just need to correct for general price increases. Correcting for inflation is important because when prices change, you cannot directly compare money figures from one year with figures in past years. A simple example makes this idea clear. A recent annual report trumpets that in a major restaurant company systemwide sales had a 10-year compound annual growth rate of 7.94 percent. A copy of the yearly sales figures and the associated sales growth is reproduced in Table 10.1.

TABLE 10.2   **Inflation-Adjusted Major Restaurant Systemwide Sales (in billions of constant dollars)**

Note: Inflation adjustment was done using the Bureau of Labor Statistics' inflation calculator.

Year	1990	1991	1992	1993	1994	1995	1996	1997	1998	1999	2000	Avg.
Sales	$24.8	$25.2	$26.9	$28.1	$30.2	$33.8	$34.9	$36.1	$38.0	$39.8	$40.2	
Change		1.6%	6.7%	4.5%	7.5%	11.9%	3.3%	3.4%	5.3%	4.7%	1.0%	**5.0%**

Overall, the average growth rate is 7.94 percent per year. The problem with this figure is that inflation has eroded money's value over time. Since food was cheaper in 1990, selling $1 worth of food a decade ago required more effort than selling $1 worth in 2000, when food was more expensive. Using the CPI each year's sales figures are adjusted in Table 10.2, with the procedure shown at the end of this chapter, to remove the effect of inflation.[1]

The adjusted table shows that, after accounting for inflation, sales only grew an average of 5.0 percent each year. Removing inflation's effects reduces sales growth by 3 percentage points a year. Since no United States annual report shows financial figures adjusted for inflation, this restaurant chain is doing nothing wrong. Nevertheless, unless you adjust financial statements for inflation, a true picture of a company's financial health will not emerge.

My simple rule is that whenever you have price information extending over more than five years, remove inflation's effects by deflating the numbers with the CPI. While it is also easy to adjust figures using the PPI, this index is less commonly used to adjust for the effects of inflation.

The Producer Price Index—How the Government Tracks Your Competitors

To track the prices of specific products or services, the best source is the Producer Price Index (PPI). Most business managers' only contact with the PPI is when they hear the monthly news report about how prices at the producer or wholesale level changed. The PPI, however, is much more than a single business indicator. Currently, the PPI program records and releases over 10,000 separate price indexes each month, covering almost every manufactured product and most services. This incredible level of detail means the government is probably already tracking your industry or product's price for you.

The simplest and fastest method of getting PPI information is to open the "Prices" chapter in the *United States Statistical Abstract* (pick the "Statistical Abstract" link on the Census Bureau's homepage (**http://www.census.gov**).

[1] All figures were changed into 2000 dollars.

FIGURE 10.1
Producer Price
Index Homepage

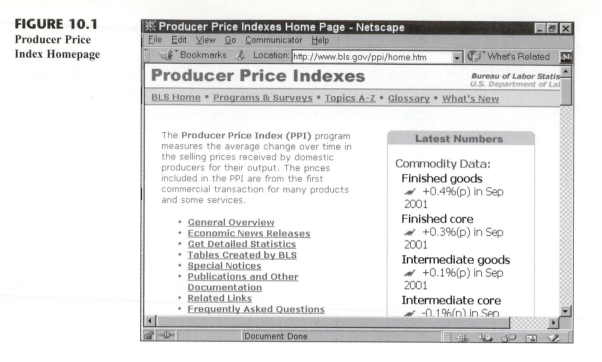

Each edition of the *Abstract* contains three key tables. The first two tables have the same title: Producer Price Indexes, by Stage of Processing. The first one shows yearly price changes for very broad categories like fuel or capital equipment, while the second reports price changes for particular commodities. The third table, entitled Producer Price Indexes for the Net Output of Selected Industries, shows yearly price changes for many large industries.

Unfortunately, because it takes the Census Bureau time to compile and publish the *Abstract,* the tables do not contain current information. For managers who need more timely information and do not like computers, the best way to get current monthly information is to purchase a subscription to the BLS periodical entitled the *PPI Detailed Report.*[2] This report, printed once each month and once at year's end, contains reams of detailed price tables.

If you need information now, or do not want to purchase a subscription, all of the price tables in the *PPI Detailed Report* are available for free online at the PPI homepage (**http://www.bls.gov/ppi**), shown in Figure 10.1.

To use PPI data you first have to understand that PPI information comes arranged in two different forms: by industry and by commodity. Because there

[2]Subscriptions are ordered from the United States Government Printing Office (**http:// bookstore.gpo.gov**).

are so many different PPI series, you can save a lot of time by first determining if your information is located under the industry or commodity branches. To see the list of industries covered, first pick the link labeled Industry Data which is found under the bullet Flat Files (FTP) in the Get Detailed Statistics section of the PPI homepage. Then scan down the list of files until you see the link "pc.product." Double click on these words to see if the product you are interested in tracking is on the industry list. If it is, write down the associated PPI code.

If you do not have any luck with the industry list, go back to the PPI homepage and pick the link labeled Commodity Data under the bullet Flat Files (FTP). Then scan down the page until you find the file "wp.item," which contains the codes and names of all commodities tracked by the PPI. Since some products appear in slightly different forms on both lists, always check both files to see which better fits your needs.

While it is impossible to list all 10,000 indexes in this book, a few examples will give you an idea of the detail provided by the PPI. Let's say you work for an insurance company and are thinking about the profitability of various policy lines. The PPI not only tracks the monthly price of homeowners' policies written nationwide, but also has separate indexes for California, New York, Texas, Florida, and Pennsylvania. The PPI also tracks auto insurance rates by providing a national index plus separate indexes for the 10 largest states. Beyond homeowners' and auto insurance, the PPI also maintains separate insurance indexes for policies like fidelity, inland marine, medical liability, and product liability. With this extensive information it is easy to monitor prices for almost every type of widely held insurance policy.

Insurance is not a unique case. The PPI tracks almost every business category at a fine level of detail. If you work for a retail appliance store like Circuit City, Best Buy, or another chain and want to know how good your purchasing department's negotiators are, the PPI can help. Using the PPI, it is easy to track the prices stores pay for appliances and home electronics. For example, the 1999 PPI summary report shows that the wholesale cost of projection TV sets fell by 7.2 percent over the year but upright vacuum cleaners rose by 0.7 percent. With this level of detail, it is easy to compare how your actual costs changed compared to other retailers.

Once you know your product or service's PPI code, the most direct method of getting producer price data is to use the online table-generation software. To use this software, choose one of the links under the Create Customized Tables link on the PPI homepage.

The Create Customized Tables (one screen) section of the PPI homepage contains three picks: industry data, industry data discontinued, and commodity data. Do not use the discontinued series since all information stops in

FIGURE 10.2
Top Level
Commodity
Custom Table
Creation Screen

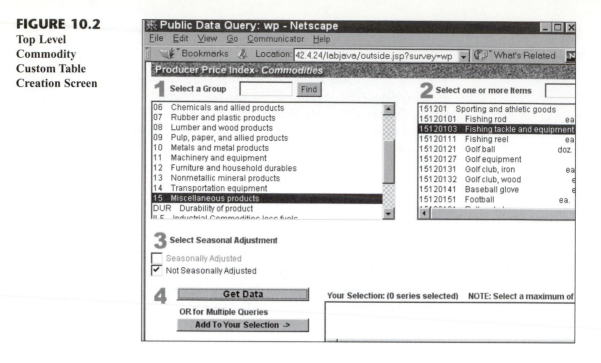

1997. Instead, pick one of the other two selections based on your information needs.

Now let's answer the scenario where you produce fishing gear and are interested in raising your prices by 5 percent. You can find how prices have changed for fishing tackle and equipment producers by picking the Commodity Data link and working through four steps. The first step asks you to choose the commodities major group. Fishing tackle is under the product category "15 Miscellaneous products." Highlighting this category creates a detailed list of all the miscellaneous items in the scroll box labeled "Select one or more Items." The line we want is "120103 Fishing tackle and equipment," which is found after toys and games but before golf equipment and firearms (see Figure 10.2).

The third step asks you to choose between "Seasonally" and "Not Seasonally Adjusted data." While broad high-level series are available both ways, the majority of finely detailed categories, like fishing tackle, are only available "Not Seasonally Adjusted."

When you push the Get Data button at the page's bottom, a large chart of information, reproduced in Figure 10.3, is produced.

To see how much the annual fishing gear index has changed, scroll to the right. The far right column lists the annual (labeled **Ann**) index values. For example, in 1999 the index was 138.4 while in 2000 the index stood at 142.2,

FIGURE 10.3
Results of PPI
Custom Table
Creation

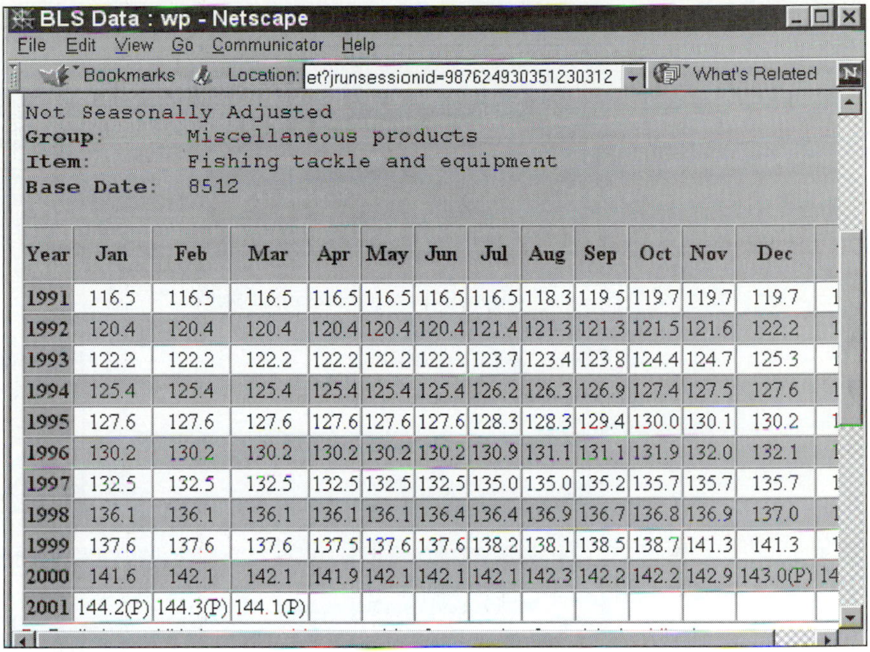

Year	Jan	Feb	Mar	Apr	May	Jun	Jul	Aug	Sep	Oct	Nov	Dec	
1991	116.5	116.5	116.5	116.5	116.5	116.5	116.5	118.3	119.5	119.7	119.7	119.7	1
1992	120.4	120.4	120.4	120.4	120.4	120.4	121.4	121.3	121.3	121.5	121.6	122.2	1
1993	122.2	122.2	122.2	122.2	122.2	122.2	123.7	123.4	123.8	124.4	124.7	125.3	1
1994	125.4	125.4	125.4	125.4	125.4	125.4	126.2	126.3	126.9	127.4	127.5	127.6	1
1995	127.6	127.6	127.6	127.6	127.6	127.6	128.3	128.3	129.4	130.0	130.1	130.2	1
1996	130.2	130.2	130.2	130.2	130.2	130.2	130.9	131.1	131.1	131.9	132.0	132.1	1
1997	132.5	132.5	132.5	132.5	132.5	132.5	135.0	135.0	135.2	135.7	135.7	135.7	1
1998	136.1	136.1	136.1	136.1	136.1	136.4	136.4	136.9	136.7	136.8	136.9	137.0	1
1999	137.6	137.6	137.6	137.5	137.6	137.6	138.2	138.1	138.5	138.7	141.3	141.3	1
2000	141.6	142.1	142.1	141.9	142.1	142.1	142.1	142.3	142.2	142.2	142.9	143.0(P)	14
2001	144.2(P)	144.3(P)	144.1(P)										

Not Seasonally Adjusted
Group: Miscellaneous products
Item: Fishing tackle and equipment
Base Date: 8512

an increase of just 2.7 percent. Using these data and the percentage change formula, you now can calculate exactly how much your competitors have increased prices over any time period.

The other choice, Industry Data, in the Create Customized Tables (one screen) section of the PPI homepage shows how prices change by industry instead of by product. Let's assume you work for a book publishing company and want to know how the prices of business books have changed. Producing a custom table for industrial prices is simpler than commodity prices, because only three items are needed. Figure 10.4 shows that the first selection asks for the high level industry. Select book publishing (SIC code 2731), which is toward the middle of the list. The second selection asks you to choose the portion of the industry, which in this example is #33, business books. Selecting Get Data shows that the index for business books rose from 121.5 in 1998 to 136.3 in 2000, a price jump of approximately 12 percent over two years.

The one drawback of using online PPI data is that the table generator searches both current and discontinued data series. While the PPI program currently releases just over 10,000 series, the database contains more than 19,000. It is fairly easy to tell when you have selected a discontinued index since the data stop well before the current year. For example, the PPI presently releases 50 different book publishing series, but the database contains over 90 series. Another example of discontinued price series is fishing gear. The

FIGURE 10.4
Industry Custom
Table Creation
Program

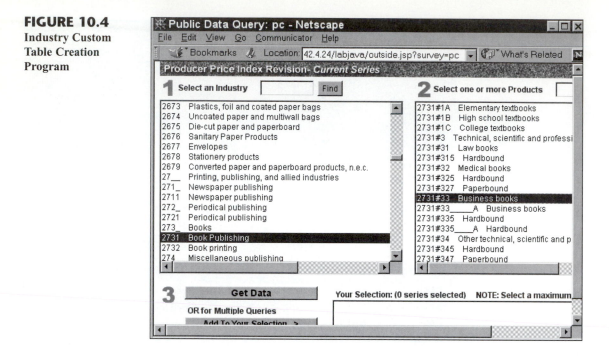

customized tables program allows you to ask for the prices of rods and reels separately, even though the rod and reel indexes were canceled in the mid-1970s and replaced by a combined index.

**Practice
Question**

You work for the vitamin division of a pharmaceutical company. The marketing department suggests raising vitamin prices, while the sales force is adamantly opposed. Using the industry data series, check how much vitamin prices changed over the last year.

**Practice
Question**

Vitamins are found in both the industry and commodity lists. Use the commodity data series to check how much adult multivitamin prices have changed. How different are answers from the commodity and industry databases?

Consumer Prices and Inflation

In addition to tracking the prices of individual products and services, many managers need to know how the overall price level is changing. Changes in the overall price level, called inflation, are important because many union contracts, rental agreements, and leases contain inflation adjustment clauses. When inflation increases, businesses that signed these contracts automatically pay more money. Additionally when inflation increases, the Federal Reserve

TABLE 10.3
Percentage of Various
Categories in CPI as
of December 2000

Percentage	Category
30.3%	Shelter/housing
5.1%	Fuel/utilities
4.6%	Household operation
9.6%	Food at home
5.7%	Food away
1.0%	Alcohol
17.6%	Transportation
5.8%	Medical care
4.5%	Clothing
5.9%	Entertainment
5.3%	Communication/education
4.8%	Other

combats the problem by raising interest rates. This makes it more costly for businesses to borrow money. Hence, managers in businesses with heavy debt loads need to understand and monitor consumer prices to predict future interest expenses.

Tracking changes in the cost of living is the main function of the Consumer Price Index (CPI). The Bureau of Labor Statistics, using a four-step process, produces the CPI. First, the Bureau uses information from the Consumer Expenditure Survey, which was discussed in Chapter 6, to determine exactly what the typical household purchases. This list of items and the corresponding quantities is commonly called the *market basket of goods*.

Then, "shoppers" are sent out to stores and other retail outlets to price all the goods the typical household purchases. The prices found in stores are used to determine how much the market basket of goods costs. This provides a baseline cost-of-living estimate. Shoppers are then sent back to the same or similar stores each month to reprice all items in the basket. The fourth and final step is to calculate the percentage difference between the current price and original price of the entire market basket. This number is the inflation rate. Table 10.3 gives an idea of how much each major consumer category contributes to the overall CPI.[3]

While this description is quite simple, the actual task of collecting and calculating the CPI is monumental. Each month a total of 21,000 supermarkets, gas stations, department stores, and other retail establishments are visited in

[3] The source for these numbers is **ftp://ftp.bls.gov/pub/special/requests/cpi/Usri2000.txt**.

85 different urban areas. In addition, housing costs are estimated from a separate survey of approximately 60,000 renters, landlords, and homeowners.

Before reading about where to find CPI information, business managers need to understand that there is currently a major debate about whether the CPI overstates inflation. Politicians are concerned because a number of very big government programs, such as Social Security and the tax code, contain inflation adjustment clauses. When prices go up, Social Security payments and the standard tax deduction automatically increase, causing government spending to increase and government revenue to fall. Some of the reasons why the CPI might overstate inflation are discussed in the following paragraphs.

1. Substitution bias: When prices increase, consumers often switch or substitute items. For example, if fish increases in price and beef does not, then many consumers will switch from fish to beef in an attempt to control their grocery expenses. Since the CPI is based on a fixed basket of goods, substitution is not possible. Hence, when fish prices increase, the CPI records an increase in consumer's grocery bills, even when it did not actually occur.

2. Introduction of new goods: The CPI is very slow to include new items in its market basket. It usually picks up new goods when the basket is recalculated roughly every 10 years. For example, cellular telephones joined the CPI in 1999, many years after being widely used in the marketplace. Many new items, like VCRs, camcorders, and computers, start off at a high price and then rapidly fall in price as they gain market acceptance. By missing this introductory phase, the CPI overlooks the dramatic reduction in new product prices.

3. Quality changes: While the CPI makes some attempts to correct for quality changes, it often underestimates the amount of quality increases. For example, medical technology has made many rapid improvements and innovations over time. Since the CPI does not adjust for medical improvements, all increases in medical prices are attributed to cost inflation. While the CPI backs up complaints that health care costs are soaring out of control, many people in both the government and business miss the key point that some of the increase stems from an improvement in care, not just inflation.

Research by the Boskin Commission[4] suggests that correcting the CPI for all these problems would lower inflation by about 1.1 percentage point a year. Nevertheless, even with some problems the CPI is still extremely useful for tracking how the overall price level is changing.

---

[4] The report's official name is "Final Report of the Advisory Commission to Study the Consumer Price Index." The report is stored online at the Social Security archives (**http://www.ssa/gov/history**).

How to Use the CPI

There are two different inflation adjustment formulas used to adjust prices over time. The first formula deals with business problems expressed in rate terms. For example, the interest on bank loans and salary raises is often stated not in absolute dollar amounts but in percentage or rate terms. These rates are nominal or current value numbers. Nominal numbers can be recalculated into real or inflation-adjusted values by using the following inflation rate formula:

$$\text{Real Rate} = \text{Nominal Rate} - \text{Inflation Rate}$$

For example, let's say the inflation rate is 2.7 percent and the interest rate on your bank loan is 8.5 percent. In inflation-adjusted terms, the bank is being repaid not at 8.5 percent but at 5.8 percent (8.5 percent − 2.7 percent). For another example, let's assume it is salary review time. Your manager compliments you for an excellent job and boosts your pay by 3 percent. After adjusting for inflation, he raised your standard of living by only 0.3 percent, which instead of being a compliment is actually a slap in the face.

The second formula adjusts old prices into current terms. This formula is the one used to adjust the major restaurant's systemwide sales at the beginning of the chapter. The formula, shown below, allows you to compare prices from two different years or time periods.

$$\text{Current Price} = \text{Old Price} \cdot \frac{\text{New CPI Value}}{\text{Old CPI Value}}$$

For example, the movie business constantly brags about new box office records that are smashing all previous totals. The hit *Titanic* currently stands at the top of the all-time list with $601 million in sales.[5] Ranked much lower on the list, with sales of $200 million, is *Gone with the Wind*. The problem with comparing these movies is that movie ticket prices were much higher when *Titanic* was released in 1997 than in 1939 when *Gone with the Wind* packed movie houses. Using the above formula you can convert *Gone with the Wind* figures into 1997 dollars. The average value of the CPI in 1939 was 13.9, while in 1997 the average CPI value was 160.5.[6] Inserting these values into the formula gives:

$$\$2.3 \text{ billion} = \$200 \text{ million} \cdot \frac{160.5}{13.9}$$

[5] One place to find the top grossing movies is **http://movieweb.com/movie/alltime.html**. This URL also discusses why lists of movie receipts are not adjusted for inflation.

[6] Calculations are done using values found on the CPI homepage under the link labeled Table Containing History of CPI-U United States All Items Indexes and Annual Percent Change from 1913 to Present.

FIGURE 10.5
Consumer Price
Index Homepage

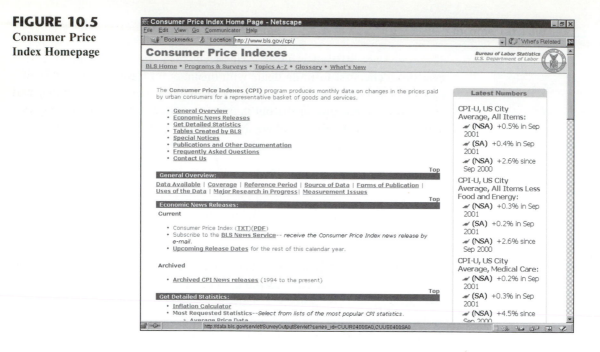

After adjusting for inflation, *Gone with the Wind* grossed $2.3 billion in 1997 dollars, which is almost four times what *Titanic* earned at the box office. While not every business needs to compare information back to the 1930s, the same formula applies when adjusting prices that are only a few years out of date.

Quick CPI Information

The simplest place to find CPI information is online at the CPI homepage, located at **http://www.bls.gov/cpi**. The homepage looks like Figure 10.5.

If you need to quickly adjust a number, pick the link labeled Inflation Calculator under the Get Detailed Statistics heading.[7] This calculator fills in the following statement: "$_____ in _____ (year) has the same buying power as $_____ in _____ (year)." You need to fill in both year boxes and one of the dollar amount boxes. When you hit Calculate, the sentence is completed. For example, my grandfather earned a $1 a day during the Great Depression. How much would Grandpa earn today? Fill in the sentence by saying "$1.00 in 1935 (year) has the same buying power as $_____ in 2001 (year)." Hit Calculate, and the computer completes the sentence with the value $12.93.

[7] The Bank of Canada has a similar inflation calculator for adjusting Canadian numbers. Look under the "Inflation" topic at **http://www.bankofcanada.ca**.

A second place that CPI information is readily available is in the *Statistical Abstract's* section entitled "Prices." This chapter contains two key CPI tables. The first table, entitled Consumer Price Indexes for All Urban Consumers (CPI-U) for Selected Items and Groups, lists the index values for almost 100 different items or categories. Using this table, it is easy to see which items have gone up dramatically in price (private elementary and high school tuition rose 384 percent from 1980 to 2000) and which items have not (interstate telephone calls were down 18 percent over the same period). The second key table is entitled Cost of Living Index-Selected Metropolitan Areas. This table compares consumer prices for almost 200 different cities to the national average. Using this table it is easy to see exactly how much more it costs to live in high-cost cities like New York (2.35 times the national average in 2000) versus low-cost cities like Jonesboro, Arkansas (87 percent of the national average in 2000).

Some business managers, especially those in the financial services industry, need to receive inflation information more quickly than the *Statistical Abstract* delivers. To get the latest inflation information, you can get the Bureau of Labor Statistics' press releases via e-mail. To subscribe, go to the CPI homepage and pick the link labeled Subscribe to the BLS News Service under the Economic News Releases section.

For people already overwhelmed by e-mail, each day all current and past press releases are available online under the News Releases section. Either method will give you more details than the headlines that flash across the wire services and faster information than waiting for the next *Statistical Abstract*.

Practice Question

The original 1977 *Star Wars* movie's gross receipts were $461 million. The 1999 Star Wars movie *The Phantom Menace* had gross receipts of $431 million. Comparing just the raw numbers suggests the two films were roughly equal box office hits. If the 1977 receipts are corrected for inflation, which film did better?

Practice Question

The 1997 hit movie *Titanic* took in $601 million. How does its receipts compare after adjusting for inflation to the original 1977 *Star Wars* gross of $461 million?

Detailed CPI Information

Like the PPI, the CPI includes a large number of very detailed price indexes that track the costs of an extensive array of products. Each month all of the current price indexes are printed in a periodical entitled the *CPI Detailed Report*. This report not only lists each index value but also contains four tables (P1 to P4), which show the actual prices recorded by shoppers. The first three

P tables list the price of gasoline, electricity, and other energy sources for the country, each region and 14 major cities per month. Table P4 lists the average retail food prices in the country and major regions by month. The detail in this table is phenomenal. For example, you can read that the price of a pound of chocolate chip cookies rose by a nickel from November to December or that a dozen grade A large eggs cost 25 cents more in the northeast than in the midwest.

All information found in the *CPI Detailed Report* is also online at the CPI homepage under the heading Tables Created by BLS. Under this section are two key selections. First, the Table Containing History of CPI lists every annual and monthly CPI value since 1913. Using this table and the formulas described earlier in the chapter, business managers can adjust for the consequences of inflation for almost any time period. Second, the links beginning with Consumer Price Index Detailed Report are PDF versions of the most recent printed report. Given the sheer quantity of information, it is relatively difficult to find one or two pieces of data in either the hardcopy or electronic version of the *CPI Detailed Report.*

A quicker way to find CPI data for particular items uses the Create Customized Tables (one screen) function on the CPI homepage. This selection runs the same data retrieval application shown earlier in the PPI section. The Create Customized Tables (one screen) selection contains the following choices:

- Average Price Data.

- Consumer Price Index—All Urban Consumers (Current Series).

- Consumer Price Index—Urban Wage Earners and Clerical Workers (Current Series).

- Department Store Inventory Price Index.

The first selection, Average Price Data, contains the information found in the four P tables that list the actual prices that CPS shoppers recorded for energy and food. Few business managers outside of retail trade need anything in the last selection, entitled the Department Store Index. The important selections are the second and third choices, which end in (Current Series). There is little difference between the second pick, which tracks all urban consumers, and the third, which tracks urban wage earners. While both contain the same underlying data, the third item gives more weight to purchases made by clerical and other blue-collar workers. While 75 years ago blue-collar and white-collar workers consumed different items, today there is relatively little difference in the tastes and purchases between these families. Given that tastes are converging, it is not important which line you pick. I personally use the second pick, which tracks all urban consumers since it covers a broader demographic group.

Let's answer the second scenario, in which you need to budget money for purchasing computer software. You know how much you spent last year per person in your division. How much will you spend this year? One way to answer the question is to calculate the change in software prices and then adjust last year's amount. Using Create Customized Tables, price changes for software are easily determined.

First, on the CPI main page, pick under Create Customized Tables (one screen) the link Consumer Price Index—All Urban Consumers (Current Series). This enters you into a four-step process, illustrated in Figure 10.6. The first screen asks you to select a particular geographic area. Since most detailed data series of business interest are available only for the entire United States, select U.S. city average.

The second step is the key, since it allows you to pick the item of interest. Scroll through the list and familiarize yourself with all the different price series the CPI tracks. Broader indexes are at the top, while more detailed indexes are at the list's bottom. For this example, highlight the line labeled Computer software and accessories.

The third step asks you to choose Seasonally Adjusted or Not Seasonally Adjusted data. Most of the detailed data series of business interest are

FIGURE 10.6
**Consumer
Price Index
Public Data Query**

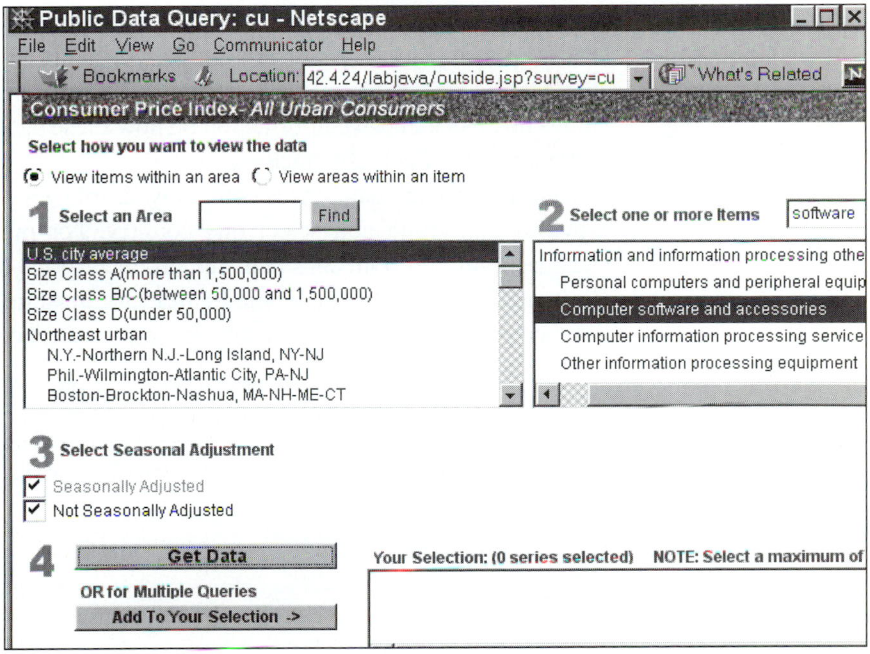

available only in unadjusted form, so select this for our example. For the last step pick the Get Data button.

The resulting table shows that software prices fell from 1998 to 1999 by 7.4 percent and from 1999 to 2000 by 3.4 percent. This suggests that the dramatic fall in software prices is over, and your software budget per person can shrink slightly. If you need to see other years or want the display formatted differently, use the Reformat selection found above the output.

Practice Question

Your broker just called and recommended buying stock in a video rental chain. The broker's research department just raised its forecast of the stock's future price by 25 percent based on expectations of much higher profit margins. You are skeptical. What has happened to video rental fees in the last few years?

Practice Question

Given you are not interested in purchasing stock in the video rental chain, your broker wants to know if he can recommend cable television companies. Intrigued, you want to know how cable television rates have changed over time.

Information for Other Countries

Every major country in the world tracks and releases some type of consumer and producer price index. Some of these indexes capture prices changes only in key urban areas, while others are nationwide in scope. Price indexes for approximately 50 countries are found in the International Monetary Fund's (IMF) Special Data Dissemination Standard (SDDS) database. This database, located at **http://dsbb.imf.org/country.htm**, not only provides price index values but also extensive information on how these data were created and what information they actually track.

Using the SDDS database is extremely simple. Go to the link shown in the previous paragraph and select one country. For our example, let's select Canada. A link for both consumer and producer price indexes (spelled indices by the IMF) is available under the Real Sector heading. Picking the consumer link brings up the following documentation for Canada.

> Prices are obtained from special surveys providing, on average, 60,000 monthly price quotes for about 650 representative commodities. The prices are collected in 15 to 76 locations depending on the price behaviors of the specific commodity, from approximately 7,000 outlets, and are collected over the first three weeks of the month.

Canadian consumer price data are then found by selecting the link "DATA Access to Canada's statistics." Picking this link provides the latest and previous month's price index, plus the percentage change over the past year. In addition to these values, each category is linked so you can jump directly to more price index data available at Statistics Canada's website. Unfortunately, these online tables provide only general price index information, not the specific changes experienced by narrowly defined products or services. To see lower level details, look at Statistic Canada's monthly periodicals *The Consumer Price Index* and *Industry Price Indexes*.[8]

Summary

CPI and PPI data help managers in two ways. First, using the detailed series produced by both programs, managers can track prices each month for thousands of products and services. The exact price indexes are stored on the PPI homepage (**http://www.bls.gov/ppi**) and CPI homepage (**http://www.bls.gov/cpi**). The second way price information is used is to calculate the overall inflation rate. For most managers, the fastest way to adjust a figure for inflation is to select the Inflation Calculator on the CPI homepage. Plugging values into this tool quickly adjusts any price for any time period from 1913 to the present. If you need data for countries outside the United States use the IMF's SDDS database, located at **http://dsbb.imf.org/country.htm**.

[8] Specific issues of the Canadian CPI periodical can be download electronically in PDF format. The price when this book was written was C$8.00 per issue. The industrial price index periodical currently is available only in paper form, but most of the information is stored on the CANSIM II database.

Chapter

11

Human Resources

How much should I raise employees' salaries? Are my benefits costs increasing in line with other companies? What salary should I offer a new worker? This chapter shows managers where to find information to answer these and other common human resource questions.

Are you paying your workers too much or too little? The first part of the chapter shows how to track wage and salary changes, key information for pay reviews. Then the chapter examines two detailed wage surveys. By using these surveys you can avoid offering new workers starting rates that are too high or too low. Additionally, using these surveys ensures your staff is competitively paid, which reduces turnover. The chapter concludes with sources of information on benefits, which are becoming a bigger portion of the total compensation package. Using all this information ensures you have the hard numbers needed to solve many human resource problems.

In this chapter's first scenario, it is time for you to give staff in the phone-call center their annual salary increase. Because overall company revenues have been down the last few quarters, you are unable to be overly generous. However, a booming labor market means that if the company is perceived as being cheap, most of the phone staff will leave. What is an appropriate increase? The second scenario is more personal. You know how much you are paid. Are you over- or underpaid compared to others doing a similar job?

Salary Review Time: How Much Should the Typical Worker's Pay Change?

Most firms change wages and salaries once or twice a year at a designated review time. During a review, stellar workers usually get big raises, poor performers small raises, and everyone else gets the "standard" raise. The common management problem is figuring out how much the standard, or typical worker's, pay should change. Using the Employment Cost Index (ECI), calculated each quarter by the Bureau of Labor Statistics (BLS), this question is answered easily.

The ECI is actually three different indexes: an index that measures wage and salary changes, an index measuring changes in employee benefits costs, and a third index, which combines wage and benefit information. The key index to use for determining standard raises is the wage and salary series. The wage and salary series tracks regular earnings before payroll deductions, bonuses, and cost-of-living adjustments.[1] This means the ECI wage series shows how worker's base pay rates are changing, not how the total amount they are paid is changing.

Each quarter, at the end of March, June, September, and December, ECI survey staff contacts over 6,000 private and publicly held businesses and about 800 state and local government units and asks each detailed questions about their workers' pay. Because the ECI collects information from the same businesses for roughly five years, it provides an accurate measure of how pay changes from quarter to quarter.

It is important to note that the ECI does not tell you the exact amount to pay workers. Since it is an index, it shows only how pay is changing over time. For example, it shows that pay increased 5 percent last year. If you do not understand indexes, read Appendix 1, "What Is An Index," at the back of this book before continuing. Once you understand indexes go to the Compensation Cost Trends homepage **(http://www.bls.gov/ect)**, shown in Figure 11.1, to track pay changes.

One easy method of following pay changes is to read the quarterly ECI news release. This release is the first choice in the Economic News Releases section.[2] Read the news release at least once to understand which detailed occupations and industries are covered by the ECI.

Another method for tracking pay changes is to create custom ECI tables. Let's answer the first scenario, about pay adjustments for the phone staff handling your reservations hotline. You can create custom tables by picking Create Customized Tables (one screen), which is found under the Get Detailed Statistics heading on the ECI homepage, and completing the following six steps.

---

[1] The wage series also excludes premium pay for overtime and weekend work, shift differentials, and nonproduction bonuses.
[2] The news release link, Employment Cost for Employee Compensation, tracks the actual cost per hour of benefits and wages.

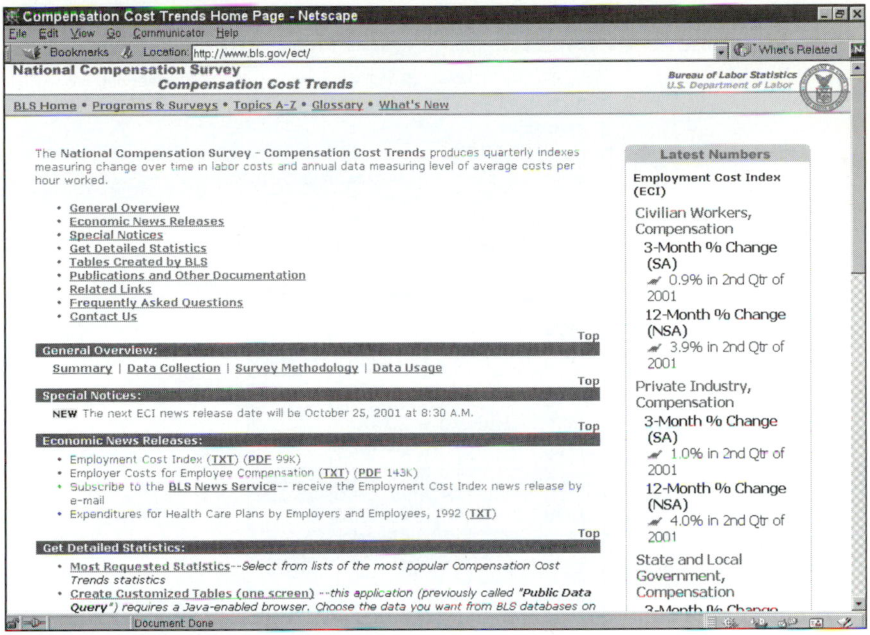

FIGURE 11.1
Compensation Cost Trends Homepage

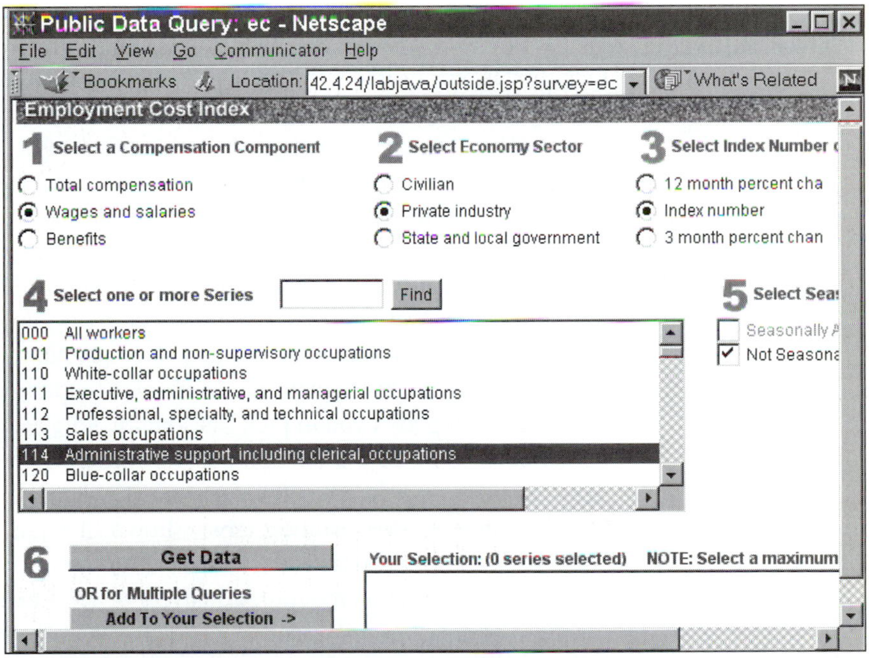

FIGURE 11.2
Compensation Cost Trends Customized Table Creation Screen

The Create Customized Tables screen, shown in Figure 11.2, first asks you to choose between the three ECI series. Select Wages and Salaries since this option records only base pay.

FIGURE 11.3
Employment Cost Index Output

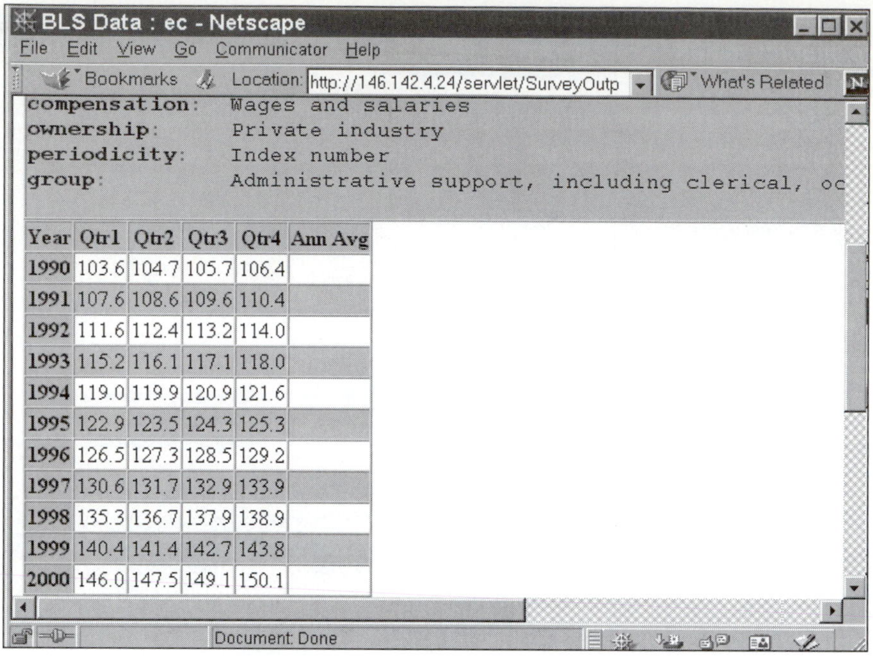

BLS Data : ec - Netscape

compensation: Wages and salaries
ownership: Private industry
periodicity: Index number
group: Administrative support, including clerical, oc

Year	Qtr1	Qtr2	Qtr3	Qtr4	Ann Avg
1990	103.6	104.7	105.7	106.4	
1991	107.6	108.6	109.6	110.4	
1992	111.6	112.4	113.2	114.0	
1993	115.2	116.1	117.1	118.0	
1994	119.0	119.9	120.9	121.6	
1995	122.9	123.5	124.3	125.3	
1996	126.5	127.3	128.5	129.2	
1997	130.6	131.7	132.9	133.9	
1998	135.3	136.7	137.9	138.9	
1999	140.4	141.4	142.7	143.8	
2000	146.0	147.5	149.1	150.1	

The second step asks you to select Civilian, Private industry, or State and local government. Select Private industry if your business is neither military nor government related. The third step allows you to select 12-month percentage change, 3-month percentage change, or the index itself. What you choose for this step is based on your personal needs. I find working directly with the index easier, so in this example, let's select that.

The fourth step is the key. It allows you to pick exactly what type of workers you are interested in tracking. If you have not read the news release, scroll through the list and familiarize yourself with all the occupations and industries. To answer our scenario, find and select occupation number 114 labeled "Administrative support, including clerical, occupations."

The fifth step asks you to pick Seasonally Adjusted or Not Seasonally Adjusted data. Most of the data of business interest are available only in unadjusted form, so select this for our example. Then for the last step, pick the Get Data button. The resulting table, shown in Figure 11.3, reveals that the wage and salary index for clerical and administrative occupations rose from 143.8 to 150.1 between the fourth quarters of 1999 and 2000. This means pay for these occupations increased by $(150.1 - 143.8)/143.8 = 4.4$ percent in the past year.[3] How much should you increase phone staff wages? I would boost phone staff pay by 4.4 percent, which matches the market, and explain that

[3] Remember the percentage change formula, which was described in Chapter 2, is (new value − old value) / old value.

until revenues start increasing the company cannot be more generous. To determine the wage increase for another group of employees, use the fourth step to pick a different occupational or industrial group.

**Practice
Question**

As soon as you finished giving the phone center staff a raise, the sales force asked how much of an increase it was getting. How much did wages increase for individuals in sales occupations last year?

What Is the Pay for a Particular Job?

While the ECI is very useful for knowing how much pay rates change, where can you find information on the actual wage and salary rates? Managers often need to know exactly how much people are paid for various jobs when creating new positions, filling positions at new levels, or just ensuring current pay rates are not out of line.

Theoretically, pay is based solely on an employee's value to the company. Workers directly impacting the company's bottom line or holding special skills and knowledge theoretically should receive high pay. Marginal, incompetent, and relatively unskilled workers should receive low pay. Unfortunately, since accurately assessing a worker's skills and effect on company profits is very difficult, most managers often pay workers roughly what other companies are paying.

Many managers know about other companies' pay by reading recruitment agency or headhunter salary surveys. These salary surveys, unfortunately, have a number of drawbacks. First, most cover only a select group of occupations. Second, the information often comes from companies that use recruitment agencies, not a nationally representative random sample. Since primarily large companies use recruitment agencies and since large companies typically pay more than small and medium-size businesses, these salary surveys are tracking only the best-paid workers, not all workers in any occupation. Hence, it is important to look beyond private surveys for pay information.

The Bureau of Labor Statistics provides two different ways to determine how much other firms pay their workers: the Occupation and Employment Statistics (OES) program and the National Compensation Survey (NCS). The Occupational Employment Statistics (OES) survey is an annual mail survey done during the last three months of each year. Each year the survey is mailed to about 400,000 businesses. The survey's goal is to measure, at the national, state, and local levels, the number of people employed in each occupation and how much they are paid.[4]

---

[4] While BLS disseminates this wage information, much of the work is actually done by each state's local employment security agency, which also manages the unemployment insurance systems. These state agencies use the survey to track local labor market conditions.

FIGURE 11.4

Occupational
Employment
Statistics Homepage

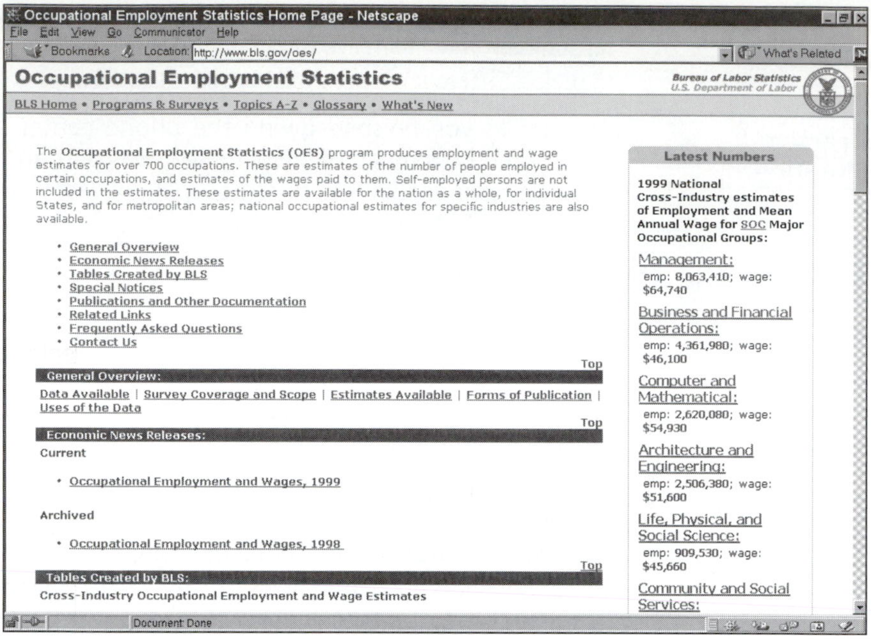

Wage and salary data from the Occupational Employment Statistics survey are found on the OES homepage **(http://www.bls.gov/oes)**, pictured in Figure 11.4.

Once at the OES homepage, you can easily find the base pay rates for any specific occupation. As an example, let's look at how much accountants earn. To find accountants' pay, pick the Tables Created by BLS link on the homepage. This brings up the screen shown in Figure 11.5 that contains for each year of OES data the following three entries: National estimates, State estimates, and Metropolitan Area estimates.

To find how much accountants earn, first choose national estimates under the year of interest. For this example let's pick 1999 National estimates. This brings up a page, shown in Figure 11.6, which contains the broad occupational categories such as: management, business and financial operations, and computer and mathematical occupations.

To find wages for any occupation, you must move from these broad occupational categories down to a very specific job. For example, to find accountants and auditors first pick Business and Financial Operations Occupations and then scroll down the list until you find 13-2011 Accountants and Auditors.

After picking the link labeled 13-2011 Accountants and Auditors, you will see the page shown in Figure 11.7 containing the job description and the pay ranges of accountants and auditors. In the 1999 OES survey, the top

FIGURE 11.5

Year and Area
Selection for
Occupational
Employment
Statistics

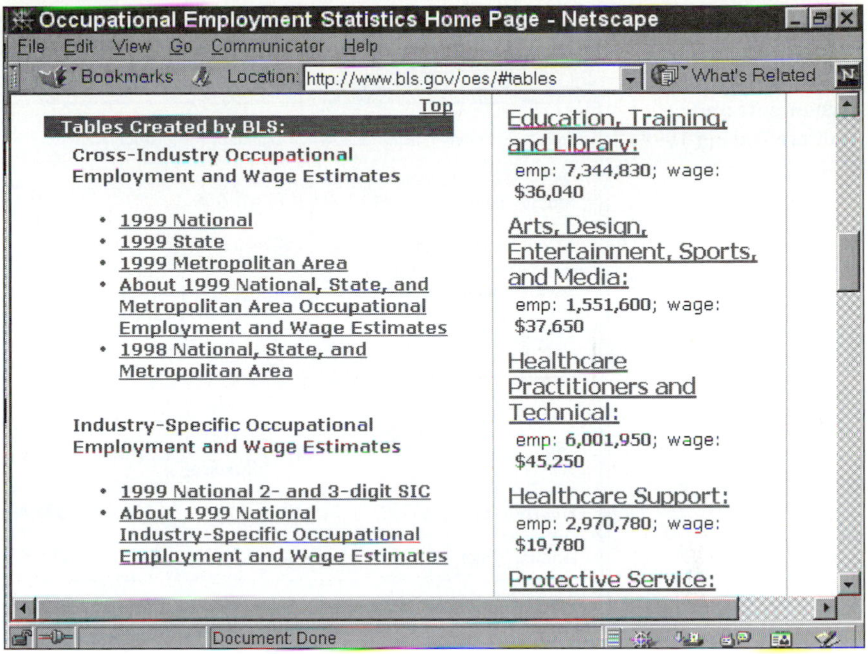

FIGURE 11.6

Occupational
Selection for OES
Data

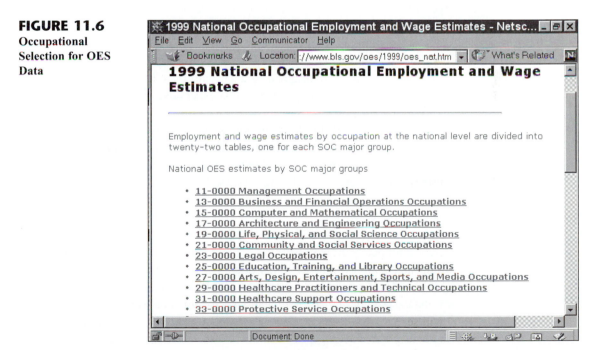

FIGURE 11.7
OES National Pay
Estimates for
Accountants and
Auditors During 1999

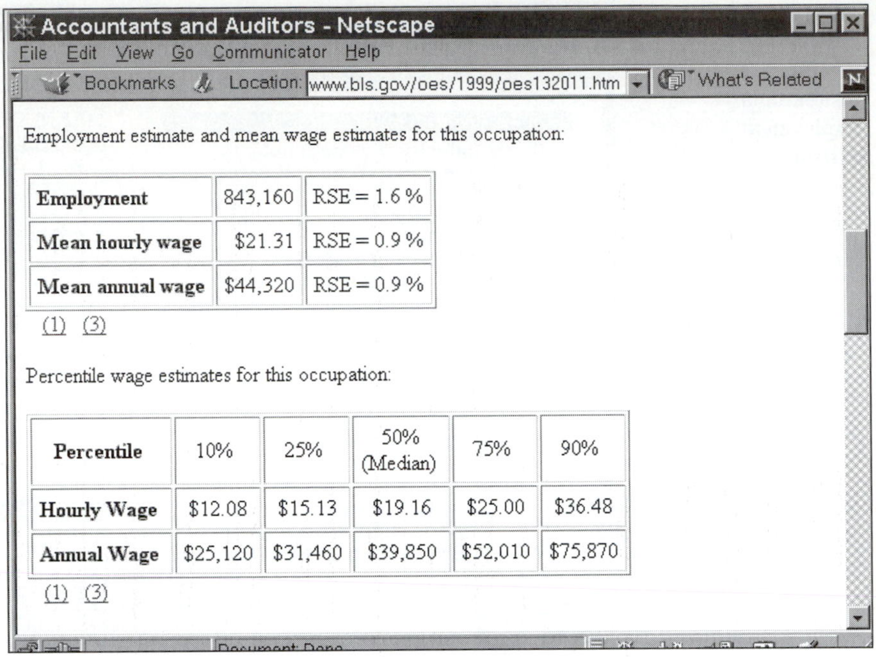

Employment estimate and mean wage estimates for this occupation:

Employment	843,160	RSE = 1.6 %
Mean hourly wage	$21.31	RSE = 0.9 %
Mean annual wage	$44,320	RSE = 0.9 %

(1) (3)

Percentile wage estimates for this occupation:

Percentile	10%	25%	50% (Median)	75%	90%
Hourly Wage	$12.08	$15.13	$19.16	$25.00	$36.48
Annual Wage	$25,120	$31,460	$39,850	$52,010	$75,870

(1) (3)

10 percent of all accountants earned at least $75,870 per year while the average (median) accountant earned $39,850, or about half the earnings of the top 10 percent.

Besides national information, the OES program also releases wage data for both the state and local levels. To find this information go back to the OES homepage (**http://www.bls.gov/oes**) and again pick Tables Created by BLS. Now instead of choosing National estimates, choose either state estimates or metropolitan area estimates.

For example, using the Metropolitan Area selection you can find out how much accountants are paid in the greater Boston area. The choices under Metropolitan Area are almost identical to those under National estimates. The only difference is that immediately after picking Metropolitan Area you get one extra screen that contains a list of major cities organized by state, as shown in Figure 11.8. Move down the list until you find Massachusetts and then pick Boston.

Boston's occupational hierarchy is identical to the national sequence, with Accountants and Auditors (SOC Code 13-2011) located under Business and Financial Operations Occupations. After following this path you will see that during the last quarter of 1999 the greater Boston area had 19,510 accountants and auditors, with average annual earnings of $46,240, or about $6,500 more than the national average. See Figure 11.9 for these numbers.

FIGURE 11.8
OES Metropolitan Area Data Selection

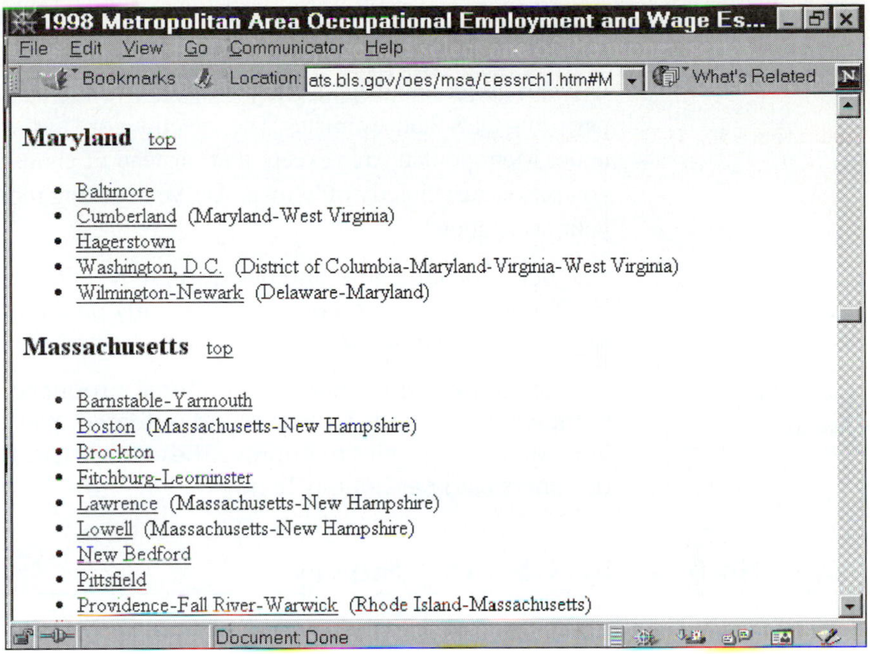

FIGURE 11.9
OES Data for the Boston Area

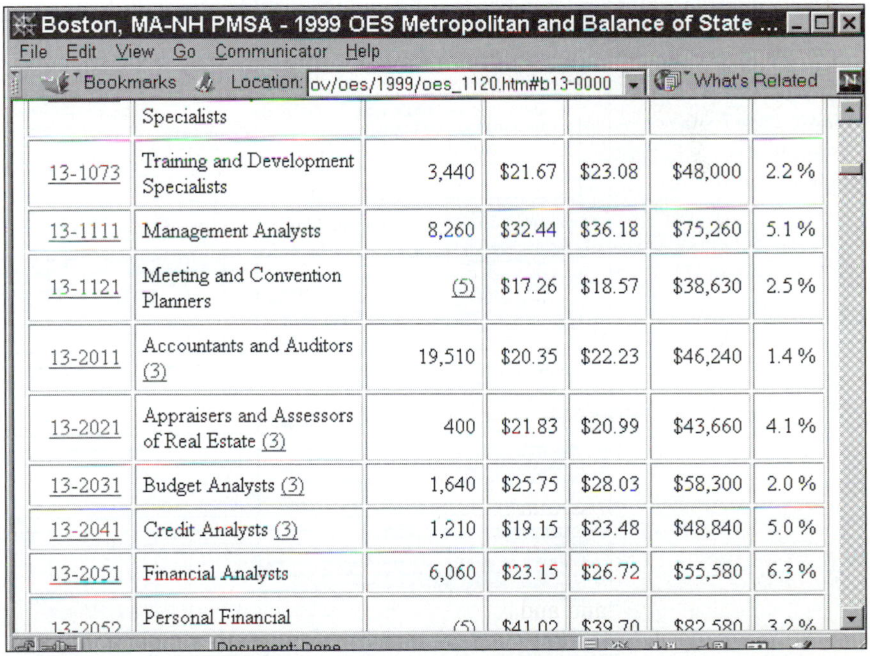

	Specialists					
13-1073	Training and Development Specialists	3,440	$21.67	$23.08	$48,000	2.2 %
13-1111	Management Analysts	8,260	$32.44	$36.18	$75,260	5.1 %
13-1121	Meeting and Convention Planners	(5)	$17.26	$18.57	$38,630	2.5 %
13-2011	Accountants and Auditors (3)	19,510	$20.35	$22.23	$46,240	1.4 %
13-2021	Appraisers and Assessors of Real Estate (3)	400	$21.83	$20.99	$43,660	4.1 %
13-2031	Budget Analysts (3)	1,640	$25.75	$28.03	$58,300	2.0 %
13-2041	Credit Analysts (3)	1,210	$19.15	$23.48	$48,840	5.0 %
13-2051	Financial Analysts	6,060	$23.15	$26.72	$55,580	6.3 %
13-2052	Personal Financial	(5)	$41.02	$39.70	$82,580	3.2 %

Now answer the chapter's second scenario. How does your pay compare to others with the same job description? Go back to the OES homepage (**http://www.bls.gov/oes**) and again choose Tables Created by BLS. Try checking your pay using OES State estimates. The selections are just like the ones encountered under Metropolitan Area except that, instead of choosing from a list of cities, you pick states directly off a map. Are you earning more or less than others in your occupation?

Practice Question	You need to hire some engineers in Denver for your mining operation. How much are mining engineers currently paid and how many are working in the Denver area?
Practice Question	The brochures and other sales material produced by your Texas-based company consistently look drab and outdated. You are thinking about hiring a graphic designer to improve these materials. How much are graphic designers paid per hour in Texas?

Limitations of the OES Pay Survey

The primary drawback to OES data is immediately seen by looking at Figure 11.10, which is a sample page from the survey. The survey does not ask businesses the exact wage paid to every worker. Instead, to make the forms easy to fill out, the survey just asks how many workers in each occupation fall into a particular wage range. Hence, the survey does not find out precisely how

FIGURE 11.10

Sample Page from Occupational Employment Survey

much accountants or computer programmers at your company are paid. Instead it only records how many workers fell in range F ($17.00 to $21.49 per hour in 1999), or range I ($34.50 to $43.74 per hour) and so forth.[5]

The second drawback to OES surveys is that they exclude both the self-employed and owners-partners of unincorporated firms. While this is not important for many occupations, the highest paid accountants are either partners of an accounting firm or self-employed. Hence, OES wage information for accountants does not fully represent what all accountants are paid, only those who are company employees.

Other Wage and Salary Information

To address the limitations of the OES, the Bureau of Labor Statistics recently created a new survey that collects information on the wages, salaries, and benefits of workers. This survey is called the National Compensation Survey (NCS). The NCS is now run yearly and tracks pay in 154 cities, the 48 contiguous states, and nationwide. The NCS is different from the Occupational Employment Statistics (OES) because it records the exact amount of money paid per worker, rather than grouping workers into 1 of 11 pay ranges.[6] Additionally, this survey collects benefits information, which is missing from the OES.[7]

The NCS is particularly useful for managers who need to justify paying a worker well above or well below an occupation's average salary. The NCS provides justification because it tracks the pay given to many different experience or grade levels within an occupation. For example, while the OES has one group called accountants and auditors, the NCS classifies accountants into 10 different levels. By breaking down each occupation into different skill categories, the NCS provides pay data needed for hiring both senior and junior-level employees.

The NCS levels vary according to the occupational category. The lowest level for any job is 1, while the highest is 15. The level for each job is created by assigning points to 10 different key factors: knowledge needed, supervision received, use of guidelines, job complexity, scope of work, type of personal contacts, purpose of contacts, physical demands, type of working environment,

---

[5] The survey does not use just one set of pay ranges: instead, there are a very large number of OES surveys and pay ranges tailored for different types of businesses.

[6] Another difference is that NCS forms are filled out at each company by BLS staff that do face-to-face interviews with company representatives. The OES is mailed out to businesses. Since the NCS requests an extensive amount of detailed information, it tracks only a small sample of jobs at each selected company.

[7] Currently the NCS does not release benefit information, but it will in the next few years.

FIGURE 11.11
National
Compensation
Survey Homepage

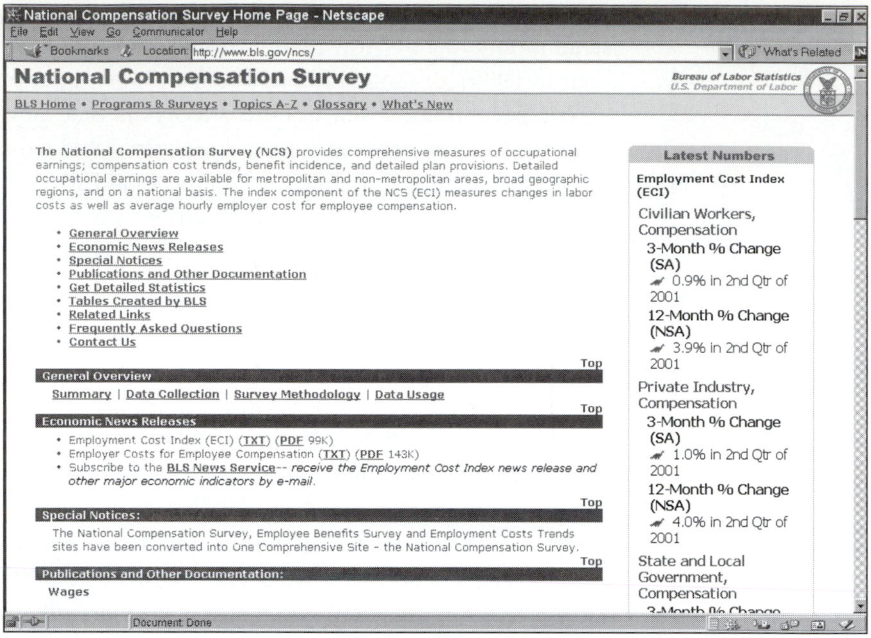

and amount of supervisory responsibility.[8] Basically, the higher the level, the more demanding the work.

Pay information from the NCS is available online at the NCS homepage **(http://www.bls.gov/ncs)**, which is shown in Figure 11.11.

Once at the NCS homepage, you have two choices for getting wage information: custom tables and preprinted books. All NCS books are available online at the NCS homepage under the link Publications and Other Documentation. This brings up the following six selections under the Wages heading:

1. National Summary

2. National Bulletin

3. Census Divisions

4. Localities

5. NCS Supplemental Tables

6. Archives

[8] For example, the amount of knowledge an employee needs for a job is broken down into 9 steps, ranging from no training or experience up to mastery of an entire professional field. The higher the level of knowledge needed, the more points given. After computing the points for the 10 different factors, the points are put into a formula to produce the job's level. The exact details of the formula, the point breakdown for the 10 factors and examples of "leveling" a job are all found in the BLS book *Evaluating Your Firm's Jobs and Pay,* available at this book's website.

TABLE 11.1
Accountant's and
Auditor's Pay and
Hours Worked

	Hourly Earnings (mean)	Error Range (in pcnt.)	Hours Work per Week (mean)
All levels	$22.10	3.2%	38.8
Level 5	$16.28	3.3%	37.7
Level 6	$18.18	4.0%	39.2
Level 7	$18.66	2.1%	38.8
Level 8	$19.96	2.5%	39.9
Level 9	$22.83	4.1%	39.0
Level 10	$26.68	2.4%	39.7
Level 11	$29.09	4.1%	39.0
Level 12	$34.31	6.0%	39.7

Source: *2000 National Compensation Survey, BLS Bulletin 2548,* Table 2-4, page 48.

To show you how to use NCS data, let's look at how much accountants and auditors are paid nationally. Pick the National Bulletin link under Publications and Other Documentation. Currently this brings up a PDF publication entitled *National Compensation Survey: Occupational Wages in the United States, 2000 Bulletin 2548.* Pay for auditors is found in this publication in Table 2-4, entitled Selected occupations and levels. Table 2-4 includes not only mean earnings for each level but also an error range, which shows the precision of each earning's estimate.

The relevant portion of NCS data are shown in the Table 11.1. NCS data reveal that in 2000 very junior accountants (level 5) earned just $16.28 per hour, while the most senior accountants (level 12) earned $34.31 per hour. Adjusting these data to account for inflation since 2000 boosts these wages even higher.

In addition to wage information, NCS tables also include the average number of hours worked per week. The table's last column shows that accountants' work hours do not vary much based on seniority and experience. While hours do not vary, the middle column shows that the earnings estimate's precision varies dramatically, particularly at the highest levels.

The NCS also has a custom table creation program under the Get Detailed Statistics link. This program, while simple to use, does not provide either error range information or information on hours worked per week. To use this program pick the Wages (NCS) link under Create Customized Tables (one screen) on the NCS homepage **(http://www.bls.gov/ncs)**. This will bring up the screen shown in Figure 11.12.

In the first step, you select the geographic area of interest. Data are available for both individual cities and the entire country. The second step allows you to pick exactly the type of workers needed. Scroll through the list until you find

FIGURE 11.12
National
Compensation
Survey's Create
Customized Tables

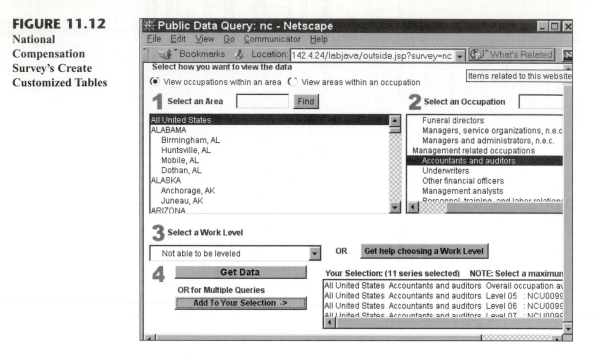

the specific occupation of interest. In the third step, choose a work level from very junior (a low number like 3) to very senior (a high number like 14). Since there are only small differences between levels, you should also collect data for nearby levels. To do this, highlight a single work level and then press the Add To Your Selection button. When all the work levels are chosen, press the Get Data button to see the results.

The NCS is an amazing source of very detailed wage and salary information. Unfortunately, because it takes a long time to gather such incredible detail, the NCS's major drawback is its lack of timely information. While data on specific cities appears relatively quickly, the latest detailed set of national information is usually released a few years after it is collected. You should use national NCS data cautiously when dealing with occupations undergoing rapid wage and employment changes, such as computer and other high-technology positions.

Practice Question

You just received a detailed bid from a general contractor to rebuild corporate headquarters. Overall, the bid is much higher than expected and certain parts do not make sense. One item that catches your eye is that the hourly rate for general plumbing work is only half the electrician's rate. You wonder whether plumbers are paid that much less per hour than electricians. Use the NCS to find the pay rate for plumbers and electricians.

Practice Question

Your company employs a small group of long-haul truckers to transport items from the factory to the distribution centers. Given this small group is the most crucial link in your supply chain, you want to ensure they are paid fairly. How much do junior and senior truck drivers earn?

Benefits Information

Fifty years ago most workers received their pay and little else. Today, benefits such as health insurance, vacation time, retirement plans, and stock options, constitute a large part of most workers' total compensation. Unfortunately, while the importance of benefits has exploded, the amount of information about these trends has not kept pace. For example, the first national survey by the United States government to track how many workers get stock options began in 2000.[9] Until the NCS starts releasing benefits data, currently the only way for managers to examine benefits is by using the Employment Cost Index.

The Employment Cost Index (ECI) is actually three different indexes: a wage and salary index, discussed at the beginning of this chapter; an index measuring changes in employee benefits; and a third, which combines wage and benefit information. The ECI benefits index tracks the cost paid by businesses for vacations, holidays, sick leave, insurance, retirement plans, Social Security, workers' compensation, and unemployment insurance. In addition, the benefits series captures all premium pay for overtime and weekend work, shift differentials, and nonproduction bonuses. Because the ECI benefits index includes overtime pay, the index goes beyond what most human resource managers think are the true costs of benefits.

To examine changes in benefit costs changes, pick Get Detailed Statistics on the Employment Cost Trends homepage (**http://www.bls.gov/ect**). Then select the link labeled Create Customized Tables (one screen) to enter into the same six-step process previously done to determine how much to raise telephone staff pay. Let's use the customized table function to see how benefit costs are changing compared to wages for the telephone staff.

Since the screen image is almost identical to the telephone example, it is not repeated here. The first step asks you to choose among the three ECI series. Instead of picking Wages and Salaries, now pick Benefits. The second step asks you to select either Civilian, Private industry, or State and local government; select Private industry. The third step allows you to select 12-month

---

[9] The first results are found in the United States Department of Labor news release #00-290. The data show that 1.7% of all private industry employees received stock options in 1999 and 2.4% of all private companies offered some form of options to their workers.

percentage change, 3-month percentage change, or the index itself. Again, working directly with the index is easier, so select that. The fourth step allows you to pick exactly what type of workers you are interested in tracking—choose White-collar occupations. In the fifth step where you can pick either Seasonally Adjusted or Not Seasonally Adjusted data select the unadjusted form. Finally, press the Get Data button to see the results shown in Figure 11.13.

What does this table mean? The table shows you how much benefits costs have risen from year to year. To calculate how much benefits rose from 1999 until 2000, insert the 1999 fourth quarter value and the 2000 fourth quarter value into the percentage change formula $[(161.5 - 152.5)/152.5]$. The result (5.9 percent) means that for every \$100 the typical private company paid white-collar workers, like your telephone staff, in benefits during 1999, they paid \$105.90 one year later. Using the custom table function, it is easy to see if your benefits costs have risen faster or slower than other companies.

Practice Question

You notice that your benefits costs have skyrocketed for your blue-collar workers in the last year. Are other companies having a similar problem?

FIGURE 11.13
ECI Benefits Index for White Collar Workers

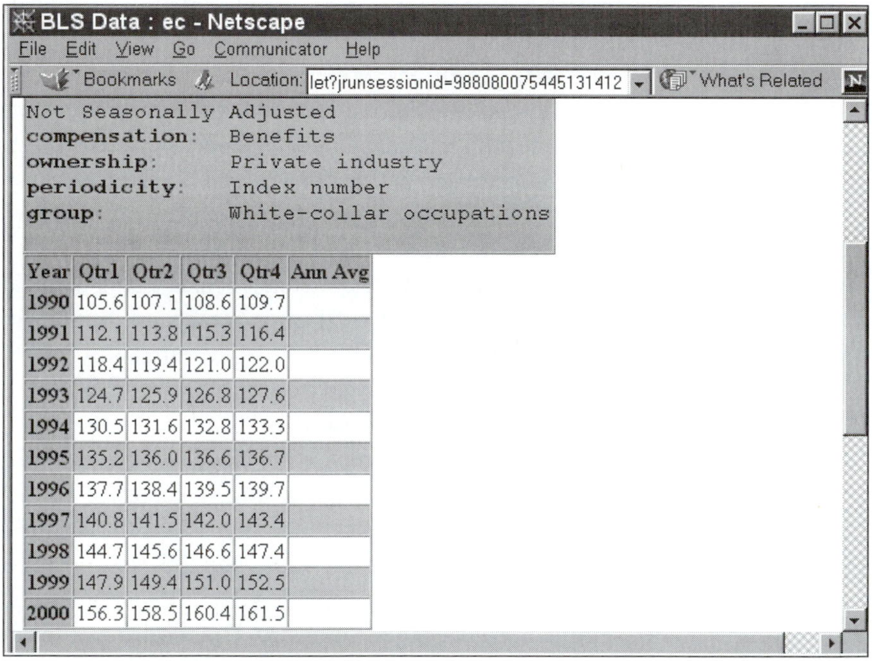

```
BLS Data : ec - Netscape                                           _□×
File   Edit   View   Go   Communicator   Help
    Bookmarks    Location: let?jrunsessionid=988080075445131412    What's Related   N
```

Not Seasonally Adjusted
compensation: Benefits
ownership: Private industry
periodicity: Index number
group: White-collar occupations

Year	Qtr1	Qtr2	Qtr3	Qtr4	Ann Avg
1990	105.6	107.1	108.6	109.7	
1991	112.1	113.8	115.3	116.4	
1992	118.4	119.4	121.0	122.0	
1993	124.7	125.9	126.8	127.6	
1994	130.5	131.6	132.8	133.3	
1995	135.2	136.0	136.6	136.7	
1996	137.7	138.4	139.5	139.7	
1997	140.8	141.5	142.0	143.4	
1998	144.7	145.6	146.6	147.4	
1999	147.9	149.4	151.0	152.5	
2000	156.3	158.5	160.4	161.5	

Information for Canada

Where do you go for human resource information for Canada? Human Resources Development Canada (HRDC) and Industry Canada (IC) have jointly created a website at **http://employers.gc.ca** that consolidates almost all publicly available Canadian human resource information into one location. The site, called Human Resources Management, provides information on hiring, layoffs, staff relations, pay, benefits, training, labor law, and many other topics for the entire country and for individual provinces. Additionally, the site has many common forms, such as the record of employment,[10] temporary work permits for noncitizens, and a variety of tax forms. The site does not contain wage and salary data for individual occupations, since the Canadian government currently does not collect this information on a regular basis.[11]

Summary

When you are faced with questions like "How much should I raise people's salaries?" or "Are my benefits costs increasing in line with other companies?" look at United States data from the Employment Cost Index (**http://www.bls.gov/ect**). ECI information comes out quickly and is very easy to use.

When faced with questions like "How much money should I offer a new worker?" or "Are my workers getting competitive wages?" you have two choices for information: the OES or Occupational Employment Statistics survey (**http://www.bls.gov/oes**) and the NCS or National Compensation Survey (**http://www.bls.gov/ncs**). OES pay data are based on a wide sample of workers, while NCS pay data break workers into finely delineated skill and experience levels. Both are very useful for determining appropriate wages. By using all three information sources, you will have the hard numbers needed to answer many difficult human resource questions. If you need information for Canada, use the Human Resources Management site located at **http://employers.gc.ca**.

[10] The record of employment allows the government to track which workers are eligible for unemployment insurance if they are laid off.

[11] Statistics Canada has gathered some information on the wages and salaries paid for various occupations via the Provincial Wage and Salary Survey, which was run in Manitoba, Saskatchewan, and Alberta in 1996, Prince Edward Island and Saskatchewan in 1998, and Ontario and New Brunswick in 1999.

Chapter  12

Labor Market Information

Is it difficult for everyone to find help, or is it just my problem? How many workers are employed in a specific field? These are some of the many key labor market questions for managers. Using the information in this chapter, you will understand where to find the data you need to make staffing decisions.

In the chapter's first scenario, you need to figure out how quickly the college-educated workforce is growing. In the second scenario you are staffing a new high-technology company and want to know how many computer scientists are working and searching for work in the various states that have large amounts of high-tech employment, such as California, Texas, Massachusetts, and Washington.

Employment and Unemployment Statistics

The key sets of labor market statistics are the monthly employment and unemployment numbers. The employment statistics are important because they tell you how many people are working in a given area, and for most people working is the primary method of earning money. Hence, areas where employment rates are high tend to spend more than areas where the percentage of people employed is lower.

Unemployment rates are also important because they show business managers how easy or hard it is to find workers. Businesses in areas with high unemployment usually have an easy time filling vacant positions and rarely need to increase pay. Conversely, managers in low unemployment areas often have

TABLE 12.1

Status of Individuals in the Labor Force

Employed	Unemployed	Out of the Labor Force
Worked 1 hour or more for pay or	Not employed and	Not employed and
Worked 15 hours or more in family business for no pay or	Made active effort in the past 4 weeks to find work or	Not unemployed
On vacation from paying job or	Waiting to start new job in less than 30 days or	
On strike from paying job or	Temporarily laid off and waiting for recall	
On sick leave from paying job		

lengthy searches for appropriate candidates and need to rapidly increase their staff's pay.

The Current Population Survey (CPS) produces employment and unemployment statistics each month for the United States. This survey, discussed earlier in Chapter 5, is the one that includes supplemental demographic and income questions each March. The CPS interviews slightly more than 50,000 randomly selected households every month. Once a household is selected, it is interviewed eight times and then dropped from the survey.

The primary goal of the survey is to classify each adult in the household into one of three categories: employed, unemployed, or not in the labor force. Table 12.1 shows exactly how individuals are classified in each category. In oversimplified terms, the employed have a paying job, the unemployed want a paying job, and those not in the labor force neither have nor are looking for a paying job.

Conceptually, the biggest problem is classifying people who want a job, searched for a job a while ago, but currently have given up hope of finding work. These discouraged people are almost but not quite unemployed. Since they did not actively search for work, official statistics classify them in the out of the labor force category. Nevertheless, many tabulations separate discouraged workers from all other individuals in the out of the labor force category so that you can add them to your calculations if it is important.

When CPS data are used to discuss the labor market, they are almost always reported as rates. These rates are simple percentages calculated using the following three formulas:

1. Number in the Labor Force = Number Employed + Number Unemployed

2. Employment Rate = Number Employed / Number in the Labor Force

3. Unemployment Rate = Number Unemployed / Number in the Labor Force

FIGURE 12.1

Graph of United States Unemployment Rate from 1900 to Present

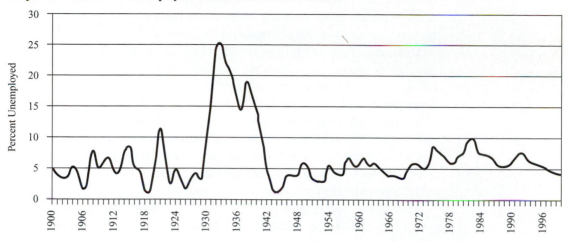

Using these formulas it is easy to track what has happened over time to the unemployed. The unemployment graph in Figure 12.1 shows that the worst time for looking for work was during the Great Depression, with one out of every four persons unemployed in 1934. Two of the best times for workers were 1918 and 1944. Both years were during major wars, when unemployment was 1.4 percent and 1.2 percent of the labor force, respectively. During the 1990s, the United States was involved in a long-term cycle of shrinking unemployment. The unemployment rate in 2000, at 4 percent, was the lowest level since 1969.

Quick Labor Force Data

There are three methods for finding labor force data to track employment and unemployment. If you need simple information, like the unemployment rate three years ago, look in the *Statistical Abstract* (pick the Statistical Abstract link on the Census Bureau's homepage **http://www.census.gov**). Each *Abstract* has a chapter labeled "Labor Force, Employment and Earnings," which contain many useful tables. The first table in the Labor Force chapter, entitled Employment Status of the Civilian Population, provides managers with basic information about the labor market, by listing the number employed, unemployed, and not in the labor force each year. The table called Civilian Labor Force and Participation Rates, with Projections shows managers that in the future the government is predicting a sharply rising number of workers aged 45 to 54 and a falling number aged 35 to 44. Finally, tables reporting Characteristics of the Civilian Labor Force by State and Civilian Labor Force by Selected Metropolitan Area are useful for planning where to site labor-intensive portions of your business, such as stores and production facilities.

Unfortunately, even the most recent *Statistical Abstract* publishes information that is two or three years out of date. The Bureau of Labor Statistics (BLS) provides more timely information in a monthly publication entitled *Employment and Earnings.* Unlike the *Statistical Abstract,* which provides only yearly data, *Employment and Earnings* reports labor force statistics each month and in greater detail. For managers without ready access to this periodical, the magazine's key tables are available online at **http://www.bls.gov/cps**. Selecting this URL and scrolling down to the section entitled Tables Created by BLS provides the choices shown in Figure 12.2.

Most of these precreated tables contain data only for the past two years or past 13 months. To create tables of values over a longer period, just select "Historical data for series in the monthly Employment Situation news release" under the Get Detailed Statistics heading of the CPS homepage (**http://www. bls.gov/cps**). This will bring up a list of 10 items which track key employment and unemployment indicators. For example, if your business relies heavily on college-educated workers, pick the third line labeled "Employment status . . . by educational attainment" to track this segment of the labor market. Picking the Employment status . . . by educational attainment line brings up the grid shown in Figure 12.3 to fill in.

FIGURE 12.2
List of Online Tables from Employment and Earnings

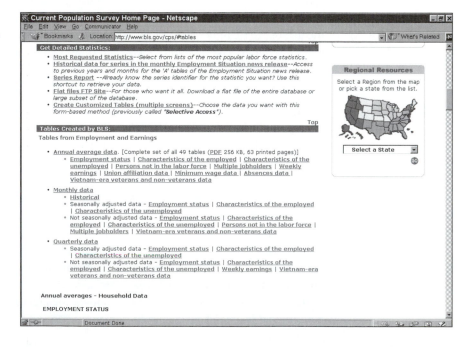

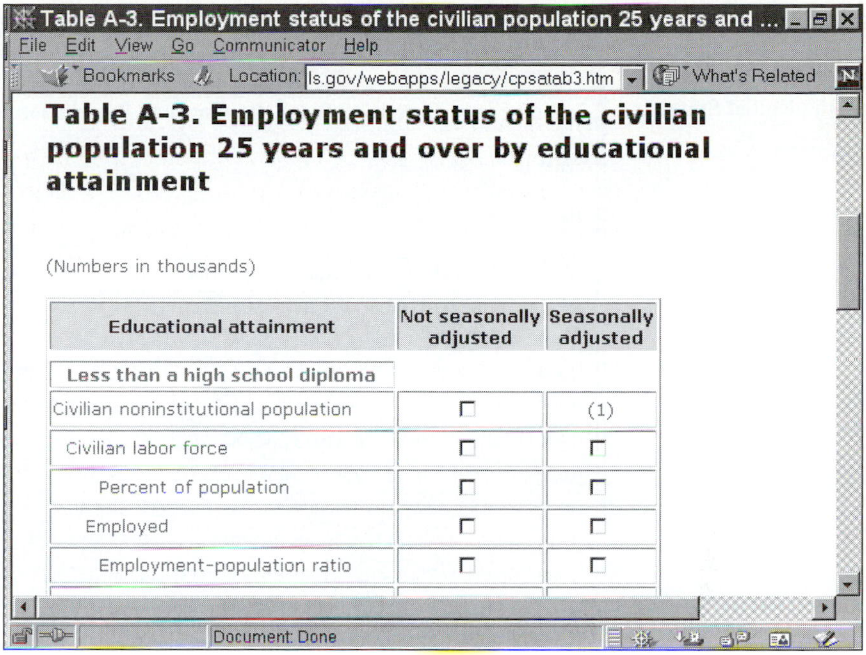

Table A-3. Employment status of the civilian population 25 years and over by educational attainment

(Numbers in thousands)

Educational attainment	Not seasonally adjusted	Seasonally adjusted
Less than a high school diploma		
Civilian noninstitutional population	☐	(1)
Civilian labor force	☐	☐
Percent of population	☐	☐
Employed	☐	☐
Employment-population ratio	☐	☐

FIGURE 12.3
Employment Status of the Civilian Population

To find the number of college-educated workers, scroll down the page to the section of the box for college graduates, and check the box in the column labeled Seasonally adjusted (right-hand column) and in the line entitled "Employed," and finish by picking "Retrieve data" at the bottom of the page. The resulting table, shown in Figure 12.4, answers the first scenario and reveals that the number of working college graduates grew from 26.8 million in January of 1992 to over 35.5 million by January of 2000, an increase of about 3.6% per year.

Practice Question

Your best friend was laid off almost four months ago and is getting very discouraged about finding a good job. She believes almost no one looks as long as she has. Is she right? How many people have been unemployed 15 or more weeks?

Practice Question

How many workers hold multiple jobs?

Custom Tabulations

In addition to looking at prepared tables, you can also create custom labor force tabulations using the FERRET system. FERRET, which stands for Federal Electronic Research and Review Extraction Tool, allows you to check for very specific employment and unemployment information by extracting data directly from the monthly Current Population Survey (CPS) database.

FIGURE 12.4
Number of College Graduates Working in the United States

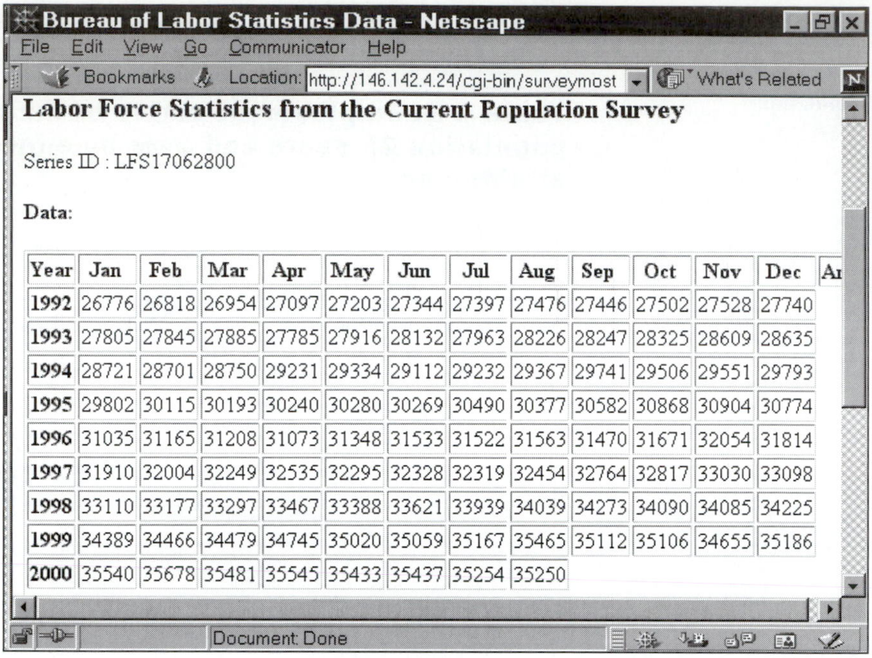

Labor Force Statistics from the Current Population Survey

Series ID : LFS17062800

Data:

Year	Jan	Feb	Mar	Apr	May	Jun	Jul	Aug	Sep	Oct	Nov	Dec	Ar
1992	26776	26818	26954	27097	27203	27344	27397	27476	27446	27502	27528	27740	
1993	27805	27845	27885	27785	27916	28132	27963	28226	28247	28325	28609	28635	
1994	28721	28701	28750	29231	29334	29112	29232	29367	29741	29506	29551	29793	
1995	29802	30115	30193	30240	30280	30269	30490	30377	30582	30868	30904	30774	
1996	31035	31165	31208	31073	31348	31533	31522	31563	31470	31671	32054	31814	
1997	31910	32004	32249	32535	32295	32328	32319	32454	32764	32817	33030	33098	
1998	33110	33177	33297	33467	33388	33621	33939	34039	34273	34090	34085	34225	
1999	34389	34466	34479	34745	35020	35059	35167	35465	35112	35106	34655	35186	
2000	35540	35678	35481	35545	35433	35437	35254	35250					

FIGURE 12.5
FERRET Survey Selection Screen

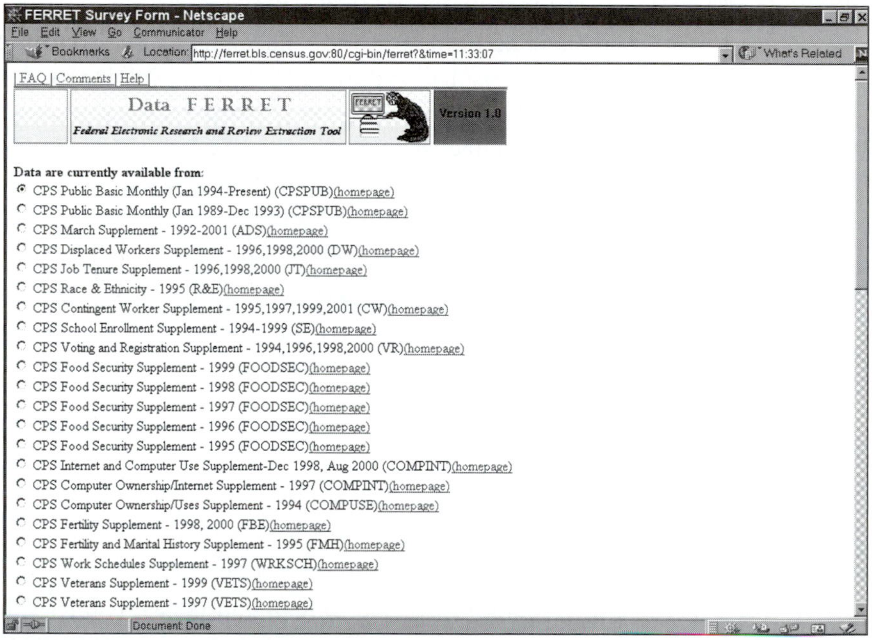

FERRET contains not only the monthly CPS but also a number of other government surveys. The picture in Figure 12.5 shows part of the list of surveys currently available on FERRET. While many of the surveys are supplements to the CPS, FERRET is slowly adding other non-CPS surveys like the Survey of Income and Program Participation (SIPP) and the American Housing Survey.

Since the process of using the FERRET system involves navigating through many windows, keep in mind that the windows are designed to get you to:

- Pick one data set to analyze.

- Select a small number of variables.

- Create a SAS command to do the analysis.

- Output your custom tabulation.

To create a custom tabulation for the monthly CPS, there are nine steps, most of which are very simple. To show exactly what is happening, we will answer the chapter's second scenario, in which you wanted to know how many computer scientists are employed, unemployed, and not in the labor force in various states that have many high-tech companies. To keep the problem simple, we will only look at California and also examine just one month: March 2001. To find the answer for other major states, just rerun the analysis using a different state code. If you want a yearly answer, select all 12 months and average the results.

1. Go to the Internet URL **http://ferret.bls.census.gov.**[1]

2. Read the introduction and choose Get FERRET Data at the bottom of the page.

3. Register by typing in your e-mail address and pick Continue.

4. Select a survey (see the previous picture). To analyze labor market information, choose the survey labeled CPS Public Basic Monthly from the list and pick Continue.

5. Pick the general types of data you want to search. FERRET provides some introductory text about the survey you selected. After reading the text, pick Continue to advance to the primary control page, which looks like Figure 12.6.

The top part of the CPS control page asks you to pick the month(s) and year(s) to analyze. Until you are comfortable using the system, just select one month-year combination at a time. For our example March 2001 is selected.

The middle part of the CPS control page allows you to pick the general categories of variables you want to examine. You will see the eight choices listed in Table 12.2.

---

[1] Note: Spelling of FERRET is not consistent on this site.

FIGURE 12.6
FERRET Date and Group Selection Screen

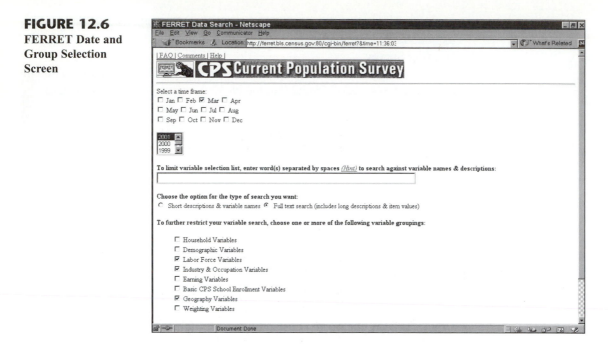

TABLE 12.2
Monthly CPS Variable Categories and a Brief Explanation

Category	Explanation
❑ Household Variables	Number and relationship of people living together
❑ Demographic Variables	Sex, age, race, and ethnicity
❑ Labor Force Variables	Working, looking for work, discouraged
❑ Industry and Occupation Variables	General to specific job titles and industries
❑ Earning Variables	Pay
❑ Basic CPS School Enrollment	Household members attending school.
❑ Geography Variables	Select particular areas of the country
❑ Weighting Variables	Corrects output so survey represents the nation

For tracking labor market conditions, the three most important categories to select are: Labor Force Variables; Industry and Occupation; and Geography. Check off these three boxes now to continue working through the scenario. The bottom part of this page allows you to control the amount of information each category displays. It has three items: Edited, Unedited, and Recodes. For most uses the default selections are all you will need. When satisfied with your choices pick Continue to advance to the next page.

FIGURE 12.7
FERRET Detailed
Industry and
Occupational
Selection

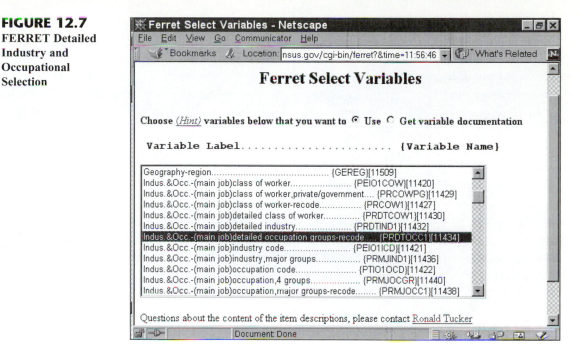

TABLE 12.3
Most Useful Monthly
CPS Geography
Variables

Census region	Geography-region....................................{GEREG}[11509]
State level	Geography-FIPS state code...............{GESTFIPS}[11511]
Major urban area	Geography-consolidated MSA code...{GTCMSA}[11501]
Urban area	Geography-MSA code...........................{GTMSA}[11506]
County	Geography-FIPS county code...................{GTCO}[11503]

Note: If you do not choose any geographic variables, FERRET automatically selects the entire nation. The list of CMSA, PMSA, or FIPS codes used for selecting particular geographic areas is found at **http://www.bls.census.gov/cps/ bmetro96.htm.**

6. Select specific variables of interest for your tabulation. The next page, shown in Figure 12.7, is the crucial one since it allows you to select a small number of specific variables for analysis.

The problem is that the list of variables that meet the previous control page's criteria is often overwhelming. Tables 12.3 through 12.6 contain the most useful variables for answering most human resource questions. Each table goes from broad categories at the top to very specific categories at the bottom.

When picking variables, keep two ideas in mind. First, do not be overly specific. Because only 50,000 households participate each month, there is a very

TABLE 12.4
Most Useful Monthly CPS Labor Force Variables

Employed and unemployed	Labor force—employed/unemployed............{PREXPLF}[11299]
4 labor force status	Labor force—employment status, recode...{PREMPNOT}[11297]
7 labor force status	Labor force—employment status.......................{PEMLR}[11287]

TABLE 12.5
Most Useful Monthly CPS Occupation Variables

4 occupations	Indus.&Occ.-(main job)occupation, 4 groups....................{PRMJOCGR}[11440]
14 occup.	Indus.&Occ.-(main job)occupation, major groups-recode..{PRMJOCC1}[11438]
46 occup.	Indus.&Occ.-(main job)detailed occupation group-recode.{PRDTOCC1}[11434]
~500 occup.	Indus.&Occ.-(main job)occupation, code............................{PTIO1OCD}[11422]

TABLE 12.6
Most Useful Monthly CPS Industry Variables

23 industries	Indus.&Occ.-(main job)industry, major groups..{PRMJIND1}[11436]
52 industries	Indus.&Occ.-(main job)detailed industry...........{PRDTIND1}[11432]
~230 industries	Indus.&Occ.-(main job)industry code.................{PEIO1ICD}[11421]

low probability the survey will accurately count the number of unemployed movie theater projectionists in Pittsburgh, for example, even though it is easy to ask FERRET to calculate the number. Start by picking broad categories, check your answers, and then refine your search criteria. Keep the number of observations (*obs*), stated at the very end on the results page, around 100 or higher to ensure the answers are statistically accurate.

To select variables in FERRET you have the following choices:

- To select or delete a single line, just move the mouse, click, and the line will highlight.

- To highlight or remove a highlight from multiple lines, hold down the control (CTRL) key and pick the lines of interest.

To calculate how many computer scientists there are in California, hold down the control key and select the following three lines:

FIGURE 12.8
FERRET Screen to Limit the Ranges of Selected Variables

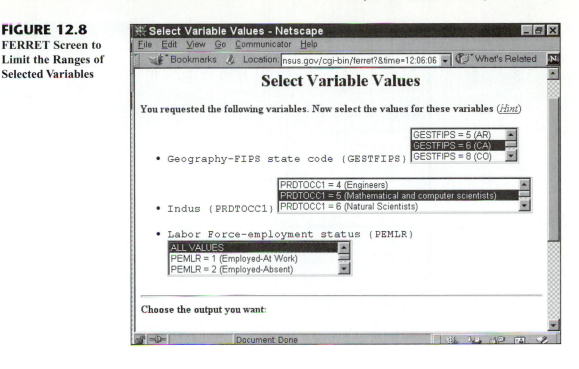

Geography-FIPS state code...{GESTFIPS}[11511]

Indus.&Occ.-(main job)occupation, major groups-recode... {PRDTOCC1}[11434]

Labor force-employment status............…...........................{PEMLR}[11287]

Be careful, because many of the lines look alike and it is easy to make a mistake.

7. Pick the specific range to analyze for each variable. The next page, shown in Figure 12.8, allows you to select only part of each variable's values. In our example we want to examine only California. Using this page we limit the GESTFIPS variable to CA, which is the two-letter abbreviation for California. We also limit PRDTOOC1 to "= 5 (Mathematical and Computer Scientists)." If you do not want to limit a variable, like the PEMLR data, either leave the box blank or untouched so that all possible values are returned or select ALL VALUES.

The bottom of the page determines how the output is returned. Most of the time you will want to choose Create crosstabs, frequencies, or SAS dataset for downloading or printing.

FIGURE 12.9
FERRET Output
Format Control

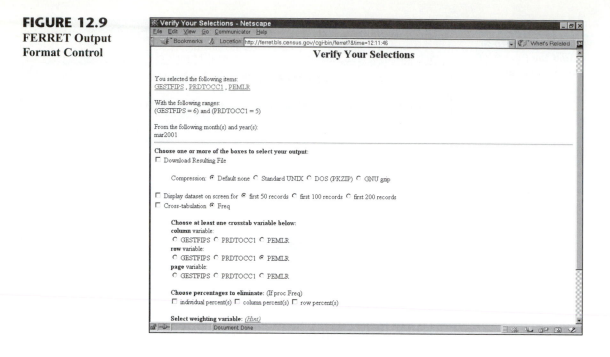

8. Customize the output tabulation. This is the last page of selections. It allows you to verify your selections by displaying the items you selected, their ranges, and the survey months being analyzed. If you do not like the choices, use the BACK button on your browser to fix the problem.

The verification page, shown in Figure 12.9, customizes the output. For our example select Cross-tabulation Freq and set the variable PEMLR as the row variable to display.

The bottom of the page asks you to Select weighting variable. Never pick unweighted when doing cross-tabulations! Weighting corrects for the special sampling features that ensure the survey covers every state in the country.

9. Look at your results. This last page shows your custom tabulation. Figure 12.10 contains the output from our example:

What does this output mean? The title says, "SAS Data Set with 105 obs was created for your query." This means that in March 2001 the CPS survey recorded labor force information about 105 individuals in California who stated they were either a mathematical or computer scientist. Because you asked for weighted results, these 105 people represent 364,231 California scientists. Not surprisingly, given the booming conditions of the software industry in California at the time, only 2,713 were without work and only 7,583 were on vacation (employed but absent from their job during the week).

FIGURE 12.10
FERRET Results

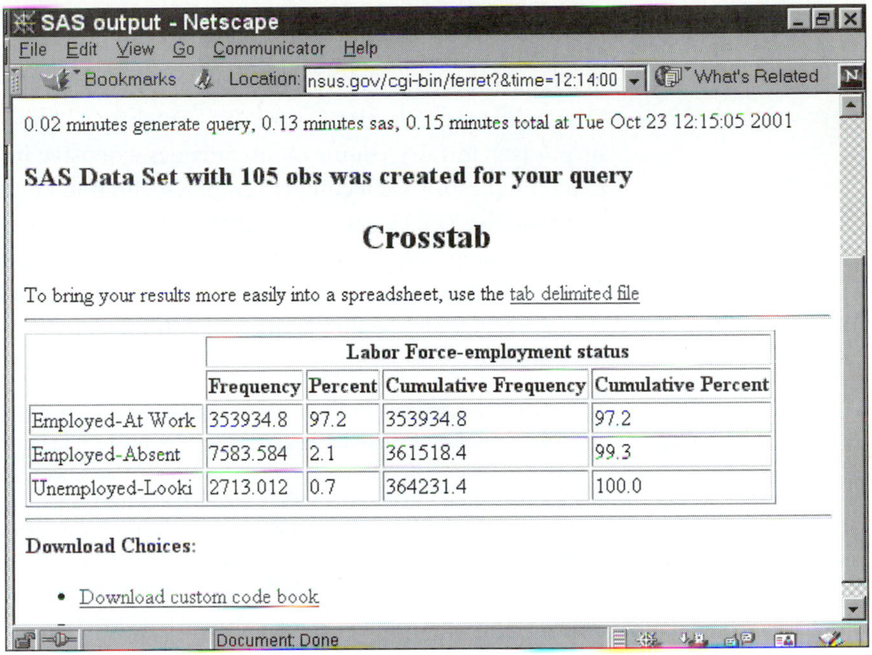

0.02 minutes generate query, 0.13 minutes sas, 0.15 minutes total at Tue Oct 23 12:15:05 2001

SAS Data Set with 105 obs was created for your query

Crosstab

To bring your results more easily into a spreadsheet, use the tab delimited file

	Labor Force-employment status			
	Frequency	Percent	Cumulative Frequency	Cumulative Percent
Employed-At Work	353934.8	97.2	353934.8	97.2
Employed-Absent	7583.584	2.1	361518.4	99.3
Unemployed-Looki	2713.012	0.7	364231.4	100.0

Download Choices:

• Download custom code book

While thinking about high technology, keep in mind that many people working with computers are not classified as computer scientists. For example, individuals doing computer programming are classified under technicians. To capture the full extent of the high-tech work force, you need more occupations than just mathematical or computer scientists.

Before ending the chapter, it is important to recognize a major drawback of the CPS for business use. The CPS does not record the number of employed job seekers, only the number of unemployed job seekers. Many computer scientists in California, while currently employed, are also hunting for a new job. Unfortunately, the current CPS questionnaire does not track these individuals' job changing desires.

Practice Question

You need a quick estimate of the number of clergy. How many are there in the United States?

Practice Question

You are responsible for hiring more teachers for the state of New York. How many teachers are currently employed or currently looking for work in the state?

Information for Other Countries

Every major country in the world tracks employment and unemployment information. Some countries track this information via the administrative records of social programs, like unemployment insurance,[2] while others conduct periodic household surveys.[3] General labor market information for approximately 50 countries is found in the International Monetary Fund's (IMF) Special Data Dissemination Standard (SDDS) database. This database, located at **http://dsbb.imf.org/country.htm**, provides extensive information on three labor market topics for each country: employment, unemployment, and earnings.

Using the SDDS database is extremely simple. Go to the link shown in the previous paragraph and select one country. For our example, let's select Canada. Then under the Labor Market heading select either employment, unemployment, or wages. Picking the employment link brings up the following documentation for Canada:

> The data are obtained from the monthly Canadian Labour Force Survey (L.F.S.), which is representative of the Canadian non-institutional population 15 years of age and older. The survey coverage excludes residents of long-term care health facilities (more than six months), members of the Canadian armed forces, persons living on Indian reserves, and those in the North West Territories and the Yukon. The survey uses a reference week concept to measure labour market activity, and the reference week is typically the week containing the fifteenth day of the month. The L.F.S. provides a number of key labour market measures that generally conform to ILO concepts and definition.

Canadian data are then found by selecting the link DATA Access to Canada's statistics. Picking this link provides the number employed, unemployed, and average weekly earnings plus the percentage changes over the past year. In addition to these values, each category is linked so you can jump directly to more detailed data available at Statistics Canada's website.

Summary

How difficult is it to find workers? How many people are looking for work? The answers to these and other questions about the United States labor market are found by looking at monthly Current Population Survey (CPS) data. While the CPS is primarily known for its role in determining the United States unemployment rate, the survey tracks many other aspects of the labor market. One of the simplest ways to access labor market information is to examine the tables printed in the monthly periodical Employment and Earnings. These tables are available online at **http://www.bls.gov/cps** under the link Tables Created by BLS. Selecting this link allows you to track the number of employed,

---

[2] For example, in Croatia unemployment is determined from administrative records maintained by the Croatian Board of Employment.
[3] For example, Great Britain's Labour Force Survey is quarterly, while Canada's Labour Force Survey is monthly.

unemployed, and out of the labor force individuals broken down by a large variety of characteristics.

If you need very specific employment or unemployment information that is not covered in these tables, such as the number of workers in a particular geographic area, industry, or occupation then use the FERRET system **(http:// ferret.bls.census.gov)** to create custom tables. While using FERRET is somewhat complex, mastering this program gives you the ability to answer very specific labor market questions.

Last, if you need information about other countries use the International Monetary Fund's Special Data Dissemination Standard database. This database, located at **http://dsbb.imf.org/country.htm**, provides extensive information on employment, unemployment, and earnings for approximately 50 countries.

Chapter 13

Tax Information

How big a bite does the tax man take from the income of individuals and corporations? This chapter first explains where to find and how to use tax data on individuals from the U. S. Internal Revenue Service (IRS). Tax data on individuals provide important information because people's spending decisions are based on their after-tax income. Taxes are important because the more taxes taken out of their total income, the less individuals have to spend.

The second part of the chapter describes information about the taxes paid by businesses. Investors, bankers, and venture capitalists care primarily about one number: after-tax earnings. One way of increasing these earnings is to reduce taxes. While this chapter does not discuss how to reduce your taxes, it does show how to determine the amount of tax typical businesses in your industry currently pay. Using this information, you can directly gauge the effectiveness of your accounting and finance department in minimizing your tax burden.

The chapter's final part explains where to find tax information for states, like Arizona, and for foreign countries, like Canada. This information shows whether another location is a higher or lower tax place to live and work.

In the first scenario you are a financial planner. Your company provides plenty of information about stocks, bonds, life insurance, and other investment options for you to sell to clients. However, before discussing where to invest clients often want to know how their tax payments compare to other's. Where do you get this kind of information?

In the second scenario, you are at a trade show, and talk at the meet-and-greet session turns to taxes. Your competitors seem to be paying rates much lower than your company. Is your current CPA firm incompetent or are your competitors skewing the truth to make themselves look better? Using the information sources detailed in this chapter, both questions are easily answered.

General Tax Information

Where can tax data be found? For the United States the best source of tax information is the Internal Revenue Service (IRS), which is a branch of the United States Department of Treasury. The most important thing to know when looking for IRS tax data is that they are not called tax information but rather statistics of income (SOI). The second important point is that the IRS does not release any information that identifies individual taxpayers or companies. This means that if all you really want to know is what your brother-in-law pays or how much your key competitor owes, you should just ask them and skip to the next chapter.

While the IRS is quick to take your money, it is slow to release data. There are a number of reasons why data are produced slowly. First, tax returns are due months after the fiscal year is over. For example, individual returns are usually prepared just before April 15, four months after the tax year finishes. This means that the IRS does not get most individual tax returns for 2002 until April of 2003.

Second, many people and businesses ask for extensions. This means that the IRS must wait until it gets all tax returns. For example, after rich individuals die, their estates must file a return to pay inheritance taxes. Tax law currently declares that estate returns must be filed within nine months of death, but six-month extension periods are available. So many extension periods are requested that the IRS waits three years before beginning to calculate estate tax information for any year.

Third, Statistical Information Services, which is the IRS office that produces the data, has a small budget. Most of its money and time are spent producing information for the Treasury Department's Office of Tax Analysis and the Congressional Joint Committee on Taxation so that the impact of congressional and presidential proposals to change the tax system can be evaluated.

The IRS releases all key tax data in book form. Much, but not all of this data, is also released online at the tax statistics homepage (**http://www.irs.gov/** and pick Tax Stats), which is shown in Figure 13.1. This homepage provides a single place to find tax information on both individuals and businesses. In addition the homepage also has information on employment taxes, estate taxes, excise taxes, tax-exempt organizations, and international tax payments.

General tax information is found on this homepage under the heading Statistical Publications. The two most useful general periodicals are the *IRS Data Book* and *SOI Bulletins.* Every year since 1993, the IRS has produced a statistical compendium called the *Internal Revenue Service Data Book.* Data from this compendium, primarily in spreadsheet format, are available by picking the IRS Data Book link, which brings up Figure 13.2.

FIGURE 13.1
IRS Tax Statistics
Homepage

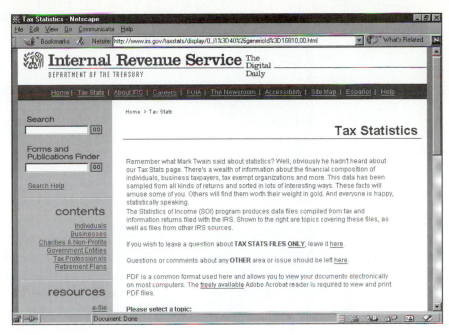

FIGURE 13.2
IRS Data Book

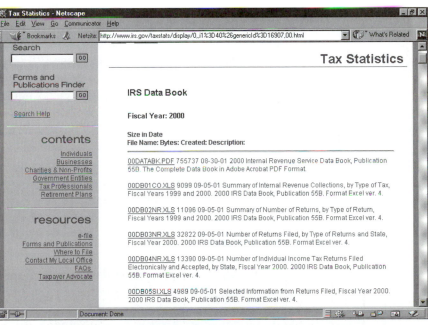

The data book has information on issues like the number and type of returns audited and how much extra tax was paid. The book's primary drawback is that many tables are broken down by IRS region. While regional data

FIGURE 13.3
SOI Bulletins

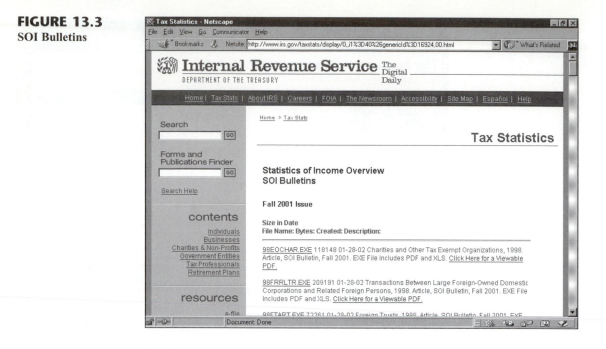

are sometimes useful, most people interested in tax information want data based on income, not location. Further, IRS tax regions do not match standard census regions, so it is difficult to combine IRS data with other information sources.

The second way the IRS provides general tax information is in the quarterly magazine *Statistics of Income Bulletin* (IRS Publication 1136). The *Bulletin,* which is available online soon after the printed version is published, provides summary information from all individual and business tax returns before the IRS releases more detailed data. Articles from the *Bulletin* are available in PDF format by picking SOI Bulletins under the Statistical Publications heading. Selecting this link brings up Figure 13.3.

Individual Tax Information

The IRS provides more detailed information on individual tax returns than what is found in the *IRS Data Book* or the *SOI Bulletin.* Each year the IRS publishes a book compiled from all individual tax returns and also releases the book online. To get data from the 1999 tax year, for example, look at the book called *Statistics of Income—1999, Individual Income Tax Returns.* The two most interesting sections of these books for financial planners and others interested in tax data are the two tables entitled "Sources of Income,

FIGURE 13.4

IRS Individual Tax
Statistics Homepage

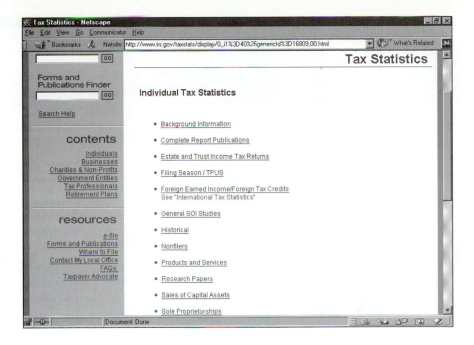

Adjustments and Tax Items, by Size of Adjusted Gross Income." The first (Table 1.4) breaks down these items for all different types of 1040 returns, while the second (Table 2.1) breaks down these items just for households who itemize their deductions (filers of IRS Form 1040 Schedule C).

To download these more detailed tables, go to the tax statistics homepage and pick the Individuals link under the Statistics by Topic subsection.[1] This will bring up Figure 13.4.

Copies of the key tables from the *Individual Income Tax Returns* are located in multiple places on this page. The easiest set to find is under the Complete Report Publications link. Picking this link brings up Figure 13.5.

Picking 99INALCR.EXE downloads a compressed file containing the major tables from the *Individual Income Tax Returns*. To view these tables, first store the compressed file on your local disk and then double-click on its name to decompress. After decompression, open the individual files using a spreadsheet package that can read Microsoft Excel files. The file called

---

[1] The IRS also produces micro data files for public use. These micro data files contain all information entered on a random selection of individual tax returns. To ensure confidentiality, all personal identifiers like names and social security numbers are removed and specific items that could identify any individual's tax form, such as very high wage or salary payments, are altered. The data, unfortunately, come out very slowly and are publicly released four to five years after the first returns are filed. They currently cost $3,300 for each year of tax records.

FIGURE 13.5
IRS Individual Tax
Statistics Complete
Reports

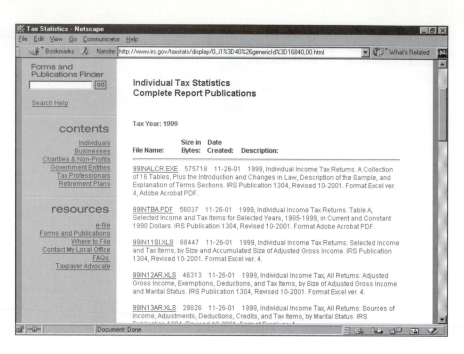

99IN14AR.XLS contains Table 1.4,[2] which holds much of the key information on individual income tax returns. This table breaks down line-by-line responses from United States tax forms in 15 different adjusted gross income (AGI) categories.[3]

This tax table provides an incredible amount of detail. For example, if you are a divorce attorney and want to know the average amount of alimony received by individuals with an AGI of $30,000 to $40,000, look at the portion of Table 1.4 shown in Figure 13.6. This reveals that the average yearly amount of alimony received in 1999 was $13,020 (418,989 returns received $5,455,497,000).

Table 2.1, found in file 99IN21ID.XLS, is similar to Table 1.4 but contains information just for individuals who itemized deductions (Schedule C filers). While the table contains interesting items like gambling losses and tax preparation fees paid, two items of more interest are charitable and home mortgage deductions. For individuals working in the nonprofit sector, charitable deduction information is useful because it gives a rough idea of total cash and

---

[2] 99IN14AR.XLS stands for 1999 tax year, individual tax return files, and table 1.4.
[3] All individual tax data are compiled from a sample of approximately 160,000 tax forms. The file 99IN14CV.XLS contains the coefficients of variation, which measures the precision of each estimate in the "ar" file.

FIGURE 13.6

Alimony Data from
Individual Tax
Returns

Table 1.4--1999, Individual Income Tax, All Returns: Sources of Income,			
(All figures are estimates based on samples--money amounts are in thousands of dollars.)			
	Alimony received		
Size of adjusted gross income	Number of returns	Amount	Number of returns
	(13)	(14)	(15)
All returns, total..................................	418,989	5,455,497	13,165
No adjusted gross income.............................	2,131	28,191	123
$1 under $5,000..	*6,702	*13,700	983
$5,000 under $10,000....................................	26,636	145,689	1,481
$10,000 under $15,000..................................	48,926	346,371	1,073
$15,000 under $20,000..................................	47,039	274,861	953
$20,000 under $25,000..................................	37,409	320,967	832
$25,000 under $30,000..................................	40,409	346,372	704
$30,000 under $40,000..................................	73,150	795,165	1,258
$40,000 under $50,000..................................	38,462	527,132	1,057

noncash contributions broken down by income.[4] For bankers selling mortgages, home equity loans, and other credit products tied to an individual's residence, the data on points paid, home mortgage deduction, and real estate taxes provide great information for creating marketing programs.

Let's finish off our financial planner scenario. Remember the clients who keep asking how their income and taxes compare to everyone else's? A good source of information for telling clients how their taxes compare to other payers is Table 1.2 in the *Statistics of Income, Individual Income Tax Returns.* To give you a rough idea of the answers available, Table 13.1 shows average income tax paid for all returns and for different income categories in 1999. The row labeled All Returns shows in that year the average household paid the federal government $9,280 in income tax.

The IRS also creates a hidden gem for business managers wanting income and tax information broken down to the five-digit zip code level. Periodically the IRS creates a set of files containing the number of households, total adjusted gross income, total income tax paid, and the total number of personal exemptions (which approximates population) by zip code. This file provides a simple method other than the census for understanding and targeting very specific geographic areas. Currently, all the 1991 files are available for free

[4] IRS data does not include political contributions, which are considered a donation by many individuals, since these contributions are not tax deductible.

TABLE 13.1
Average Tax Paid
in 1999

Adjusted Gross Income	Income Tax Paid
All Returns	**$9,280**
$1 under $5,000	$143
$5,000 under $10,000	$334
$10,000 under $15,000	$750
$15,000 under $20,000	$1,225
$20,000 under $25,000	$1,739
$25,000 under $30,000	$2,277
$30,000 under $40,000	$3,101
$40,000 under $50,000	$4,462
$50,000 under $75,000	$6,788
$75,000 under $100,000	$11,767
$100,000 under $200,000	$22,855
$200,000 under $500,000	$69,465
$500,000 under $1,000,000	$192,426

Source: Author's calculations from data found in Table 1.2 of the *Statistics of Income–1999, Individual Income Tax Returns.*

online. A sample of the 1998 files is also available online so that you can easily determine if the more recent information is worth buying. To download this information, go to the tax statistics homepage (**http://www.irs.gov/** and pick Tax Stats) and pick the Individuals link under the Statistics by Topic subsection. Then pick the Zip Codes link under the heading Geographic Areas, and the screen shown in Figure 13.7 on the next page will appear.

Under the heading Tax Year 1991 on this page, is a link to a spreadsheet containing tax and income information for each zip code. If your business needs more current information, pick the link 98ZIPCDE.XLS under the Tax Year 1998 heading. This newer spreadsheet shows you the layout of the 1998 data and contains directions for ordering the information.

Practice Question

You are interested in starting a business that helps people find renters for apartments, homes, and other property. What percentage of tax filers rented out their property? What percentage of total income did net rental payments constitute?

Practice Question

Assume you itemize your deductions. Do you pay more or less tax than other people in your AGI bracket?

Corporate Tax Information

Clearly there is plenty of individual tax information, but what about corporate tax data? Additionally, how do you answer the second scenario, in which talk

FIGURE 13.7

Individual Tax
Return Data by Zip
Code

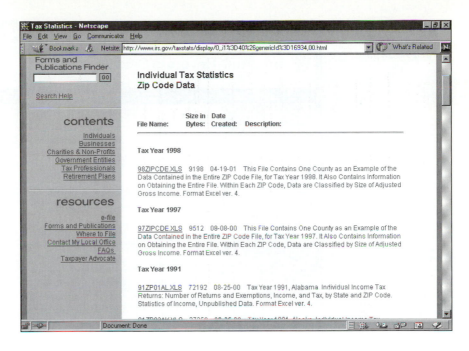

during a trade show suggested your competitors were paying a lower average tax rate than your company?

The IRS publishes details on corporate taxes each year in books with titles like *Statistics of Income—1998, Corporation Income Tax Returns.* Other volumes in the series have the same title but different year designations. Each book is published about three years after the tax year.[5] IRS tax data are also available for corporations, sole proprietorships, and partnerships. Because the vast majority of businesses are incorporated, this section focuses just on corporate information taken from IRS Form 1120. A copy of Form 1120 is located on this book's website.

The *Corporation Income Tax Returns* report breaks down all corporations by broad, or two-digit SIC or NAICS industry code. Each industry's data are reported both for all returns filed and then for only those returns filed that had net income. While there is no right or wrong choice, think carefully before choosing all returns or just those with net income. In smaller or cyclical businesses like construction, I recommend using all businesses, because during an economic downturn a significant fraction of viable businesses have no income. In large or stable sectors, like utilities, I recommend using only

---

[5] While individual tax returns are based on calendar years, business tax return information uses a July-to-June accounting period.

FIGURE 13.8
IRS Corporate Tax
Return Homepage

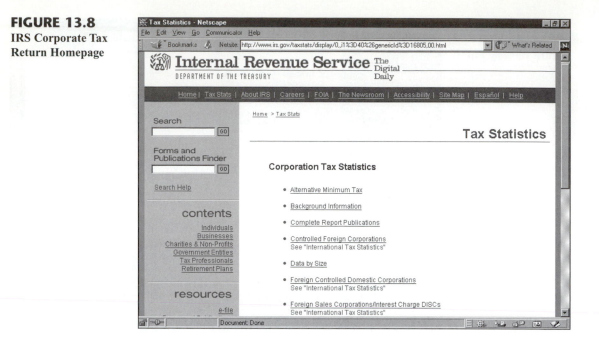

businesses with net income, because businesses with no income are very different types of companies.

Beyond these two breakdowns, the report also provides details on assets, receipts, deductions, taxable income, and income tax paid. By dividing the amount paid by the number of returns filed, you can find the average amount of income tax paid by companies in any industry. While overall averages, like income and taxes, are useful, the most interesting information lies in the detailed breakdowns. For example, deductions are broken into 17 detailed categories and reveal how much the typical firm in an industry spent on advertising, bad debts, and rent, to name only a few choices. Another place to look is the total assets category, which helps you determine the amount of cash or inventory your typical competitor holds.

The tables from these corporate fact books are also available online. To download these more detailed tables go to the tax statistics homepage (**http://www.irs.gov/** and select Tax Stats) and pick the Corporations link under the Statistics by Topic subsection. This will bring up Figure 13.8.

Identical sets of tables from the *Corporation Income Tax Returns* report are located under multiple links on this page. The easiest way to find a set of tables is to choose the Complete Report Publications. Picking this link brings up Figure 13.9.

To see the online version of *Corporation Income Tax Returns,* pick one file and download it to your local disk. Then double-click on the downloaded

FIGURE 13.9
IRS Corporate Tax
Return Reports

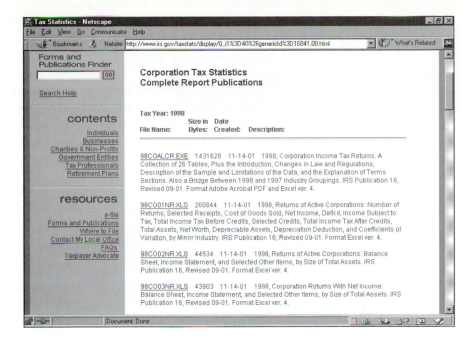

file's name to uncompress its spreadsheets. Each compressed report contains about 25 separate spreadsheet tables plus endnotes and other explanatory text provided in Adobe PDF files. This format of separate files makes it easy to cut and paste information but difficult to thumb through and find a single number.

The two most useful tables in the book and online version are Tables 6 and 7, which provide a balance sheet, income, and tax paid for each major industrial division. Table 6 covers all corporations while Table 7 includes only those with net income. To find information in the online tables, remember to scroll right when looking at the spreadsheet because the tables are very wide.

Let's make the second scenario, where you talked with your competitors about taxes, specific by assuming you own an auto dealership. To figure out the typical tax rate for auto dealerships, open up Table 7 for 1998 (98CO07NR.XLS) and scroll right until you see the column labeled Motor vehicle dealers and parts dealers (in Microsoft Excel this is column AQ).[6] Then scroll down to see that Dealers had a net income subject to tax of $3.3 billion (cell BA82) and paid $1 billion in federal income tax after credits (cell BA94) for an average tax rate of 31.3%. Because your dealership is paying close to 35 percent, you begin thinking about inviting another CPA firm to handle your taxes.

---

[6] It is much easier if the column containing the row labels is next to the income and tax numbers. Get them together by deleting all columns between *Item* and *Automotive Dealers*, or by using the split screen function in your spreadsheet program.

The finest level of detail is found in the IRS publication called the *Corporation Source Book,* which is not currently available online. This book goes well beyond the two-digit major industrial breakdown found in *Corporation Income Tax Returns* and provides information for many finely determined industrial groups.[7] For example, the automotive dealers and service stations category is broken down into three subcategories: motor vehicle dealers; gasoline service stations; and other automotive dealers. Before getting the *Source Book,* check the complete list of all major and minor industries in table 1 of *Corporation Income Tax Returns* to ensure your particular industry is one of the almost 600 the IRS covers.[8]

While purchasing the printed version of the *Source Book* is fairly expensive (around $185 in 2001), the IRS currently is willing to copy particular industry pages and notes for any year for $30, plus $1 per page copying charge. Send e-mail to the Statistical Information Services department (sis@irs.gov) for more information on getting just the pages you need.

Practice Question

After years of fighting on the corporate battleground, you yearn to retire and open a small bar and grill. Before ditching your suit and tie, you want to know how much money sole proprietors earn from running eating and drinking establishments. What kind of income can you expect?

Practice Question

Your general contractor consistently complains about how crushing taxes are ruining the building business. After listening for awhile, you are curious and want to know whether general building contractors pay more taxes than other businesses.

State Tax Information

While the IRS provides information on federal taxation, where do you go for information on state taxes? The key place to search for information below the federal level is the Federation of Tax Administrators (FTA), which consists of the tax collection agencies from all 50 states. The FTA's homepage, located at **http://www.taxadmin.org**, contains a link to every state tax

---

[7] IRS industry data are not as precise as census data. The IRS does not break apart financial data for companies engaged in multiple businesses. Instead, all financial data are included in the industry where the company has the most sales. Hence, conglomerates, such as General Electric, are included in just one industry even though they operate in many diverse fields.

[8] The industrial classification scheme before 1998 follows the SIC (Standard Industrial Classification) list, discussed in Chapter 8, except for businesses in the financial industry. Starting in 1998, the classification scheme switches to NAICS.

agency under the Links selection. If you need specific tax rates or want to compare multiple states, look under the selection Tax Rates/Surveys. Table 13.2 shows the list of key tax tables compiled by the FTA.

For planning business operations, the specific tax tables are very useful. For example, the corporate income tax rates by state table shows that while two-thirds of all states have a single flat-rate corporate tax, these flat rates range from under 5 percent to over 10 percent. Using these tax tables helps you accurately anticipate tax liabilities for business income earned in any state.

Information for Other Countries

International federations that compile tax statistics and provide direct links also exist. Tax information for all countries in North or South America is consolidated in one place by the Inter-American Center of Tax Administrations, whose abbreviation is CIAT. CIAT's website, located at **http://www.ciat.org/ ingles**, provides information on tax statistics, legislation, and how tax systems are administrated for over 30 American countries. Beyond this information, the Links button on the top of the CIAT homepage provides a simple method of directly accessing every country's primary tax authority.

Eastern European countries also have formed a group called the Intra-European Organization of Tax Administrations (IOTA), located at **http:// www.iota-tax.org**. This website provides information and links for countries like Hungary, Poland, and the Czech Republic. Last, if you need tax information on countries like England, Australia, and Canada, the Commonwealth Association of Tax Administrators website, located at **http://www.cata-tax.org**, provides a set of links to many of the British Commonwealth's official tax offices.

TABLE 13.2
List of Key Tax Tables Created by the Federation of Tax Administrators

Individual Income Tax Rates by State
Corporate Income Tax Rates by State
Social Security/Pensions Taxes by State
State Sales Taxes
State Food and Drug Sales Tax Exemptions
State Motor Fuel Excise Tax Rates
State Cigarette Excise Tax Rates
State Spirits, Wine and Beer Excise Taxes

Summary

Where can you find tax data? For the United States the best source of tax information is the Internal Revenue Service (IRS), which calls tax data *statistics of income* (SOI). While all key tax data are released in book form, most, but not all, of these data are also released online at the Statistics of Income homepage (**http://www.irs.gov/ tax_stats**). This homepage is a single place to find tax information not only on individuals and businesses but also on employment taxes, estate taxes, excise taxes, tax-exempt organizations, and international tax payments.

For tax information below the federal level, start with the Federation of Tax Administrators' (FTA) website, located at **http://www.taxadmin.org**, which contains both tax tables and links to state tax authorities. For tax information on countries located in North or South America, use CIAT's website, located at **http:// www.ciat.org/ingles**. Eastern European tax information is found at IOTA's website, located at **http://www.iota-tax.org**. Last, tax information for British Commonwealth countries is found at CATA's website, located at **http://www.cata-tax.org**.

14

Information on the Economy

Where do you turn for information on general economic and financial variables like GDP (gross domestic product) and interest rates for the U.S. and other countries? This chapter shows you how to use FRED, the Federal Reserve Bank of St. Louis's Economic Database. While there are a number of online databases, this repository of national economic and financial data is the easiest to use. Compared to other information sources covered in previous chapters, using FRED is quite simple. Therefore, most of this chapter concentrates on explaining exactly what the information means and how business managers can use national economic and financial data effectively. The end of the chapter then shows how to find similar information for most of the other countries in the world.

In the chapter's first scenario, your company is considering issuing new corporate bonds to finance a corporate expansion. One major concern is that interest rates could change dramatically between the time senior management decides to issue bonds and the time the bonds are actually sold. Your assignment is to provide information to senior management on how much interest rates have fluctuated over various time frames. Where do you find this information?

In the second scenario, you are about to present a plan to improve your division's productivity. The plan's key is a major capital investment in new computers, software, and other equipment. Headquarters has typically given your division a 3 percent capital budget increase each year, which you feel leaves it at a competitive disadvantage. The fatal flaw in your presentation is that it does not contain data on other companies' spending for new equipment. Where can you find this information on short notice?

FIGURE 14.1
Federal Reserve
Economic Data
(FRED) Homepage.

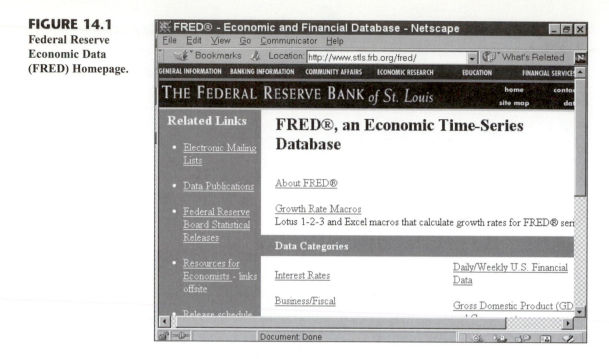

FRED: The Source for Economic and Financial Information

The St. Louis Federal Reserve (Fed) has created a simple-to-use online repository of national economic and financial data. The St. Louis Fed, which is part of the U.S. central bank, publishes the information to help individuals and businesses better understand the U.S. economy. The FRED system is located at **http:// www.stls.frb.org/fred**, and its homepage is pictured in Figure 14.1.

FRED collects labor market, interest rate, exchange rate, GDP, price, and banking sector data in one place. To find data on a particular subject, select the broad category on the homepage, scan the list of tables, and pick one. FRED returns a simple ASCII file, useful for cutting and pasting directly into a spreadsheet or word processing program.

Interest Rates: The Cost of Doing Business

For most managers, interest expenses are a key cost of doing business. For example, in the late-1990s corporations owed $3.2 trillion in short-term and $4.8 trillion in long-term debt to their creditors.[1] In a typical year, U.S.

---

[1] Interest expenses are found in the "Business Enterprise" chapter of the *Statistical Abstract* in tables entitled Corporations-Selected Financial Items. These tables also show the amount corporations paid in taxes and interest plus corporate debt holdings.

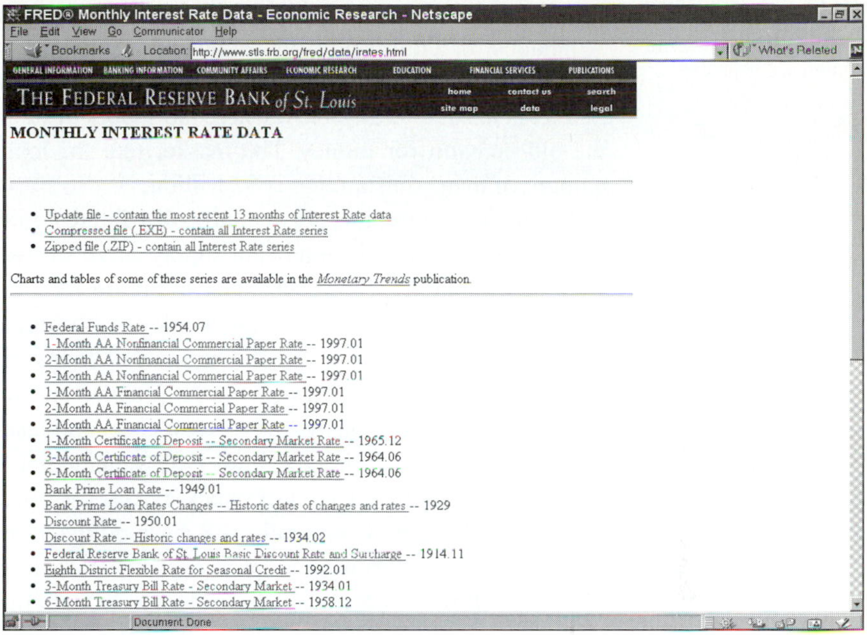

FIGURE 14.2
Interest Rate Data
from **FRED**

corporations' interest expense is more than twice as large as their tax payments. This section first shows you where to find interest rate information, provides a brief explanation of why interest rates change, and then explains why it is more important to track inflation-adjusted interest rates than unadjusted rates.

To find interest rate information, go to FRED's homepage (**http:// www.stls. frb.org/fred**) and select the database category labeled "Interest Rates." Picking this category brings up Figure 14.2, which contains over 40 different interest rate series, many extending back to the 1950s. To see the actual interest rate data just select any series.

Casual observation of any of these interest rate series shows that rates are constantly changing. Why do interest rates change so much? Two forces affect the current interest rate: the supply of and demand for loans. The supply of loans comes from individuals, businesses, and governments who have excess money and are willing to loan this money out in exchange for interest payments. The supply curve slopes up, because the higher the interest rate being offered, the more money people and businesses are willing to loan to others. In simple terms, the bigger reward entices more people to loan money.

The demand for loans comes from individuals, businesses, and governments who need money and are willing to pay to borrow it temporarily. The demand curve slopes downward because at high interest rates, few people or businesses want to borrow. In simple terms, the more onerous the cost, the less is the enticement to borrow.

Financial markets for loans work much like other markets in the economy. A balance, or equilibrium, is established where the total dollar amount of loans being offered just equals the total amount wanted. In Figure 14.3 the market is in balance at spot A, where the supply of money crosses or intersects the old demand for money. The market rate for loans is 4 percent and the amount of loans outstanding is $2 trillion.

Using the picture, it is easy to show why interest rates change. Interest rates change when either the demand or supply curve shifts. Let's first take the case where the demand for loans changes. In Figure 14.3, the demand for loans has shifted up and to the right reaching a new equilibrium at B. At point B the new interest rate is 6 percent and the amount of loans outstanding increases to $3 trillion. An upward right shift means that at every interest rate people desire more loans than previously, and interest costs increase. One dramatic upward right shift occurred during the late 1990s when demand for margin loans, used to buy shares in the soaring U.S. stock market, skyrocketed no matter how interest rates changed. Conversely, the sharp pullback in high-technology share values during 2000 caused a downward left shift in margin loan demand, as investors left the stock market regardless of margin interest rates.

Interest rates also change when the supply curve shifts. When the supply curve shifts downward and to the right, the amount of loans being offered expands at every interest rate, and overall interest costs decrease. The supply curve does this when the Fed runs an expansionary monetary policy or when banks decide the risk of making business loans has fallen. Upward left shifts of the

FIGURE 14.3
Simplified Supply and Demand Interest Rate Graph

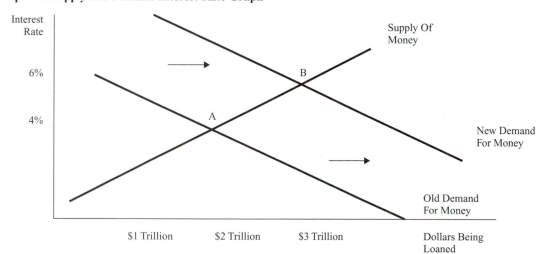

supply curve occur when the Fed tightens monetary policy or when banks collectively become more cautious.

The important point for managers to take from this discussion is that interest rates change because of government policy, investor sentiment, and general business decisions. Given that all three factors are constantly changing, sometimes it is difficult to discern exactly why interest rates are going up or down. Nevertheless, there are many times where it is clear which direction rates are heading. For example, if the Fed is tightening monetary policy (upward left shift of supply curve) and businesses are still expanding quickly (upward right shift of demand curve), like in the later part of 1999, interest rates begin to rise quickly, while the value of new loans originated stagnates.

The second important point for managers to understand is that all interest rates shown in the financial press or in the FRED database are nominal rates, which are not adjusted for inflation. What managers really want to track, however, are real, or inflation-adjusted, interest rates. A simple example shows why. Let's assume inflation is growing at 5 percent per year. If you borrow money at 8 percent, you are really paying just 3 percent to use the money. The actual cost is 3 percent because the lenders need 5 percent more money after one year just to have the same amount of purchasing power as when they lent you the money. After removing the 5 percent to account for inflation, the lender's real increase in purchasing power for making the loan is just 3 percent. In general the real interest rate formula, which is what managers need to know, is equal to the nominal rate minus the inflation rate.

Real Interest Rate $=$ Nominal Interest Rate $-$ Inflation Rate.

Why is it important to know this formula? The graph in Figure 14.4 plots the U.S. prime rate in both real and nominal terms since 1960. The prime rate is the rate large U.S. banks charge their best, or prime, customers. The key point in this graph is that just because nominal interest rates are rising does not mean that real interest rates are also rising. Look carefully at the figure from 1960 to 1980. During this period, nominal rates rose but real interest rates were actually falling. The cost of borrowing money after accounting for inflation was going down, not up, for business managers.

Using FRED's interest rate database, it is easy to answer the chapter's first scenario, in which your company is interested in issuing new corporate bonds. The finance committee wants you to calculate how much corporate bond rates fluctuate over different six-month periods. To get the data, scroll down FRED's Monthly Interest Rates list and pick the item labeled Moody's Seasoned Aaa Corporate Bond Yield—1919.01.[2]

---

[2] The 1919.01 numbers at the end of title signify the year and month when the series starts.

FIGURE 14.4

Real and Nominal U.S. Prime Rate from 1960 to 2000

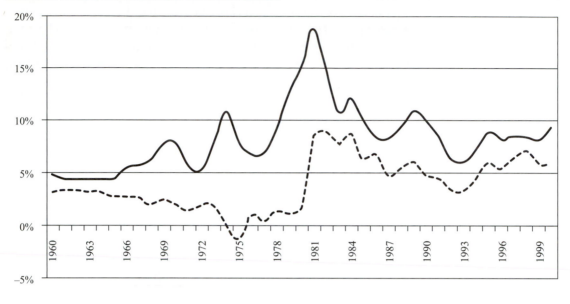

Prime Rate ------ Inflation Adjusted Prime Rate

Looking at six-month changes, you will see that the biggest increase in corporate bond yields occurred from September 1979 to February 1980. During this period rates jumped from 9.44 percent to 12.38 percent, a rise of almost 3 percentage points. The biggest fall occurred from June to December 1982, when corporate bond rates plunged from 14.81 percent down to 11.83 percent, a drop of over 3 percentage points. While these changes are dramatic, you inform the committee that interest rates tend to move in one direction for long periods of time. When interest rates are moving down, the typical (mean) drop over six months is only 0.27 percentage points, while the typical six-month rise is only 0.32 percentage points. Both of these changes are well within the committee's parameters.

Practice Question

You are thinking about buying a home. What were the highest and the lowest interest rate recorded by FRED for 30-year conventional mortgages?

Practice Question

You work for a large regional homebuilder whose leaders are perplexed about the current housing market. When the company first started building homes, interest rate changes had a big effect on customers. Now, no matter what happens to interest rates, people just keep buying. You suggest that instead of looking at current mortgage rates, the company

FIGURE 14.5
Monetary Policy
Data from FRED

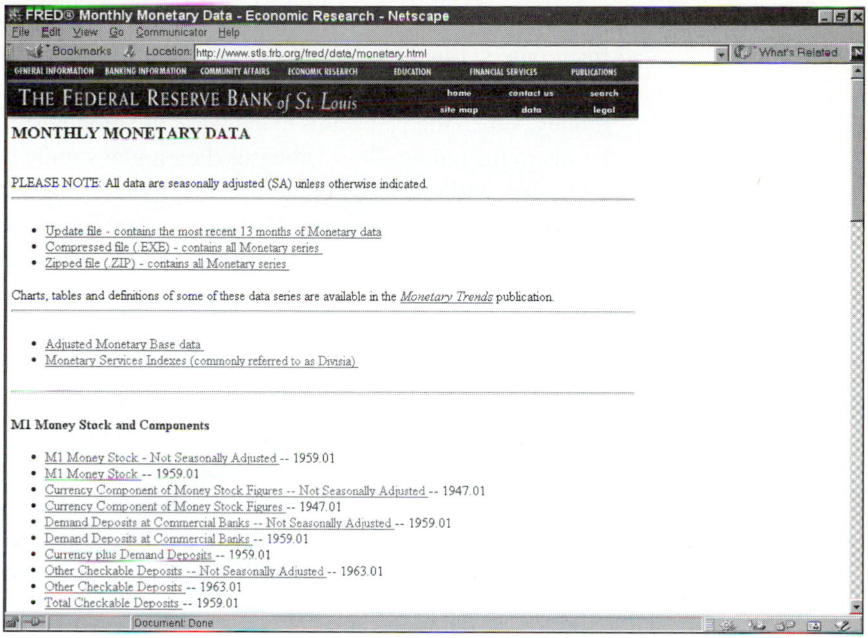

should be examining real, or inflation-adjusted, rates. Your discussion is intriguing and the president wants to see a graph of inflation-adjusted 30-year mortgage rates right away. What does the graph look like?

The Money Supply: How the Fed Affects Inflation

The second key set of economic information found on FRED is the category Monetary Aggregates. These data track monetary policy changes by the Federal Reserve (Fed), which is the nation's central bank. Monetary policy just means how the government uses money and interest rates to influence inflation and the economy. Picking the monetary category brings up Figure 14.5.

While most managers constantly hear about the Fed raising and lowering the discount rate, the more important way that the Fed affects the economy is by changing the money stock, or the money supply. The country's money stock is simply the quantity of money available in the economy and is determined by adding up the amount of all money in the bank accounts and possession of individuals, businesses, and government. The Fed changes the amount of money being held through *open-market operations*. This is just a fancy term for the Fed purchasing or selling U.S. government bonds on the open market.

When the Fed wants to increase the money stock, it buys government bonds from banks, businesses, and individuals. Buying bonds increases the money supply because the public trades bonds to the government in exchange for money. When the Fed wants to decrease the money supply, it sells government bonds to the public. This decreases the money supply because the public gives up money and receives bonds.

Look again at the simplified interest rate supply and demand diagram drawn at the beginning of this chapter. When the Fed is increasing the money stock, the supply curve shifts right and downward. This lowers interest rates, reduces borrowing costs for businesses, and leads managers to expand their companies. When the Fed is decreasing the money supply, the supply curve shifts upward and to the left. This raises interest rates, which makes borrowing more expensive. When borrowing is more expensive, businesses curtail expansion plans, reducing inflationary pressures.

Monetary data are key series for managers in highly leveraged companies, interest-sensitive industries, and those working in financial services, because in all these situations successfully predicting the direction of future interest rate changes dramatically improves profitability.

While all Fed watchers agree that money supply changes influence interest rates, inflation, and the economy, there is no universal agreement on whether a narrowly or broadly defined money supply definition is most important. The FRED system provides data on the four most important money supply series: M1, MZM, M2, and M3.[3] Table 14.1 below shows the types of money included in each measure, plus its value in December 2001. Finding more recent

TABLE 14.1
Federal Reserve Money Supply Series

Name	Types of Money Included	Amount in December 2001
M1	Cash, coins, checking accounts, and travelers checks	$1.2 trillion
MZM	M2 – small time deposits + institutional money market mutual funds	$5.7 trillion
M2	M1 + saving deposits + small time deposits such as CDs < $100,000 + money market funds	$5.5 trillion
M3	M2 + large time deposits such as CDs >= $100,000, reverse purchase agreements, and Eurodollar deposits	$8.1 trillion

[3] While the financial press often refers to M1, M2, and M3, the MZM term is relatively unknown. MZM stands for money at zero maturity and includes high-yield savings accounts with no withdrawal limiations.

values for any money supply series is easy. Simply pick the Monetary Aggregates link on FRED's homepage and select one of the money series.

In general, managers do not care about the exact amounts of each type of money supply. More important is the percentage change in each type of money supply. As a rough approximation, future inflation in a country is equal to the change in the money supply minus the change in economic growth. In equation form, this formula is:

$$\text{Future Inflation Rate} \approx \text{Money Growth Rate} - \text{Country's Growth Rate.}$$

For example, if the economy is growing at 3 percent per year and the money supply is growing at 7 percent per year, then future inflation will be roughly 4 percent. If the economy is growing at 4 percent and the money supply is growing at 4 percent, then inflation tends to disappear. While there is not universal agreement over which money measure to use in this formula, I recommend using M2, which is neither too broad nor too narrow. The end of this chapter discusses how to calculate the country's growth rate using GDP data.

The FRED system also contains a number of very useful special series that deserve mention for bankers, traders, and other financial managers. On FRED's Monetary aggregates page, shown earlier, are links to data for tracking the amount of travelers checks outstanding, savings deposits, and retail money market funds. If you are a bank manager, these series provide a simple way to compare how your accounts are growing versus all other banks.

Practice Question	Travelers checks are big business for a number of financial firms, like American Express. How many dollars worth of travelers' checks are currently outstanding?

Other Business Data

FRED's Business/Fiscal selection also contains many useful series. The top section of data in this category contains annual and monthly information on the size of the federal debt and government's deficit/surplus. The federal deficit/surplus is simply the difference between federal government receipts and payments in a given year. When the federal government spends more in a year than it receives, it runs a deficit; conversely, when it spends less than it receives the difference is called a surplus. The federal debt is just the sum of all deficits and surpluses since the country was founded.

These numbers are useful first because when the government runs a persistent deficit, selling bonds often finances the deficit. Unless the Fed attempts to counteract the sales, this causes interest rates to rise. To see why, look again at the simplified interest rate supply and demand graph drawn at the beginning of this chapter. When the government runs a deficit, it sells bonds to the public and receives money. This means the money supply curve shifts upward and to the left. This increases interest rates for business, choking off expansion plans. Hence, U.S. government budget changes affect the future direction of interest rates.

Scrolling down the Business/Fiscal page (partly shown in Figure 14.6) reveals monthly data on many series constantly discussed in the business press. For example, FRED contains the Commerce Department's monthly retail sales and housing starts figures, which are useful for tracking the financial health of department stores and the construction industry. The same page also contains auto and light truck sales figures, which are released each month by the Bureau of Economic Analysis and can be used for tracking the automotive industry. Additionally, the page contains the Federal Reserve's series on consumer debt service payments as a percentage of income. These data are very useful for understanding the indebtedness of the typical U.S. consumer. Spend just a few minutes reading all the different titles listed on FRED and you will see that it contains almost all of the key economic series used to understand the state of the economy.

FIGURE 14.6
Business Data from FRED

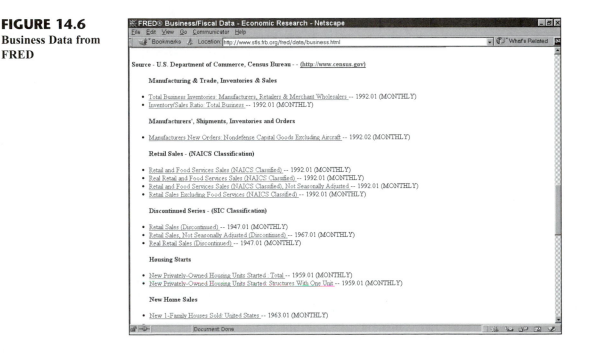

Practice Question	Your company builds major home appliances, like dishwashers and stoves, the vast majority of which are installed in new homes. You want to understand the potential size of the market. How many new homes are sold each month?
Practice Question	You are the credit manager for a large department store. You know a great deal about your customers' credit and income histories but know little about how your customers compare nationally. How much do typical consumers pay each month on their debts as a percentage of their income?

How Much Is the Country Producing? Gross Domestic Product (GDP) Information

How much does a country produce and how fast is the economy growing? The single most important piece of information used to answer these questions and to judge how well the economy is performing is GDP, which stands for gross domestic product. GDP is the total market value of all final goods and services currently produced within a country in a given period of time. The easiest way to explain what this definition means is to break it down into parts.

GDP is the total market value: Since GDP combines all items, the easiest way to value everything is using the price at which each item is sold in the market. If the price of apples is twice the price of oranges, then each apple sold contributes twice as much to GDP as each orange sold.

Of all: This idea means that GDP encompasses everything produced and sold in the economy. It is a comprehensive measure. Unfortunately, official GDP statistics do not include activities from the illegal or underground economy, since by definition governments do not know how much is being produced. Nevertheless, the goal of GDP is to include all other transactions.

Final: Many companies produce intermediate products, that are only used by other companies. These business-to-business sales are not counted because if they were, GDP would be double-counting the value of many products. Only items that are sold to the final consumer are counted in GDP. The final consumer does not have to be an individual; it could be a corporation or even the government. The key idea is not who buys the product or service but that the product or service is not resold.

Goods and services: GDP includes not only the physical output of a country, like the number of cars, planes, and trains it produces, but also services like doctor visits, insurance sales, and college lectures. What is the difference between goods and services? Goods are items, which can be resold after a purchase, like cars. Services, like having your teeth cleaned, are difficult or impossible to resell.

FIGURE 14.7

Gross Domestic
Product (GDP) Data
from FRED

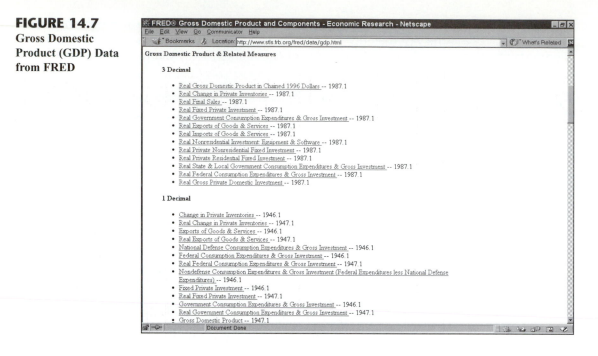

Currently produced: GDP includes only things made in the time frame under examination. Used items, no matter what their resale price, are not included in GDP calculations.

Within a country: GDP measures the amount produced inside the country's boundaries. There is a closely related concept called GNP (gross national product). The key difference between the two concepts is that GDP measures what is produced within a country regardless of the nationality of the individual or company producing the good or service. GNP, however, measures what citizens of a country produce, no matter where in the world those individuals are located. Because of the difficulties in tracking citizens' economic activities when they are abroad, many countries have switched away from GNP measures and replaced them with GDP.

Finding GDP information on FRED is easy. Pick Gross Domestic Product and Components on FRED's homepage (**http://www.stls.frb.org/fred**) and then select the series you are interested in viewing. The top section of the GDP page is shown in Figure 14.7. The important idea to keep in mind before using GDP figures is that they *must* be adjusted for changes in prices. Do not look at nominal GDP, but instead use *real* GDP information, which is adjusted for inflation. By adjusting for inflation, you are removing growth from GDP that occurs only because prices are increasing.

FIGURE 14.8
Real U.S. GDP
during the Great
Depression

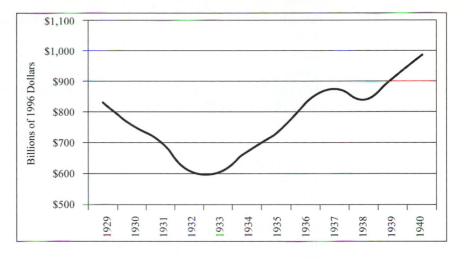

The FRED database automatically takes care of GDP inflation adjustments in any series that starts with the word *real*. Unless you know exactly what you are doing, only choose GDP measures from FRED that begin with *real*.[4]

Using FRED's gross domestic product information, it is easy to answer the chapter's second scenario, in which you need data on other companies' spending for new computers, software, and other equipment. One of the main components of GDP is private investment. Private investments are broken down into three groups: business investments in structures and buildings, business investments in equipment and software, and residential investment.

To see exactly how much other companies are investing, choose Real Nonresidential Investment: Equipment and Software. The data show that from 1998 to 1999 companies increased their spending after inflation by 11.5 percent, while from 1999 to 2000 spending increased by 8.3 percent. With figures like these it is easy to show that 3 percent yearly capital budget increases have left you at a severe competitive disadvantage.

Another way GDP data are useful is to help predict future sales. The key to predicting sales is to figure out if your company's sales lead, lag, or match the business cycle. The business cycle is just the idea that the economy goes through periodic ups and downs. This up-down pattern is simple to see in Figure 14.8, which graphs real GDP during the Great Depression. Only the Great Depression is shown because it is the clearest example of both the up and down portions of the business cycle.

To see if your sales lead, lag, or match the business cycle, first divide your company's sales by either the CPI or PPI to remove inflation's effects. Then

[4] Unlike the monthly series, FRED's GDP dates, like 1998.02, stand for year and quarter.

plot your quarterly sales against quarterly real GDP values. If your peaks and troughs come before those in GDP, then your sales cycle leads GDP. Your sales match GDP if the pattern is roughly the same. If the peaks and troughs in sales come after, or lag GDP, your sales cycle is behind the business cycle. Once you know how your sales compare to GDP, then listening to media reports both about GDP and predictions about GDP will give you a clear idea of how your sales will change in the future.

Practice Question

Overall your company's sales growth is excellent. The only sales laggard during the late 1990s is the division selling products to state and local governments. The division head's standard response is that state and local governments are not expanding as quickly as other economic sectors. After hearing this explanation one too many times, you decide to investigate the issue yourself. Did state and local government spending lag the rest of the economy during the late 1990s?

Information for Other Countries

Where do you turn for information on financial variables, interest rates, and other general economic data for countries outside the U.S.? Central banks throughout the world provide statistical information that is extremely similar to the Federal Reserve. The Bank for International Settlements (BIS), headquartered in Basel, Switzerland, maintains the list of all central banks. The BIS is an international organization, which is the bank for the world's central banks. The BIS website, located at **http://www.bis.org**, has an entry on its homepage entitled Links to Central Banks. This selection brings up hot links to over 110 central banks ranging from Albania to Zimbabwe.

As an example, select Canada's Bank of Canada—Banque du Canada (**http:// www.bankofcanada.ca/en**). This link brings up a homepage preloaded with key statistics like the current exchange rate between the Canadian and U.S. dollar, the current Canadian prime interest rate and the interest rate on long-term Canadian bonds. In addition, picking the Bank's link entitled Rates and Statistics, shown in Figure 14.9, brings up many of the same categories found in FRED, such as interest rates, monetary data, prices, exchange rates, and stock market values.[5] The key difference between the Bank of Canada's page and FRED is that the Bank's variables focus on Canada, not the United States.

---

[5] If you need to adjust Canadian figures for price changes use the Inflation Calculator. This calculator works just like the one on the BLS website, discussed in Chapter 10, but adjusts figures based on Canadian data.

FIGURE 14.9
**Bank of Canada's
Rates and Statistics
Homepage**

Copyright Bank of Canada.

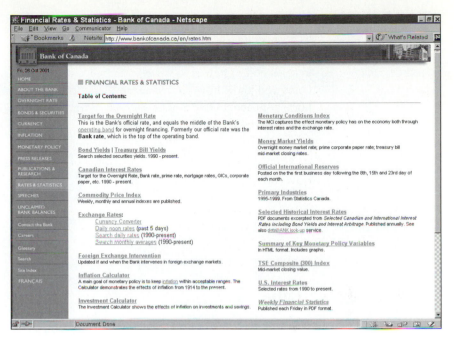

Summary

If you need general information on labor markets, interest rates, exchange rates, GDP, prices, and the banking sector, turn to FRED (**http://www.stls.frb.org/fred**). FRED is the Federal Reserve Bank of St. Louis's Economic Database and is a simple-to-use online repository of national economic and financial data. To find information on a particular subject, select the broad category on the homepage, scan the list of tables, and pick one. FRED returns a simple ASCII file, useful for cutting and pasting directly into a spreadsheet or word processing program. If you need this information for countries outside the U.S., go to the Bank for International Settlements' website (**http://www.bis.org**) and use its list of Links to Central Banks to find almost any country.

Chapter

15

Exporting and Importing

Just a few decades ago, foreign trade was not particularly important to the U.S. economy. As recently as 1970, the United States exported only $57 billion of goods and services, worth roughly 5.5 percent of GDP. By 2000, however, the United States exported $1.1 trillion of goods, worth 11 percent of GDP.[1] The doubling of exports as a percentage of the country's GDP over the last 30 years is just one dimension of the growing interdependency of foreign countries and United States businesses.

Where do you turn for export and import information? This chapter first shows you how to track the exports and imports of specific products. Then the chapter overviews where to find tariff schedules. The chapter also describes the Import and Export Price Indexes, which track how prices change, and ends with an overview of foreign exchange rate information. Together these sources provide most of the key information that businesses need to compete globally.

In this chapter's first scenario, you are a budding artist and entrepreneur who creates sculptures evoking the Wild West. Your best customers are European tourists who constantly ask why you do not sell your work abroad. You are interested in testing the export market but your banker wants facts, not tourist hearsay, before extending you any credit. Where do you get information on the value of sculptures exported?

In the second scenario, you work in accounting and recently began noticing a sharp rise in air travel costs to Japan. Your company has a universal coach

---

[1] Calculate these ratios with information from the *Statistical Abstract*. Export information and GDP data are found in the section entitled Income, Expenditures and Wealth, in a table labeled *GDP in Current and Real Dollars*.

class only policy, but you suspect that employees flouting the rules are responsible for increasing the average ticket price paid per trip. Where can you find information to determine if your suspicion is right or wrong?

Trade Classifications

Before using trade data you must understand the trade classification systems, because almost all export and import information are released using these codes. The primary system used worldwide is the SITC. SITC stands for the Standard International Trade Classifications and is maintained by the United Nations. The goal of the SITC is to ensure that every item traded between countries is classified and given an identifying number.

Like the NAICS and SIC industrial coding systems discussed earlier, the SITC trade codes are arranged in a hierarchy. Each commodity or service is given a numeric code. The fewer the digits, the more aggregated or broader the commodity's level, while the greater the number of digits, the finer the level of disaggregation. For example, the highest level SITC code is one digit while the lowest international level is five digits. Below is an example of how SITC codes change from the broad food category down to the very specific category of goose livers, which are used for making pâtè to spread on crackers.

- SITC Code 0 is   Food and Live Animals

- SITC Code 01 is   Meat and Meat Preparation

- SITC Code 012 is   Meat, Other than Bovine (Cows)

- SITC Code 0123 is   Meat and Parts of Poultry

- SITC Code 01233 is   Fatty Livers of Geese or Ducks

In this example, the one-digit SITC code covers all food products, while the lowest-level five-digit SITC code applies to a very specific food item. The 10 broadest SITC categories, or sectors, are shown in Table 15.1.

Where do you go for the full list of SITC codes? One of the best sources for all types of trade information is the United States International Trade Commission, or USITC. The commission has created a special website devoted just to providing trade data (**http://dataweb.usitc.gov**). This website is pictured in Figure 15.1.

To find the list of detailed SITC codes, pick the Lookup for HTS/SIC/SITC/NAICS/End-Use descriptions link located under the ITC Trade DataWeb heading. This brings up the screen shown in Figure 15.2.

To find an SITC code, click on the circle next to the appropriate level of detail and push the List Items button. This will create a table of SITC codes and descriptions. To begin answering our first scenario, in which you are a

TABLE 15.1
High-Level SITC
Groups and
Associated One-Digit
Codes

SITC Sector	Code
Food and Animals	0
Beverages and Tobacco	1
Raw Materials, except Fuel	2
Fuels	3
Oils, Fat and Waxes	4
Chemicals	5
Manufactured Goods	6
Machinery and Transport	7
Miscellaneous Manufactures	8
Coins, Gold and Other Items	9

FIGURE 15.1
United States
International Trade
Commission's Tariff
and Trade Homepage

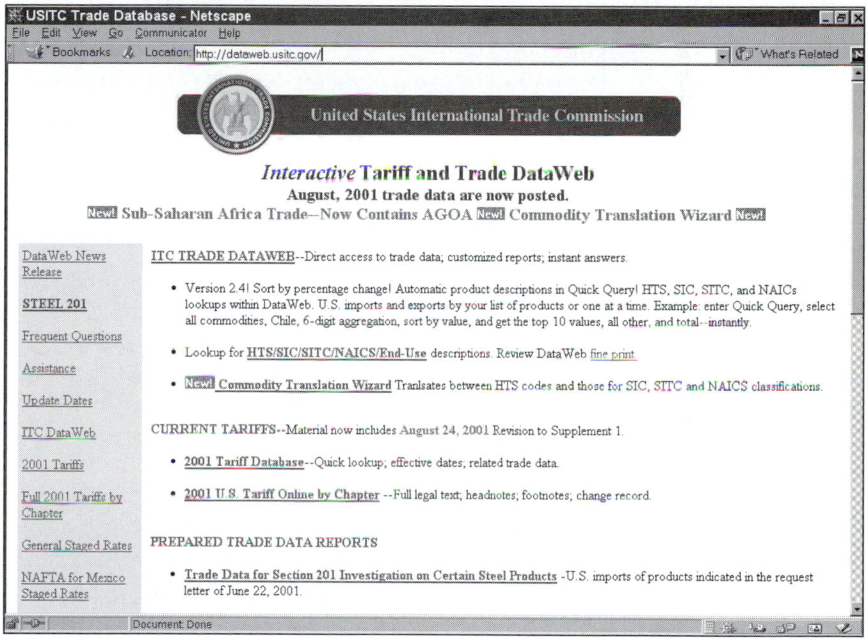

budding artist interested in exporting your statues and sculptures, let's find the SITC code for sculptures. Searching through all four-digit SITC entries shows the relevant code is 8963.[2]

**Practice
Question**

Motorcycles are no longer driven just by the young and restless. While the demographics of motorcycle owners are changing rapidly, the repairing

---

[2] Both Netscape Navigator and Microsoft's Internet Explorer have a Find in Page command under the Edit function, which allows you to search for words, like sculpture.

FIGURE 15.2
**International Trade
Classification
Description Lookup**

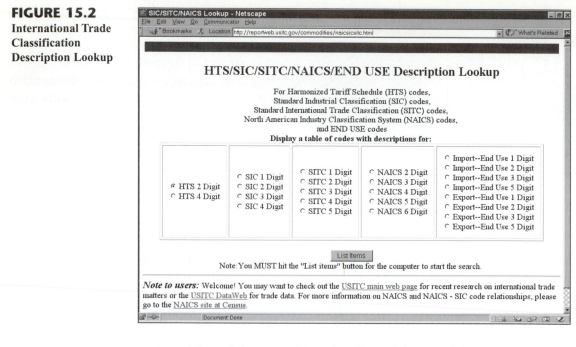

and servicing of these machines is still reminiscent of the 1950s. You are writing a business plan to create a standardized chain of motorcycle repair shops, similar in concept to the national muffler replacement business. To find information about motorcycle imports, you need the relevant SITC code. What is it?

**Practice
Question**

You have built a good business importing beer from Australia and are now thinking of expanding by importing wine. What is wine's four-digit SITC code?

How Much Is Exported and Imported?

How much is exported and imported? Where do you find information on tracking exports and imports of specific products? The United States has excellent information on exports and imports of all types of goods. While much of the information discussed earlier in the book comes from surveys that sample a portion of the population, export and import information comes directly from Customs Service forms. Except for smuggled and illegal items, these customs forms record everything valued at more than $250, which is brought in or out of the country.[3]

---

[3] A copy of the U.S. export form, called the Shipper's Export Declaration, is found on this book's website. There is no single form used for U.S. imports.

For businesses needing in-depth data on exports or imports by port of entry, by destination, or by originating port, these customs forms provide excellent information. The chief drawback to using official export and import figures is that they include ***all*** shipments, whether a commercial transaction occurs or not. For example, U.S. aid for disaster relief and arms shipments to a foreign government for political reasons are both counted as exports, even when no money is ever expected in return. This procedure artificially inflates export trade figures.

Another problem with using foreign trade data is that the information focuses almost entirely on goods and ignores services. While in the 1950s and earlier, trade in goods was king, today exports of consulting, banking, insurance, and other services are very important parts of international trade. Unfortunately, since no business consultant fills in a Shipper's Export Declaration before jetting off to Europe on assignment, the amount and quality of data on services pales in comparison to the information on goods.

These problems aside, trade figures are still very useful business tools. If you need trade figures, go back to the United States International Trade Commission's DataWeb homepage, pictured earlier, and pick ITC Trade DataWeb. As an example of how to use the DataWeb system, let's answer the chapter's scenario in which you are a budding sculptor interested in exporting your work. How much sculpture (SITC code 8963) did the United States export last year? Which countries bought the sculptures? The first step to using the DataWeb is to create an account, which is free to all users, and log in. After a successful login, Figure 15.3 is shown.

This page lets you decide whether to track import or export data and the rough time frame needed. First, pick United States Total Exports under the Select Trade Type heading on the left-hand side. Then pick Quick Query in the middle and press the Proceed button. Pressing proceed brings up the Query Design Page, pictured in Figure 15.4.

While this page looks very complex and scary, you can safely ignore most of the selections. The only two default values that most managers need to change are the Enter a Commodity Number section on the left side and the Select Country Aggregation section in the bottom right. Entering a commodity number is simple. Just input the SITC code you looked up earlier (8963 for sculptures) and make sure the SITC button below that number is selected. Most managers want to see exports or imports broken down by importing or exporting country, so make sure you choose Display All Countries Separately in the Select Country Aggregation box, instead of the default, which aggregates, or lumps, all countries together.

At the very bottom of the page (not shown) press the Proceed To Next Step button. This will bring up another complex form that enables you to modify how the output is displayed. For beginning users, all the default values work

FIGURE 15.3
Top Level DataWeb
Page

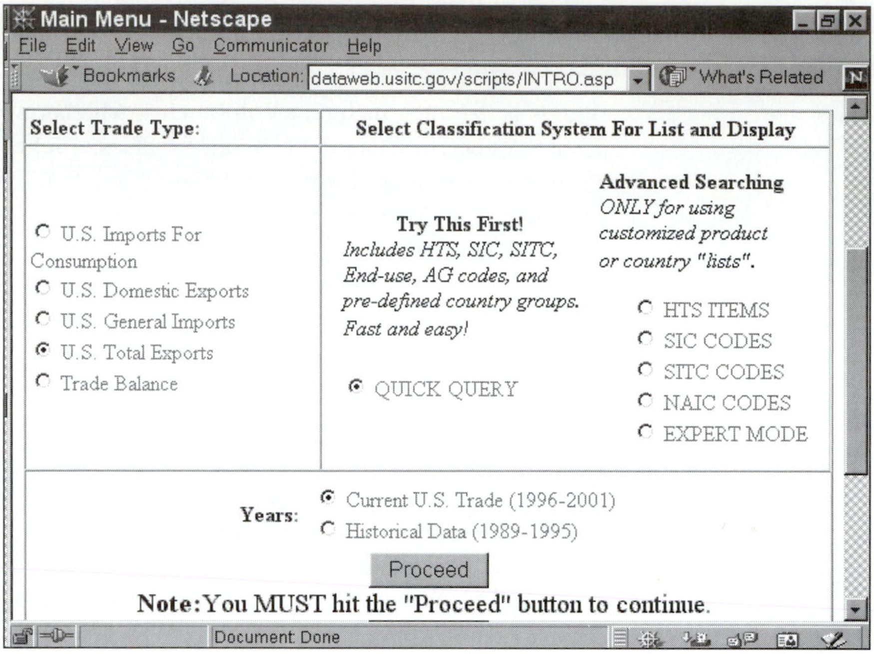

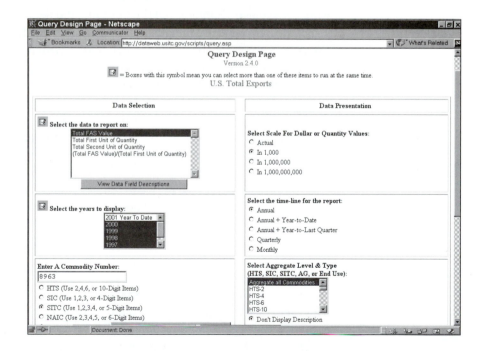

FIGURE 15.4
DataWeb Page
Used to Choose
Traded Items

fine. Ignore all the choices and just press the Run Report button at the bottom
of the page. The report that is generated is partially shown in Figure 15.5.

FIGURE 15.5
DataWeb Output

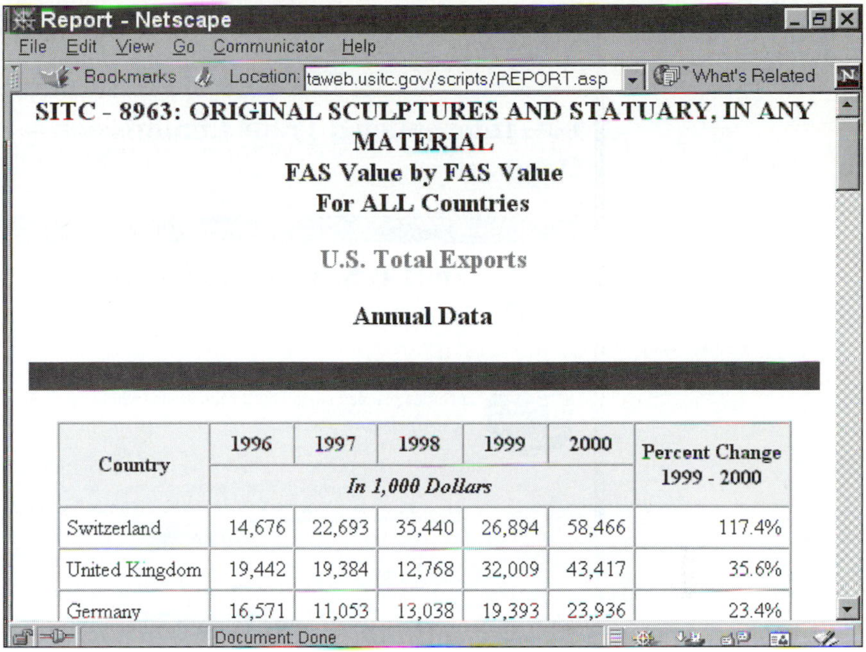

```
Report - Netscape                                              _ □ ✕
File   Edit   View   Go   Communicator   Help
   Bookmarks    Location: taweb.usitc.gov/scripts/REPORT.asp  ▾     What's Related   N
```

SITC - 8963: ORIGINAL SCULPTURES AND STATUARY, IN ANY MATERIAL
FAS Value by FAS Value
For ALL Countries

U.S. Total Exports

Annual Data

Country	1996	1997	1998	1999	2000	Percent Change 1999 - 2000
	In 1,000 Dollars					
Switzerland	14,676	22,693	35,440	26,894	58,466	117.4%
United Kingdom	19,442	19,384	12,768	32,009	43,417	35.6%
Germany	16,571	11,053	13,038	19,393	23,936	23.4%

```
                     Document: Done
```

The very bottom of this report shows that from 1996 to 2000 the United States exported between $122 million and $195 million of sculptures each year. The top three importing countries were the United Kingdom, Switzerland, and Germany. Because these data support your sales pitch, your banker reluctantly agrees to extend a small credit line so that you can begin exporting sculptures.

Practice Question

In a previous practice question, you were creating a business plan targeting motorcycles and found the relevant SITC code. Using this code, determine how large the motorcycle import and export markets are currently.

Practice Question

In a previous practice question, you were thinking of expanding your business by importing wine from Australia. How much wine does the United States import from this country?

Tariffs

One of the most confusing parts of exporting or importing products is that there is no uniform tax or duty. It seems almost every product has a special tariff rate. Moreover, tariff rates vary depending on the product's country of origin. For example, if you import men's cotton dress shirts[4] from a Mexican

[4] Men's cotton shirts are SITC code 84371 and harmonized trade schedule product number 61051000.

FIGURE 15.6
United States Tariff
Database Homepage

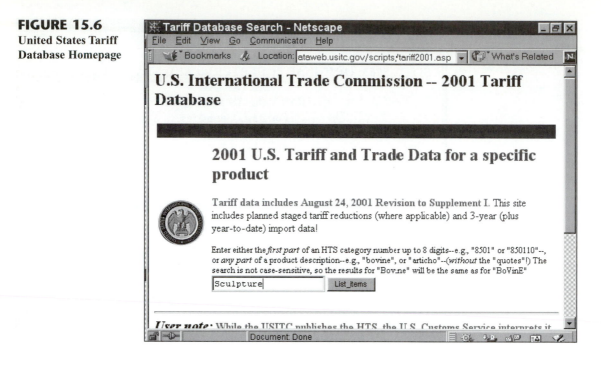

shirt factory, there is no tariff. Import shirts from a nation with normal trade relations (NTR) or most favored nation (MFN) trade status, and the rate is 20.2 percent. Import the shirt from a country that did not negotiate a preferential trade agreement, and the import duty is 45 percent.

Where do you find the list of all U.S. tariffs for imports? The list is published annually by the federal government's Office of Tariff Affairs and Trade Agreements in a book entitled the *Harmonized Tariff Schedule of the United States Annotated (HTSA)*. Because tariff rates are constantly changing as new agreements are reached and old agreements expire, using the online version ensures that the information is up to date. To see the online version of the HTSA, go to the USITC's DataWeb site (shown previously) and pick the most current tariff database link.

Selecting this link brings up a screen filled with a legal warning, which tells you the interactive database is not the official guide for U.S. tariff rates. After proceeding past this screen, the interactive database displays a very simple query form, shown in Figure 15.6, that asks you to type the product's description in the search box. In our example type in the word "sculpture."

Pressing the List_items button brings up all the items for which tariff and trade information are available. The 2001 Tariff Database contains two types of statues and sculptures: 97030000, which tracks sculptures and statues purchased by private individuals and businesses; and 98100040, which tracks

FIGURE 15.7
United States Tariff for Sculptures

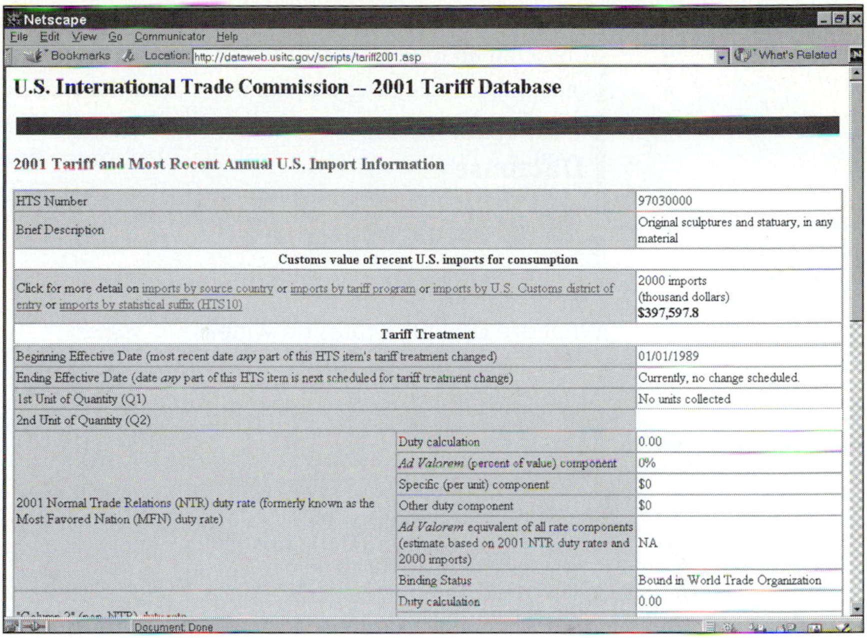

U.S. International Trade Commission -- 2001 Tariff Database

2001 Tariff and Most Recent Annual U.S. Import Information

HTS Number		97030000
Brief Description		Original sculptures and statuary, in any material
Customs value of recent U.S. imports for consumption		
Click for more detail on imports by source country or imports by tariff program or imports by U.S. Customs district of entry or imports by statistical suffix (HTS10)		2000 imports (thousand dollars) **$397,597.8**
Tariff Treatment		
Beginning Effective Date (most recent date *any* part of this HTS item's tariff treatment changed)		01/01/1989
Ending Effective Date (date *any* part of this HTS item is next scheduled for tariff treatment change)		Currently, no change scheduled.
1st Unit of Quantity (Q1)		No units collected
2nd Unit of Quantity (Q2)		
2001 Normal Trade Relations (NTR) duty rate (formerly known as the Most Favored Nation (MFN) duty rate)	Duty calculation	0.00
	Ad Valorem (percent of value) component	0%
	Specific (per unit) component	$0
	Other duty component	$0
	Ad Valorem equivalent of all rate components (estimate based on 2001 NTR duty rates and 2000 imports)	NA
	Binding Status	Bound in World Trade Organization
	Duty calculation	0.00

sculptures for public or nonprofit institutions. Select 97030000 and press the Detail button to see Figure 15.7. Reading over the duty rates show that sculptures for private use are not taxed, no matter from where they are imported.

Tariffs for Other Countries

While businesses importing goods into the United States have a single book listing all relevant duties and tariffs, where is information on the tariff rates used by other countries?[5] The World Customs Organization (**http://www.wcoomd.org**) is one of the international bodies seeking to coordinate and improve trade. On the organization's homepage, select Links to Member Administrations. This leads to a list of hotlinks for the customs authorities in most countries.

For example, selecting the link for Canada brings you directly to Canada's Customs and Revenue Agency (**http://www.ccra-adrc.gc.ca**). To find Canada's tariff code, the fastest method is to use the search button and look for Customs Tariff. Canada has placed its entire tariff code online in PDF files. Since the entire tariff code is a huge document, the online version is separated into about

[5] WorldTariff (**http://www.worldtariff.com**), a Federal Express company, simplifies and translates into English the world's tariff and duty information, but their prices are outside this book's range.

100 sections. Instead of wading through this massive code, a quicker method of looking up import taxes is to use Canada's Tariff Wizard. The Tariff Wizard is a simple-to-use program that is very similar to USITC's tariff database described on the previous page. To find the Tariff Wizard, go to Custom and Revenue's homepage and select the Electronic services button. The Tariff Wizard is currently found under the Customs heading's Business link.

Practice Question	What are U.S. tariff rates on motorcycle imports?
Practice Question	What are U.S. tariff rates on wine?

Import-Export Prices

How much do imported and exported goods cost? For many products and services, the best data are found in the Producer Price Index (PPI) and Consumer Price Index (CPI), discussed in Chapter 10. Both of these include many goods and services. However, there are a number of common items not covered by a CPI or PPI series because U.S. industries do not produce these goods. For example, almost all coffee and tea drunk in the United States is imported.[6] To track these types of goods and services, the International Price Index program has produced import and export price indexes since the early 1980s. The export indexes track the prices of goods and services sold by U.S. residents to foreign buyers while the import price indexes track the prices of goods and services purchased from foreign sellers by U.S. residents.

The program collects prices every month for 20,000 to 25,000 goods and every three months for 1,500 to 2,000 service items.[7] These items are then consolidated into more than 400 series for businesses to use. The drawback to these series is that individual import and export indexes are created only for items whose annual trade is worth billions of dollars.[8] This means that, unlike the PPI, it is impossible to track very specialized prices such as imported computer memory chips since the overall dollar value is not high enough to warrant a separate index.

---

[6] The March 2000 issue of *Smithsonian* magazine (pp. 24–26) has an article about the tiny Charleston Tea Plantation, which is the only domestic U.S. tea grower.

[7] For imports, the collected price basis of f.o.b. (free on board) at the foreign port. F.o.b. is the price before insurance, freight, and duty are added and represents how much the items cost abroad before sending them to this country. For exports, the collected price is f.a.s. (free alongside ship) at the U.S. port of embarkation. Once again, f.a.s. does not include the cost of transporting, insuring, or paying duty on the goods from the United States to its ultimate destination.

[8] The actual cutoffs for creating an export or import index are at least $2 billion and $1.6 billion in annual trade, respectively, as of 1995.

While it is impossible to track chip prices using these indexes, the program's hidden gems are the 22 shipping service indexes. These indexes provide very quick quarterly information on how airfreight, air passenger fares, and ocean liner freight rates to and from various parts of the world are changing. For example, Figure 15.8 shows the outbound air freight rate indexes to both Atlantic (London, Paris, etc.) and Pacific (Hong Kong, Tokyo, etc.) ports. The graph shows that Atlantic freight rates are slowly rising over time while Pacific airfreight rates plummeted during the late 1990s.

International Price Indexes are available from the Bureau of Labor Statistics at **http://www.bls.gov/iep**, which is shown in Figure 15.9.

There are three methods of accessing import and export indexes at this URL: Economic News Releases, Tables Created by BLS, and Get Detailed Statisitics. Using the News Release option, you can read the current month's release or retrieve older releases from the archives. Each press release contains the current month or quarter's figures for all major indexes, plus information on how each index has changed over the past year.

The other option is to use one of the five data retrieval methods found under the "Get Detailed Statistics" selection. For business purposes, the most useful choice is Create Customized Table (one screen). If you choose this item, you can retrieve one of over 1,500 series via a simple three-step process.

The first step is to pick an index. The easiest way to determine which index you want is to skim the tables in any press release. Three acronyms appear on the list many times. SIC stands for Standard Industrial Classification codes (see Chapter 8 for more details), SITC stands for the U.N.'s Standard International Trade Classifications (see the first part of this chapter), and BEA

FIGURE 15.8
Outbound Air Freight Rates to Atlantic and Pacific Ports (1995=100)

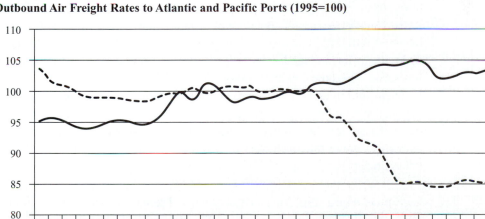

FIGURE 15.9
International Price
Indexes Homepage

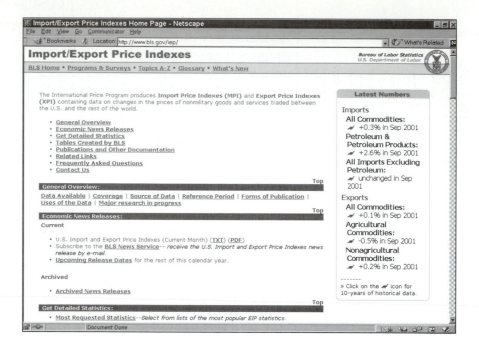

stands for the Bureau of Economic Analysis, which is the U.S. agency that publishes trade statistics.

Using Create Customized Table (one screen) shown in Figure 15.10, it is easy to answer the chapter's second scenario in which you notice a sharp rise in air travel costs to Japan. First, pick the Services International Index in the first box labeled Select an Index. Then using the second box select the series name. There are a variety of air passenger fares for U.S. carriers on the list. Since you are concerned about travel to Japan, the specific item you want is labeled EIUIU221211 Japan. The first part of this label, EIUIU221211, is the series identifier, and the last part represents the country, Japan. After selecting this series, press the Get Data button.

The resulting table (not shown) reveals that while air ticket prices to Japan bounced around between March 1994 and December 2001, there is no upward trend. These data bear out your suspicion that employees are flouting your company's universal coach class only policy, which is increasing the average ticket price paid per trip.

**Practice
Question**

Each month you ship hundreds of cases of French cheese by boat to New York. Citing rising transportation costs, your shipper has increased prices by roughly 2 percent each quarter. Are other importers facing the same cost increases?

FIGURE 15.10
International Price
Index Public Data
Query

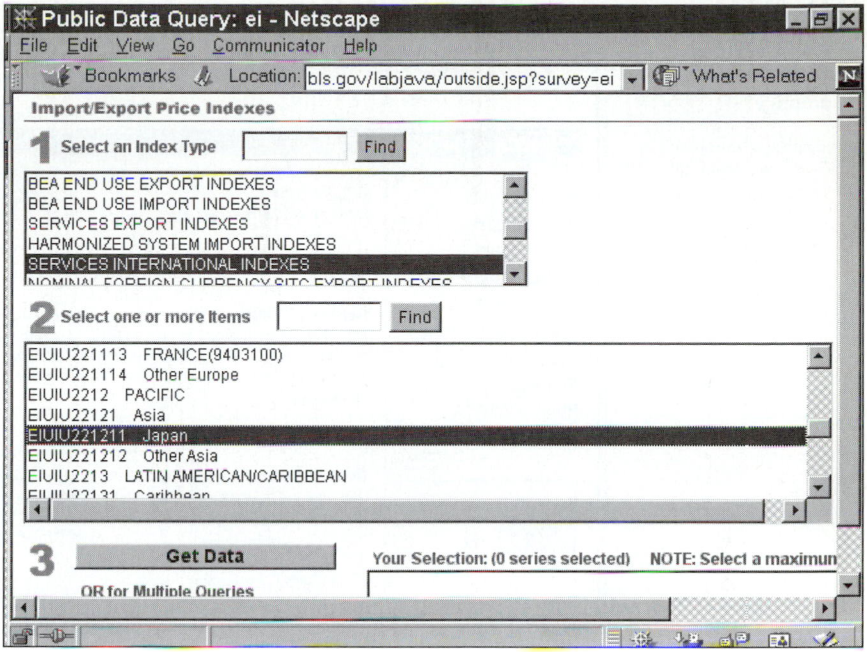

Exchange Rates

The last key piece of information needed to understand exporting and importing is foreign exchange rates. Foreign exchange rates are the price or conversion factor used to change money from one currency into another. For example, assume you are the clothing buyer for a budget department store and are offered a lot of beautiful English woolen sweaters for £80 each. Converting £80 into U.S. dollars reveals if these sweaters are appropriately priced for your store's clients.

While the current prices for converting major currencies like the British pound, French franc, and Japanese yen are found in the business section of every major newspaper, where do you find older information or conversion rates for more exotic currencies like the Bahrain dinar or Botswana pula? The best place to find currency information is the International Monetary Fund (IMF).

The IMF has excellent information because the fund was originally created solely to help countries control their exchange rates. While over time the fund has expanded its mandate and now acts as a short-term lender to countries when sources of private credit disappear, it still monitors exchange rates closely. The fund publishes the daily values of the world's top currencies in its monthly publication *International Financial Statistics.* For managers without

FIGURE 15.11
International Monetary Fund Homepage

Copyright the International Monetary Fund. Used with permission.

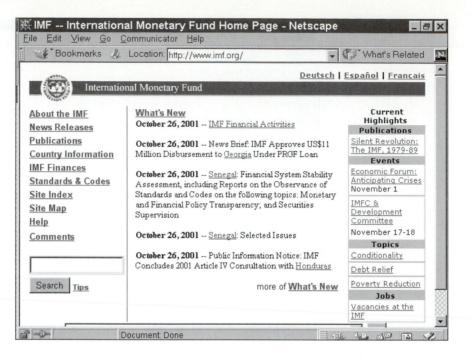

ready access to *International Financial Statistics,* currency information is also found on the IMF website, located at **http://www.imf.org** and shown in Figure 15.11.

To find conversion rates, select "IMF Finances" on the homepage's left side. This selection brings up the Finances main page, shown in Figure 15.12, which contains two choices on the left side for contemporaneous information: Current Rates and Current Month. To find historic currency information, select any year from 1996 to the present under the Data Archive heading.

Picking the Current Rates link on the IMF Finances page results in a foreign exchange table like the one shown in Figure 15.13.

To understand IMF currency tables, you need to know that all IMF currency information is denominated in a currency called SDR, or special drawing rights. SDRs are international currencies, created in 1969, that are used by the world's central banks to settle transactions. SDRs are actually a basket of the world's major currencies.[9] The current value of SDRs is shown in the top left corner of the IMF Finances page. Looking at the Finances figure you can see that on Oct. 26, 2001, each SDR was worth 1.27 U.S. dollars.

---

[9] Every five years the weights change. From January 2001 to 2006 the basket is composed of the U.S. dollar (45%), the Euro (29%), the Japanese yen (15%), and the English pound sterling (11%).

FIGURE 15.12
International Monetary Fund Financial Data

Copyright the International Monetary Fund. Used with permission.

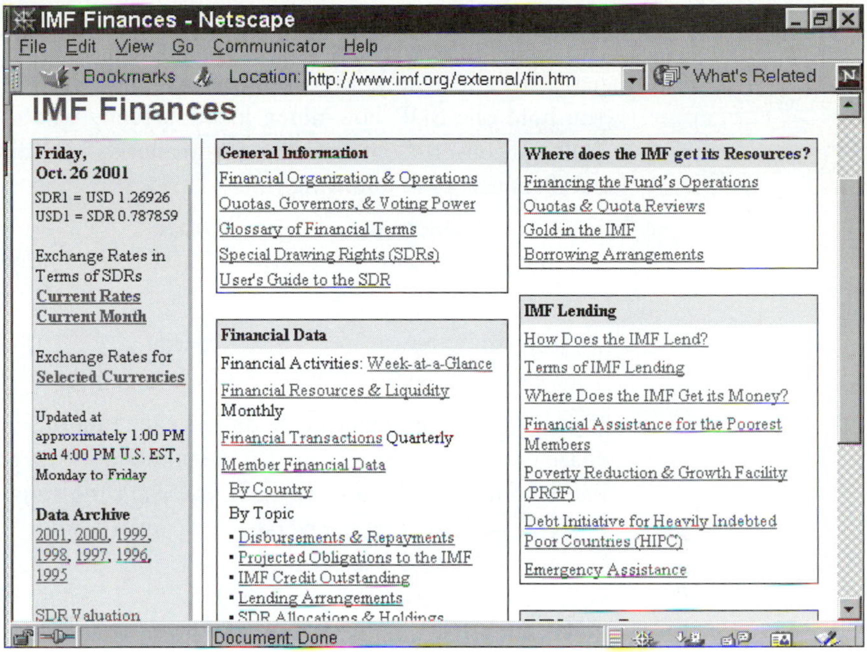

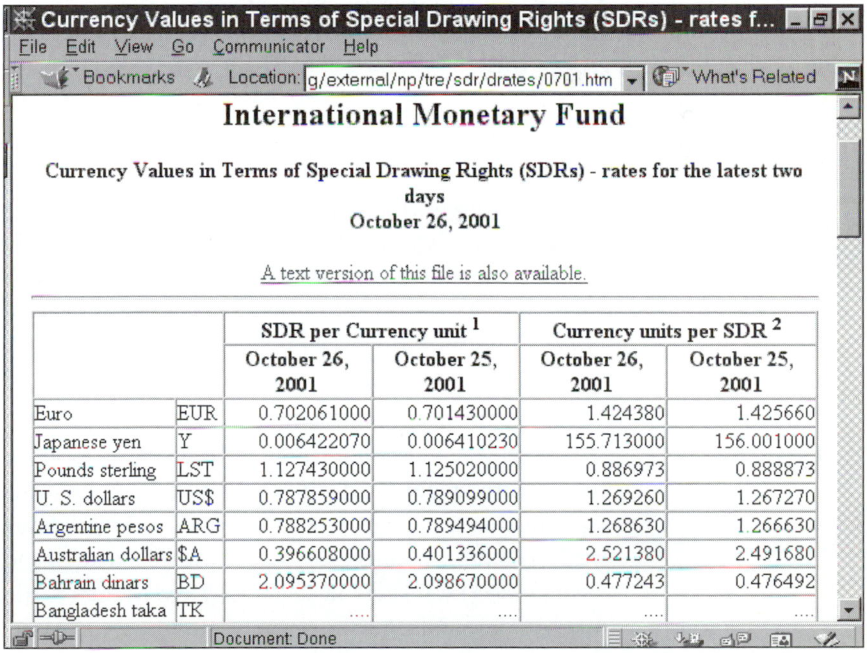

FIGURE 15.13
Foreign Exchange Rates from the International Monetary Fund

Copyright the International Monetary Fund. Used with permission.

To conserve space, all IMF currency tables show just the relation between SDRs and the local currency. The right-hand columns, labeled Currency units per SDR, are the ones I recommend using. These right-hand columns show if you hold one SDR how much local currency would be exchanged for that SDR. To convert from one currency to another, just divide the right-hand side numbers using the following rules.

United States Dollars into Foreign Currency	divide	Foreign SDR rate / United States SDR rate

or

Foreign Currency into United States Dollars	divide	United States SDR rate / Foreign SDR rate

If you want the amount of U.S. dollars each unit of foreign currency will purchase put the foreign currency in the numerator (top part) and the U.S. rate in the denominator (bottom part). If you want the amount of foreign currency one U.S. dollar will buy, reverse it.

For example, on October 26, 2001, each SDR purchased 2.52 Australian dollars, while each SDR purchased 1.27 U.S. dollars. Hence, each Australian dollar buys 0.50 U.S. dollars (1.27 / 2.52), or each U.S. dollar buys 1.98 Australian dollars (2.52 / 1.27). The same formulas work if you need to convert between two non-United States currencies. For example, say you need to convert between Bahrain dinars and the British pound. On October 26, 2001, each SDR was worth 0.48 Bahrain dinars and 0.89 British pounds. This means that one dinar buys 1.85 pounds (0.89 / 0.48), and one pound buys 0.54 dinars (0.48 / 0.89).

Practice Question

How many British pounds does one Australian dollar buy today?

Practice Question

You are in deep discussions with a Brazilian produce company for importing acerolas (also called the Barbados cherry) into the United States. Acerolas are a small fruit that looks like a cherry, tastes very different, and has a very high vitamin C content. The company is quoting you a price of 40 Brazilian reais (also called reals) per case. How much is this in U.S. dollars?

Summary

Where do you go to find export and import information? The best source for all types of trade and tariff information is the United States International Trade Commission trade data website, located at **http://dataweb.usitc.gov**. For information on other countries, go to the World Customs Organization (**http://www.wcoomd.org**) website and select Links to Member Administrations. This leads to a list of hotlinks for the customs authorities in most countries.

If you need import or export price information, the Bureau of Labor Statistics' International Price Index program, located at **(http://www.bls.gov/iep)**, has tracked these prices since the early 1980s. Finally, if you need exchange rate information go to the International Monetary Fund's website located at **http://www.imf.org** to determine conversion rates between almost any set of countries in the world.

Chapter 16

Conclusion

This book has shown you how to find, understand, and use many sources of business information. There are, however, still two final topics to discuss. The entire book has shown how to find current and past information, but where is information about the future? Second, what should you do if the sources discussed in this book do not answer your question?

Forecasting the Future

What will happen in the future? While no one has a perfect crystal ball, many business decisions are based not only on current information but also on the best guess about the future. To get information about the future, you can either generate predictions yourself or use a private company, government agency, university, or nonprofit organization's forecast.

Generating your own forecasts is no longer difficult. For those willing to go outside this book's free/nominal costs philosophy, there are a variety of software packages, such as Eviews®, which generate business forecasts based on past data.[1] However, even without buying a fancy package you can generate forecasts using the simpler methods built into most spreadsheet programs.

No matter whether you use a professional package or your spreadsheet's forecasting functions, techniques for predicting the future fall into two general categories. In the first case, predictions are created solely by examining current and past trends. For example, a best guess about how many people will be using the Internet next year can be made by extrapolating current and past usage figures. To make a prediction, first calculate or find a function that matches current and past information. For example, sales curves are sometimes

[1] Eviews is created and sold by Quantitative Micro Software (**http://www.eviews.com**).

elongated S shapes. Sales are flat during the product's introduction; after people know about the product, sales grow sharply; and then when the market reaches saturation, sales stop growing rapidly and settle down. An example of exponential functions is the price of Internet stocks during the mania of the late 1990s. There are a variety of mathematical handbooks that contain pictures of common functions. Once you find a function that matches the shape of your current and past data, it is relatively easy to estimate the function and predict future values.

A second method of predicting the future is based on the idea that the future depends primarily on the status of key economic, social, or business variables. Hence, future values depend on how much you spent advertising your product last year, the number of sales associates you hired, or the level of interest rates. For example, many people in the real estate business believe that future home sales are primarily affected by mortgage rates and the labor market situation, not by the number of homes sold in the past. The key to predicting with this method is to find the variables with the most important influence. Using statistical regression techniques, the impact of these key variables is estimated. Once the function is estimated, you can plug in expected values for these key variables to guess the future trend.

If you do not have the time, interest, or statistical knowledge to create your own forecasts, you can use prepared forecasts. The most complete list of companies in the forecasting business is found in the book entitled *World Index of Economic Forecasts.*[2] No forecasts are found in the *World Index;* instead the book lists the name, address, and type of business variables each organization, business, and consultant projects into the future. Another place to look for forecasting companies is the American Economic Association's Resources for Economists website, located at **http://www.aeaweb.org/RFE**. On the Resources homepage is a selection entitled Forecasting and Consulting, which contains a list of and links to a variety of forecasting companies.

The problem with most of the companies listed in the *World Index of Economic Forecasts* and the Resources for Economists website is that these forecasts cost a lot of money. One free source for general business forecasts are the predictions done by the Congressional Budget Office, commonly called the CBO.[3] The CBO issues economic forecasts and projections primarily to help Congress make better tax and spending decisions.

The CBO releases two types of information: forecasts, which are short-term guesses about the next 18 to 24 months, and projections, which are

---

[2] *World Index of Economic Forecasts: Including Industrial Tendency Surveys,* fourth edition, Robert Fildes editor, Gower Press, 1995.

[3] The British government also provides free economic forecasts. These forecasts are available at Her Majesty's Treasury Department website (**http://www.hm-treasury.gov.uk**) under the Economic Data & Tools link.

long-term guesses covering the next 10 years. Both forecasts and projections examine major economic variables like gross domestic product (GDP), unemployment, inflation, and interest rates. To see these forecasts, go to the CBO homepage, located at **http://www.cbo.gov**, and find Data Highlights. Under the highlights is the key pick, Current Economic Projections. The top part of the economic projections page shown in Figure 16.1, contains the CBO's short-term forecasts while the bottom part contains the CBO's long-term projections.

When using private or government forecasts, the important point to keep in mind is that there is not a good relationship between the cost and accuracy of these predictions. During periods of rapid economic and business transformation, the most expensive estimates created from sophisticated computer models can be just as wrong (or right) as rough guesses from informed business executives. Forecasts are most useful and accurate when the time frame being predicted is quite short, like next month or next quarter, and when economic conditions are relatively stable. Nevertheless, no one yet has ever consistently predicted the future accurately.

Need More Information?

What should you do if this book did not answer your question? First, the surveys, archives, and other sources discussed in this book only scratch the

FIGURE 16.1
Congressional
Budget Office
Projections

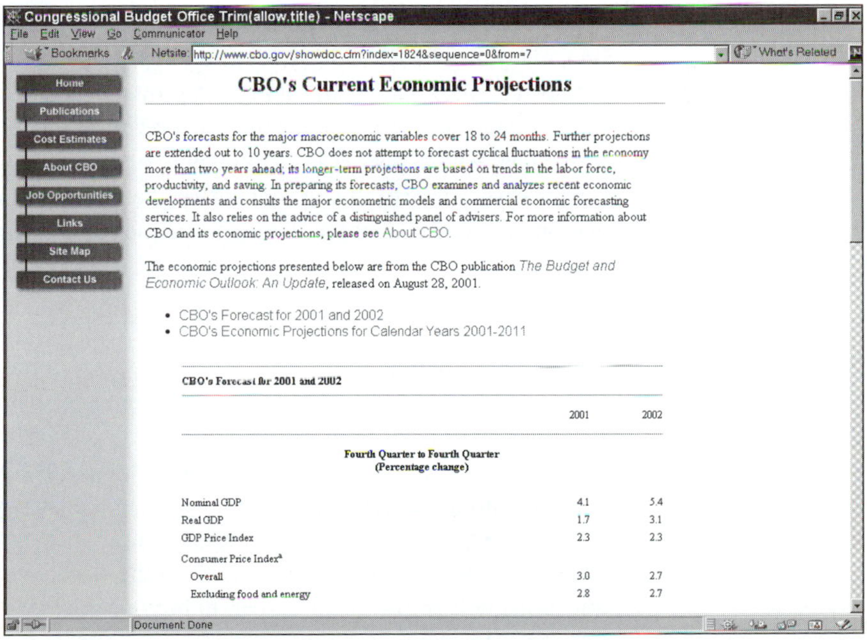

surface of what is publicly available. While it is impossible in this book to cover all sources of business information, someone probably has already collected what you are seeking. The problem is finding it. If the *Statistical Abstract* has some data relevant to your question, look at that table's footnotes. The sources cited there often lead directly to better information sources.

If you still cannot answer your question, there are other resources. First, check some of the commercial sources like Compustat®, Dialog®, Dow-Jones News Retrieval®, ABI-Inform®, and Lexis-Nexis®. If these sources fail, you can always gather the data yourself. Unfortunately, it is almost always cheaper and faster to analyze information that has already been collected than to collect it yourself and then analyze it. Another choice is to hire a consultant or consulting organization to find the answer. While the goal of this book has been to show you how to act as your own information consultant, sometimes a professional can tackle problems that are too big, complex, or scary.

If you decide to collect your own data or hire a consultant, you should first find more information about how business research is done. There is a large number of textbooks on business research methods. Two examples are Donald Cooper and Pamela Schindler's *Business Research Methods 7th edition* (McGraw-Hill) and Uma Sekaran's *Research Methods For Business 2nd edition* (John Wiley). These books have details about writing research reports, the method of doing scientifically valid research and appropriate techniques for testing hypothesis. These are all useful topics, which were not covered in this book.

Since answers to key business questions directly affect a company's bottom line, many businesses will pay for information. The increasing amount of money means that information consulting is a growing career field. The field even has its own trade association called the Association of Independent Information Professionals, whose goal is to help owners of firms doing information research (**http://www.aiip.org**). If you cannot find the information on your own, the association is a good source for finding the names of consultants willing to work on your problem.

Summary

Today, more than at any time in history, power comes from knowledge and information. By showing you the key online and offline sources of business information, this book increases your power. Using these sources gives you the ability to answer business questions quickly. Before rushing off with an answer, read the data notes, understand what the survey or census is tracking, and ensure you are not making one of the common mistakes discussed in Chapter 2, "Information Basics." Having the skills to quickly answer business questions will further your career, help your business, and make you part of the new information royalty.

Appendix 1

What Is an Index?

A number of key pieces of business information are released only in index form. For example, the Consumer Price Index (CPI), Producer Price Index (CPI), Employment Cost Index (ECI), Import-Export Price Index (IEXP), and the Index of Leading Economic Indicators are all released this way. This appendix explains how indexes are created and how to use them.

In simple terms, an index is a way of transforming sets of numbers into a simple series that quickly shows how the values have grown or shrunk over time. Within the series is one key value, called the *base,* which is set equal to 100. All growth and shrinkage is measured relative to the base.

The government reports much information in index form for three reasons. First, price and wage data often come from confidential reports on the actual price at which goods were sold, not the list price. In highly consolidated industries or occupations, there may be only one company providing the government with information. If indexes were not used, customers in these industries who negotiated high-price contracts could easily determine what others were paying. Using raw wage data, workers could determine exactly how much fellow employees were paid. Hence, by providing wage and price information only in index form, the government protects company confidentiality and encourages truthful reporting.

Another reason why untransformed numbers are not used is that indexes are a simple method of combining many products and occupations. This combination is done by weighting some items more than others. Without using different weights, changes in an index would primarily reflect price changes in the most expensive items, not items that are commonly used. For example, without weighting, the Employment Cost Index would primarily track CEO and other upper management pay, instead of representing all workers.

TABLE A.1

Example of Converting Prices into an Index Using 2000 as the Base Year

Year	Price		(Price / Base)* 100 =	Index
1999	$6.00	➡	($6.00 / $8.00) * 100 =	75.0
2000	$8.00	➡	($8.00 / $8.00) * 100 =	100.0
2001	$7.00	➡	($7.00 / $8.00) * 100 =	87.5
2002	$12.00	➡	($12.00 / $8.00) * 100 =	150.0
2003	$14.00	➡	($14.00 / $8.00) * 100 =	175.0

Finally, indexes allow the government to link prices and wages of slightly disparate products into a single series. For example, the soft drink industry used to produce 32-ounce bottles of soda but today almost universally produces drinks in 1-liter containers. Instead of providing one set of prices for 32-ounce and another for 1-liter bottles, the government combines both into a single soda index which links, or melds, the prices together. By linking the prices, a single index accurately reflects how soda prices change from month to month even though the underlying product is changing over time.

While weighting, linking, and substitution issues make creating accurate indexes difficult problems, the basic idea for creating an index is simple.[1] The key idea is: *divide all prices by the base year price and then multiply by 100.* Table A.1 above provides a simple example of transforming prices into an index for a single unchanged product, with 2000 arbitrarily picked as the base year.

To transform the product's price, shown in the second column, into an index, divide all prices by the base year price of $8.00 and multiply by 100. This produces the index series in the last column. The index is 100 in the base year and ranges from 75 in 1999 up to 175 in 2003. There is no special meaning to the numbers like 75, 100, and 175 by themselves. The key use for these numbers is in calculations that show how prices change over time. To calculate a price change just insert index values into the following formula;

$$\text{Percentage Change} = \frac{(\text{New Value} - \text{Old Value})}{\text{Old Value}} \times 100\%$$

For example, to calculate how much prices changed from 2002 to 2003, insert the 2002 value of 150 and the 2003 value of 175 into the formula like this:

$$\text{Percentage Change} = \frac{(175 - 150)}{150} \times 100\% = 16.7\%$$

---

[1] The time-consuming part of creating indexes is determining the items and associated weights. In the example, there is only one item, so the weighting problem goes away.

TABLE A.2
Example of Converting an Index Back into Prices

Year	Index		Index* Conversion =	Price
1998	90	➡	90 * 0.208 =	$18.72
1999	95	➡	95 * 0.208 =	$19.75
2000	100	➡	100 * 0.208 =	$20.80
2001	120	➡	120 * 0.208 =	$25.00
2002	125	➡	125 * 0.208 =	$26.00

Sometimes, even though you have an index, you really want to see actual prices or wages. To convert an index for a single product or occupation back into a series of prices, you need its cost at one point in time. Once you know the real value for any part of the index it is easy to convert the whole index back into money terms. The first step creates a conversion value by dividing the price at one point in time by the matching index value. Then, multiplying the conversion value by every index number regenerates the full price series.

To make these two steps concrete, let's convert the index shown in Table A.2 back into prices. Assume that in 2001 you bought this product for $25.00. Since the 2001 index value is 120, the conversion factor is ($25.00 / 120) = 0.208. Then, to convert the index back into prices, multiply every index value by 0.208. This produces the set of prices in the last column.

Practice Question

The CPI wine price index was 89 in 1980, 114 in 1990, and 147 in 1998. If the average bottle of wine cost $6 in 1998, how much did a bottle cost in 1980 and 1990?

Summary

Many key pieces of business information, like the CPI, which tracks inflation in the United States, are released only in index form. To create an index from price or other data, divide all prices by the base year price and then multiply by 100. If you have an index but want to see actual prices or other data, you need to know the actual value for one point in time. Once you know the real value for any part of the index, first create a conversion value by dividing the price or value at that point in time by the matching index value. Then, multiply the conversion value by every index number to regenerate the underlying data series.

Appendix 2

Census and Survey Details

This appendix explains in more detail how census and surveys are conducted. Most public statistical information used to answer business problems comes from census enumerations and surveys. Enumerating, or counting, everything is used when the goal is extreme precision or when the number of things to count is small or simple. For example, publicly traded companies are not allowed to release quarterly best guesses of sales and profits figures. When the Securities and Exchange Commission discovers companies that do not release true accountings, it fines them heavily.

The most famous and widely used enumeration is the United States Census of Population, which is done every 10 years (1990, 2000, 2010, etc.). The first census was done in 1790 to determine the number of congressional representatives for each state. During the early 1800s, the census was expanded to include a Census of Manufacturers to provide details on U.S. businesses.

While today the Census Bureau provides a huge variety of information on the U.S. population, for its first century of existence the Bureau had a very limited scope. Until 1902 the Census Bureau only existed as a government agency during the counting and data tabulation. Once its job was finished, the agency disbanded until the next census was started.

While in business perfection is always desired, it is usually very expensive or impossible to track everything of interest accurately. For example, while the United States Census Bureau spends huge sums trying to count every person, there is widespread recognition that millions of people are missed. In some cases the expense to track everything exceeds the benefit. For example, when airlines overbook flights they often reassign passengers to another carrier that maintains a reciprocal agreement. To save costs in the 1960s and 1970s, many carriers only sampled their reassignment tickets instead of counting the exact number of passengers swapped between airlines.

Sometimes an exact count is impossible because things do not last long enough to fully enumerate. For example, new businesses are often a prime source for creating jobs. Each year over a half million new businesses are created and almost that many existing businesses close.[1] Since over 3 million workers are affected by the hiring and firing decisions of new and dying companies, the exact numbers are important. Nevertheless, because some companies open and close quickly, it is impossible to enumerate every business, so surveying is the only method for providing information.

Surveys come in two forms: cross-sectional and longitudinal.[2] Most people are familiar with cross-sectional surveys. In these surveys, a random group of individuals is selected and asked questions about a topic such as the President's performance (Roper and Gallup Polls), crime in their neighborhood (National Crime Survey), or how often they visit a doctor (Health Interview Survey). The results are tabulated and when weighted properly represent national attitudes or experiences.

Cross-sectional surveys are very common because they are inexpensive to field. Each time the survey is run, a fresh group of respondents is chosen. While cross-sectional surveys show broad changes over time, they do not provide enough information to understand how individuals or families are changing. Additionally, whenever cross-sectional data are used to explain trends over time, a major concern is whether the results are showing the actual trend or just the changing composition of the pool of individuals or firms being surveyed.

Longitudinal surveys also select a random group of individuals or businesses to represent the nation. However, unlike cross-sectional surveys where a new group is selected every time the survey is run, longitudinal surveys go back and repeatedly interview the same group. Because they follow the same group along over time these surveys show how people or companies develop and change. For example, longitudinal surveys can show whether people develop more conservative attitudes as they grow older; examine how receiving government aid, like welfare, affects life experiences; or track exactly when companies hire or layoff workers.

---

[1] See the section entitled Business Enterprise in the *Statistical Abstract* for the table labeled Employer Firm Births and Deaths by Employment Size.

[2] There are many good books available on survey methodology that go well beyond the information in this chapter. One short but excellent book is Floyd J. Fowler Jr.'s *Survey Research Methods* 2nd Edition, published in 1993 by Sage Publications.

Longitudinal surveys also have drawbacks. First, managers must wait long periods of time before enough time series data are collected to be useful. Second, rapid changes in the population's characteristics are missed by longitudinal surveys, which do not periodically refresh their sample because the respondents represent the nation's characteristics when the survey began. Third, attrition from the survey might make the answers suspect, if those who leave have specific characteristics like being rich or going out of business.

Survey and Enumeration Methods

There are a large number of methods for running surveys and enumerations. The first is **continuous tracking.** Inventory control systems are the simplest example of continuous tracking. As new items come into a warehouse, the count for each category is increased. As items leave a warehouse, the count for each category is decreased. As long as there is no theft, spoilage, or other loss, the current count is an accurate measure of what is in the warehouse. Demographic information such as the number of births and deaths in a city is often kept using continuous tracking.[3]

The second method is **face-to-face interviews.** For these interviews, survey or census takers are sent to an individual's home or a business armed with clipboards or laptop computers to ask questions and record answers. This method has a number of advantages such as relatively high response rates, more truthful answers, and the ability for an interviewer to explain confusing questions. The biggest problem with this method is its high cost. Physically getting interviewers to the interviewee is expensive. Since many people are not always home, interviewers often must contact respondents multiple times before successfully completing an interview. For businesses, the most knowledgeable person is often not readily available. Finally, in dangerous situations, such as interviews in high-crime neighborhoods or interviews done late at night, multiple interviewers are often sent together. While this increases safety and reduces problems for the staff, it dramatically increases the survey's cost.

The third method is **phone interviews.** Phone interviews are often done out of giant call centers, which are special rooms set up with a large number of phones and monitoring devices. Phone interviews are much cheaper than in-person interviews because there is no travel time and no need for multiple interviewers for one respondent. It is also very easy to recontact households

---

[3] Continuous tracking is popular in small United States towns. I once stayed in a tiny Colorado town with a large sign proclaiming its name, elevation, and population.
The night I was there, twins were born and the proud father announced their birth by repainting the population figures on the sign.

where no one was home. While phone interviews are a low cost method of collecting data, there are a number of disadvantages. Call screening and public backlash against telemarketers result in many phone interviews having low response rates. Additionally, the lack of eye contact gives phone interviews a level of anonymity. This anonymity encourages some, but not all, people to be less truthful when answering questions over the phone rather than in person.

The fourth method is **mail surveys.** In this method questionnaires are printed and mailed out with a cover letter asking the respondent to fill in the questionnaire and mail it back. These types of surveys are done using a very small staff and at low cost, since neither phones nor a trained interview staff is needed. The biggest problem is the low response rate. The overwhelming amount of junk mail received by individuals at both home and work means many cover letters and questionnaires are never even opened, much less filled out and returned.

The fifth method is **random passerby interviews,** which are done only for individuals. Interviewers stand on a street corner or in a shopping mall and ask random individuals to fill in the survey, or an interviewer asks an entire group to fill in a survey. While this method provides face-to-face contact like in-person interviews, it is much cheaper to field since the respondents are immediately available for interviewing. The major disadvantage is that the significance of the results is highly questionable. Interviewers are never completely random in their selection of individuals. Additionally, shopping malls and street corners do not contain a random sample of people. This nonrandomness often significantly biases the results.

The last method is **captive audience surveys.** These are surveys filled out by all people currently attending an event such as a conference or class. These have the advantage of very high response rates. Sometimes, however, the response rates are too high, with examples like All-Star balloting at some baseball parks reaching well over 100 percent of paid attendance during every ball game. Beyond the response rate problems, these surveys are also statistically questionable since respondents often are led to answers. For example, during All-Star balloting many stadiums flash the names and ballot places of all local players onto the scoreboard, a tactic designed to influence the survey's outcome.

While most surveys use a single type of data collection, some use multiple methods. For example, the United States Census initially does a mail survey to every known address. If an address does not return the form, the Census Bureau switches to a phone survey. If the phone survey is unsuccessful, face-to-face interviewers attempt to complete the form. If face-to-face interviewing fails, the Census Bureau then does face-to-face interviewing of neighbors. Only if all four methods fail does the Census Bureau mark the address as vacant.

Exactly which survey method is used affects response rates, data quality, and cost. The more valuable the information, the more important it is to have an interviewer directly contact respondents. Unfortunately, the more interviewer contact, the more money the survey or enumeration costs. A rough rule of thumb that business managers should use when evaluating survey and census quality is the more interviewer contact, the higher quality the results.

Survey and Enumeration Questions

Once one of the above methods is chosen for the survey or enumeration, the survey designers must decide how to ask the questions. Business managers using survey data need to understand this part because the way questions are asked influences the results. The importance of question style and wording is shown by the old joke, "Have you stopped beating your spouse?" No matter what you say, this question forces you to admit to spousal abuse. While no survey contains questions this leading, you should always read the text of questions that are key to your analysis to check if they contain more subtle leading statements or biases.[4]

In general, surveys and census enumerations ask two types of questions: open and closed. Open-ended questions have no specific responses provided. One open-ended question is, "What do you like about your job?" A common open-ended question in individual surveys asks respondents to describe their occupation, while a similar open-ended business question asks in which industry the company operates.

Closed questions are phrased differently than open-ended questions and let respondents choose only one of a fixed set of responses. For example a closed question might ask, "Which of the following items do you like about your job: the pay, the hours, the location, or your responsibilities?" Closed questions commonly ask individuals about their age, sex, and marital status, while closed-ended business questions ask about topics like the number of employees and the company's ownership.

Each question format has advantages and disadvantages. Using a closed question format produces a survey that is completed faster, because interviewers do not have to record lengthy answers. It also enables the automatic processing of raw survey data and ensures all answers are consistent. Unfortunately, a closed format forces people to provide only answers that the questionnaire designer thought were important. Since prior to a survey or census the questionnaire designer does not know all possible choices, closed format questions often miss some information.

[4] For example, many surveys ask respondents "How much money did you earn from working?" This statement's implicit assumption that most people work causes some people without jobs to state work earnings to avoid embarrassment.

For example, one survey recently asked teenagers how often they received an allowance. The questionnaire allowed only three responses: weekly, monthly, and other. After the survey was fielded it was discovered that many teens got allowances on a daily or biweekly basis. Since these choices were not available, daily and biweekly teens were automatically lumped with teens getting money on an irregular basis.

The advantage of open-ended questions is that respondents can provide answers that survey designers did not consider. The primary disadvantage is that many hours of work are needed to translate open-ended answers into categories useful for computer processing. Some survey organizations combine both methods. First, they run a small pilot survey, which is composed primarily of open-ended questions. Then results from the pilot survey are used to create the range of closed-ended responses used in the larger final survey.

Accuracy and Precision of Answers

Business managers need to know that not all answers are accurate even if the questions are perfect. Inaccuracy arises because some respondents do not understand the question, do not know the answer, do not remember the answer, or do not want to reveal a truthful answer. Survey staff try very hard to get around these problems. Face-to-face interviews are done to increase truthfulness. Many surveys make legal promises to protect confidentiality. Cognitive testing is done to revise difficult questions into simpler forms, and question wording helps people remember or associate distant events. Nevertheless managers must remember that not all information coming from a census or survey is accurate. All information described in this book ultimately comes from humans. Since humans are imperfect, so is the information.

Because survey and census information is imperfect, how do we measure this imprecision? The key idea behind imprecision is that each answer produced by a survey is not a single number but instead a number and an associated range. For example, the average price of gasoline while this book was being written was $1.50 per gallon. However, while the average was $1.50, the actual price varied from $1.35 up to $1.80 per gallon.

Good surveys directly tell you the range or precision surrounding estimates. For example, United States unemployment rates are produced from the Current Population Survey (CPS). While the current national unemployment rate is 4.1 percent, the CPS's error range is plus or minus 0.2 percent. Therefore, while the survey's best estimate is 4.1 percent, if the survey was done 100 times, statisticians estimate that the unemployment rate would range between

3.7 percent and 4.5 percent in 95 cases.[6] A summary of the major censuses' and surveys' precision is found in the Statistical Abstract's Appendix III, which is called "Limitations of the Data." Read Appendix III before using major census and survey data to make important business decisions.

There are four statistical ideas to keep in mind when looking at survey results. First, there is no imprecision error if a complete enumeration is done accurately. Second, increasing a survey's sample size generally reduces the imprecision of estimates. This means a bigger survey has more precision than a smaller survey that is trying to measure the same thing.

Third, increasing the sample size reduces the imprecision much more for small samples than large samples. What this means for business managers is that a giant survey, asking questions to hundreds of thousands of people, is not a lot more trustworthy than a well-done medium-size survey that interviews only a few thousand. However, a well-done medium-size survey is much more trustworthy than a small survey that interviews a few hundred people.

Fourth, the imprecision is biggest when people are evenly split on a question. Hence, if about half the people in your survey are renters and half are homeowners you will have more imprecision trying to determine the exact percentage renting than if 20 percent are renters and 80 percent are owners. For business managers this means that the survey you use must contain more people if the questions have answers that are hard to differentiate. Conversely, if the questions have clear-cut answers you only need a small sample. Examples of this are political polls. In a very close race, you need to poll thousands to figure out which candidate truly has the lead, while in a lopsided contest asking only a few hundred people can accurately predict the winner.

Summary

Most business information comes from either a census or a survey. There are six major methods of gathering this information: continuous tracking, face-to-face interviews, phone interviews, mail surveys, random passerby interviews, and captive audience surveys. While each method has a unique set of advantages and disadvantages, all provide results with limitations. Read the Statistical Abstract's Appendix III to understand more about these limitations.

---

[6] To calculate the 95 percent confidence interval multiply the error range by two.

Appendix 3

Answers to Practice Questions

The best method of learning to answer business questions is practice. No matter how tempting to look at the answers first, try the problems yourself before doing so. Additional practice questions are found on the book's website (**http://www. mhhe.com** and type Zagorsky in the search box).

Chapter 2

Question: While three years ago your staff numbered 64 people, today you have just 52. What is the percentage change in your staff's size?
Answer: Use 64 as the old value and 52 as the new value in the percentage change formula. The answer is *negative* 18.75% = (52−64)/64 * 100%.

Question: In 2001 a gallon of gas costs $1.60. Adjusting only for inflation, how much should a gallon of gas have cost back in 1975?
Answer: The trick to answering this question is that $1.60 is the *Inflation Adjusted Price* found on the left-hand side of the equation, not the *Original Price*. Like the example in the chapter, put the average CPI value for 1975 of 53.8 into the *Value of CPI Originally* and put the 2001 value of 177.1 into the *Value of CPI Currently*. Then just solve for the *Original Price*.

$$\$1.60 = \text{Original Price} \times \frac{177.1}{53.8}$$

In 1975 the price of gallon of gas should have been about 50¢ a gallon. The actual price was 36¢ a gallon and is found in table 1284 of the *1977 Statistical Abstract*.

Chapter 3

Question: Your department's projected budget is due today. You want to give everyone a cell phone to improve communication. Unless you have an accurate cost estimate, the accounting department automatically eliminates the item from your request. How much is the typical cell phone bill? How long is the typical cell phone call?

Answer: Look in the *Statistical Abstract* by going to **www.census.gov** and pick the link labeled Statistical Abstract. The *Abstract* table labeled Cellular Telephone Industry contains information on cellular telephone usage. Communications and Information Technology, table 919 in the 2000 edition). The 2000 table shows that in 1999 the typical monthly bill per phone was $41.24 and the typical phone call was 2.38 minutes.

Question: You are thinking of opening a chain of small kiosks in every major United States airport and want to target the largest first. What are the five busiest airports?

Answer: Look in the *Statistical Abstract* by going to **www.census.gov** and pick the link labeled Statistical Abstract. The *Abstract* table labeled Top 40 Airports contains information on the busiest airports (Transportation–Air and Water, table 1069 in the 2000 edition). The table shows that in 1998 Atlanta's Hartsfield (34.9 million passengers) edged out Chicago's O'Hare (32.5 million passengers) as the biggest airport. Dallas, Los Angeles, and Denver with 27.7, 22.7, and 16.8 million passengers enplaned round out the top five airports.

Question: How much has the population of the Canadian town of Halifax, Nova Scotia, grown or shrunk over the past five years?

Answer: To find the population of Halifax first go to Canada's statistical website at **http://www.statcan.ca/english**. Then pick Canadian Statistics followed by Population, and then Population again. Finally, select Population, census metropolitan areas to see the size of various Canadian cities. In 1996 the population of Halifax was 341.5 thousand people, while in 2000 the population was 356 thousand. To see if the population has grown or shrunk, put these numbers into the percentage change formula, discussed in Chapter 2. Using this formula shows Halifax has grown by 4.2% = (356−341.5)/341.5 * 100%.

Question: What is the population of Dublin, Ireland?

Answer: The population of greater Dublin is 953,000 in 1996. To get this answer first go to the Irish Central Statistics Office homepage (**http://www. cso.ie**) and pick Statistics. Then on the page that comes up, find the section entitled Demography and select Principal Statistics. The link Largest Cities and Towns provides data for Dublin, plus many other key Irish cities.

Chapter 4

Question: You are the editor of a brand new magazine aimed at active older men ages 55 to 65. How big is the current market for your product? How big will this market be in 2010?

Answer: Look in the *Statistical Abstract* at the table labeled *Resident Population, by Sex and Age* (Table 13 in the 2000 edition) for this information. In 1999 the relevant lines of this table (reproduced below) show 12 million men fit your demographic profile.

Number	Age Range
6,183,000	men aged 55 to 59
4,968,000	men aged 60 to 64
889,000	men aged 65
12,040,000	**Total**

To project how big the market will be in 2010, examine the *Abstract* table entitled *Resident Population Projections by Age and Sex* (Table 14 in the 2000 edition). The middle part of this table shows that men aged 55 to 64 will grow from 11.4 million to 16.97 million. While this age range misses those exactly age 65, it suggests that your target market is growing by 49 percent in slightly over a decade. Given the total United States population (top of the table) is only projected to grow by 9.5 percent over this time period (275.3 million to 299.8 million), the active adult male population appears an excellent marketing opportunity.

Question: Your boss wants to know whether there are more Asians or Hispanics living in the Greater San Francisco Area. Which population is larger?

Answer: To answer this question examine the *Statistical Abstract* table entitled 75 Largest Metropolitan Areas—Racial and Hispanic Origin (Table 35 in the 2000 edition). The San Francisco CMSA appears near the top of the list and shows that in 1997 Asians constitute 18.8% of the population while Hispanics constitute a slightly larger 19.3%. Given how close the numbers are, I would report the exact figures and then suggest the two groups are roughly equal in size.

Question: You are offered the exclusive franchise rights for the next 10 years to either North Dakota or South Dakota. This franchise typically generates more sales in faster-growing areas than slower-growing ones. To choose wisely, determine which state has the faster growing population.

Answer: To answer this question open the P25 document entitled *Population Projections, States* (the most current document when this book was written is P25-1131) and turn to Table 1. In 2000 North Dakota's population is 662,000 while South Dakota's population is 777,000. In 10 years (2010) North Dakota's expected population is 690,000 while South Dakota's expected population is 826,000. Using the percentage change formula (see Chapter 2), North Dakota will grow 4% [(690,000−662,000)/662,000*100%] while South Dakota will grow 6.3% [(826,000−777,0000)/777,000*100%]. The calculations show South Dakota is the better choice.

Question: Your Boston-based health club is located at 39 Dalton Street, in Suffolk County. Your best clients are young professionals aged 25 to 34 who are eager for exercise. You are thinking of mailing out flyers to this market. How many flyers do you need printed?

Answer: The American FactFinder website (**http://factfinder.census.gov**) has information to answer this question. First, use the Reference Map pick to find out the census tract number for 39 Dalton Street. The tract number is 105 but you also will want to capture information from the adjoining tract number 106, which is also very close to the health club. Under the Change Selections button use the Geography pick to select these two census tracts. Data from the 2000 census show that there is 867 people aged 25 to 34 in tract 105 and 799 people in that age range in the adjoining tract 106. Overall, your club has a target audience of slightly less than 2,000 potential clients.

Question: How many renters live in your neighborhood? If you live outside the United States answer this question for the city of Upper Arlington, which is on the edge of Ohio State's campus.

Answer: Since Upper Arlington is an entire city; you do *not* need to use the Reference Map pick. Under the Change Selections button use the Geography pick and tell FactFinder you want information on a "place" in Ohio. At almost the bottom of the place list will be "Upper Arlington city." Select this and press, "show table." Data from the 2000 census reveal that renters occupy 18.7% of Upper Arlington's homes and owners occupy 81.3%.

Chapter 5

Question: How many households in Houston, Texas, earn between $50,000 and $75,000 a year?

Answer: The 1990 census shows almost 75,000 households. To find income information from the census long form, go to the FactFinder website (**http://factfinder.census.gov**). Use the Start with Basic Facts box. Use the

Show Me box to select the Income and Poverty table. Then fill in the next three boxes with a place, Texas and Houston city before pressing the Go button.

Question: What percentage of families living in the Bronx have income of less than $10,000 per year? The Census Bureau classifies this New York City borough as Bronx County.

Answer: The 1990 census shows 291,978 families lived in the Bronx in 1990. Of these families, 36,337 have less than $5,000 of income and 34,565 had between $5,000 and $9,999. This means 24%, or approximately 1 out of every 4 families in this area, survived on an extremely low amount of money. To see these numbers from the census long form go to the FactFinder website (**http://factfinder. census.gov**). Use the Start with Basic Facts box. Use the Show Me box to select the Income and Poverty quick table. Then fill in the next three boxes with a county, New York and Bronx county before pressing the Go button.

Question: Your company is beginning its Midwest expansion in either Kansas or Oklahoma. The planning committee asks you, "Which state has higher household income?"

Answer: Look in the *Statistical Abstract* at the table entitled Money Income of Households—Median Income, by State. (Table 742 in the 2000 edition). In 1998 the median income of a household in Kansas was $36,711 while in Oklahoma it was $33,727. Since in general the table shows households in Kansas receive around $3,000 more per year than those in Oklahoma, I recommend beginning the expansion in Kansas.

Question: You are marketing a new upscale apartment complex for families who earn more than $75,000. You suggest to the builder advertising not only on the local English-speaking stations but also the local Spanish-language stations. Before committing to this plan, the builder asks how many Hispanics earn over $75,000 a year.

Answer: The *Statistical Abstract* has a table entitled Money Income of Families—Percent Distribution by Income Level, Race, and Hispanic Origin. (Table 743 in the 2000 edition) This table shows the number and percentage of families earning $75,000 and over a year. In 1998 over 7.2 million Hispanic families earned this amount.

Question: You design custom vacations for the very wealthy and want to know roughly the size of your market. How many households earn more than $250,000 a year? How many families earn more than $250,000? Why is there a difference in the two numbers?

Answer: Go to the Income homepage at the Census Bureau's website (**www. census.gov**). Select Detailed Income Tabulations and first select the Household link under March 2001 (2000 Income). Picking HINC-07 Income Distribution to $250,000 or More for Households, shows that in 2000 there were 1.305 million households who earned an average of $464,461 per year. Going back and picking the Family link under March 2001 (2000 Income) and then FINC-07 Income Distribution to $250,000 or More for Families, shows that in 2000 there were 1.147 million families in this category. There are more households than families in the richest category because some high-income households are composed of multiple families. For example if a man and woman who each earn $150,000 live together but stay unmarried, the combined household income is over a quarter of a million even though each is separately under this level.

Question: You are the head of admissions for your local community college. A middle-aged white woman with a high-school degree just came in the office and wants to know if getting an associate's degree will boost her income enough so that she can start saving for a new car. What can you tell her about her probable income after earning a degree?

Answer: Go to the Income homepage at the Census Bureau's website (**www. census.gov**). Select Detailed Income Tabulations and then the Person link under March 2001 (2000 Income). At this point there are a number of different tables that provide answers to her question. For this example select PINC-03 Educational Attainment—People 25 Years Old and Over, by Total Money Income in 2000 and then select the 147th line labeled 147. Female, 25 Years and Over, Worked Full-Time, Year-Round, White. Looking at the bottom of the table shows that the median income for a white woman who is a high-school graduate in the year 2000 is $24,578 but those with an associates degree earned $30,565, a boost of almost $6,000 a year, which should more than cover gas, insurance, and car loan payments.

Question: Does it make any difference if your 38-year-old client with a PhD is a female, instead of a male?

Answer: Using FERRET to examine the March 2001 Demographic supplement, shows almost no difference in family income if you select females in the 35 to 41 age range with a PhD versus males. For example, switching from males to females reveals that families earning $25,000 are in the bottom 8% of the income distribution instead of the bottom 5%. Approximately, half of all families with middle-age females holding PhDs earned more than $100,000.

Question: You are a financial planner again and another client just walked in. This client is a divorced 45-year-old male with a bachelor's degree who earns

$65,000 a year. Before hearing the latest stock pitch, he wants to know how his income compares with others.

Answer: Using FERRET, you examine the March 2001 CPS supplement. Use the same selections as the PhD example, but add the variable Demographics, Marital status…{A_MARITL}. Then in step 7 select males who have a bachelor degree and are in the age range of 42 to 47. To increase the size of your sample, highlight not only the divorced but also the separated category when choosing the person's marital status. FERRET returns with a table based on 105 observations. Look down the left-hand column until you find $65,000 and then at the far right cumulative percentage column. The 72.9 in this column means your client is doing better than almost 73% of all other men with a similar background.

Chapter 6

Question: In which region (Northeast, Midwest, South, or West) do families spend the most on reading materials, like books, magazines, and newspapers?
Answer: Each edition of the *Statistical Abstract* contains a table labeled Average Annual Expenditures of All Consumer Units by Region. The 2000 edition (Table 733) shows that Northeasterners spend the most at $201, followed by Westerners at $173, Midwesterners at $170, and Southerners at $125.

Question: You need to move an employee from the New York City metropolitan area to the Pittsburgh area. What type of salary adjustment is needed?
Answer: Looking at the *Statistical Abstract* table labeled "Average Annual Expenditures of All Consumer Units by Metropolitan Area," shows in the 2000 edition (Table 735) that the typical consumer spent $41,103 in the New York City metropolitan area but only $36,239 in the Pittsburgh area, a drop of over 10%. Since it is hard enough to convince employees to relocate, I recommend leaving their pay alone and using the lower cost of living to help sell the benefits of relocating.

Question: The United States Poultry Council hired you to research consumer spending. They are concerned that the Pork Council's ad campaign, "Pork, The Other White Meat," is luring consumers away. They want to know if consumers are spending relatively more or less on poultry as compared to pork.
Answer: The Consumer Expenditure Survey's Multiyear tables (**http://www.bls.gov/cex**) have poultry and pork expenditures since 1984. In 1984 the typical consumer spent $119 on pork and $85 on poultry. This means that for every dollar they spent on chicken, they spent $1.40 on pork. By 1999,

however, the spending ratio has fallen to $1.15. The multiyear table shows the Poultry Council should not worry about pork ads.

Question: Many business commentators have expressed concern over the growing indebtedness of United States families. What percentage of the typical family's after-tax income was spent on mortgage interest and charges in 1985, 1990, 1995, and presently?

Answer: The Consumer Expenditure Survey's Multiyear tables (**http://www.bls.gov/cex**) have information on both after-tax income and mortgage interest payments. The following table tracks changes over time and shows in the last column that debt payments for mortgages have not grown appreciably over time.

Year	After Tax Income	Mortgage Interest	Percentage Spent
1985	$22,887	$1,382	6.0%
1990	$28,937	$1,817	6.3%
1995	$33,864	$2,104	6.2%
1999	$40,652	$2,547	6.3%

Question: As a financial planner and advisor, you are constantly asked about parents' ability to save money for their children's college education. How much money does a single person save? How much does a married couple with children save?

Answer: The answer is found in consumer expenditure survey data at the URL **http://www.bls.gov/cex**. On the CES homepage pick Tables Created by BLS and then under the heading Current Standard Tables, pick the link Composition of consumer unit. Savings each year is just income minus spending. People who spend less than they earn have positive savings while those who spend more have negative. You can compute savings by looking at the table's third line, which lists average income after taxes, and the 23rd line, which is average annual expenditure. Single persons (last column) on average in 1999 earned $26,044 after taxes but spent $25,835 for an average savings of $213 per year. Husbands and wives with children (third column) on average earned $58,763 and spent $51,154 for a savings rate of $7,609. Single parents with children (eighth column) on average earned $24,776 but spent $27,900 for a negative savings rate of $3,124. This means that while the average two-parent family is saving enough to put children through many colleges, single parents are not.

Chapter 8

Question: Your best friend whispers in your ear that pork bellies are the next hot investment trend. What are the names and URLs of the pork industry's trade associations?

Answer: To find associations, go to the American Society of Association Executives database located at **http://info.asaenet.org/gateway/OnlineAssocS list.html**, and type Pork. The site currently lists the National Pork Board (**www.porkboard.org**) and National Pork Producers Council (**www. nppc.org**).

Question: What are the SIC and NAICS codes for greeting cards?

Answer: Using the NAICS and SIC lookup at **http://www.census.gov/naics** shows that the NAICS code for greeting cards is 511191, while the SIC code is 2771.

Question: What are the SIC and NAICS codes for bookstores?

Answer: Using the NAICS and SIC lookup at **http://www.census.gov/naics** shows that the NAICS code for bookstores is 451211, while the SIC code is 5942.

Question: You are thinking about broadening your Connecticut insurance brokerage business by creating a claims adjustment subsidiary. How many companies are currently competing for business in the nutmeg state?

Answer: One way to answer this question is to go the American FactFinder at **http://factfinder.census.gov** and pick Industry Quick Reports. Using the Browse pick under Select Industry, choose NAICS industry 524291, Claims Adjusting. The tree to get to Claims Adjusting looks like:

  52: Finance & insurance
    524: Insurance carriers & related activities
      5242: Agencies, brokerages, & other insurance related activities
        52429: Other insurance related activities
          524291: Claims adjusting

Then pick Show Report to see that while there are 4,443 businesses doing claims adjusting in the entire United States in 1997, Connecticut has only 60 or 1.3% of all companies in this business.

Question: You are in living in the Pacific Northwest and searching for a little-known book about the Cascades. How many bookstores exist in Oregon and Washington?

Answer: Go the American FactFinder at **http://factfinder.census.gov** and pick Industry Quick Reports. Using the Browse pick under Select Industry, choose NAICS industry 451211, bookstores. The tree to get to bookstores looks like:

  44-45: Retail trade
    451: Sporting goods, hobby, book and music stores
      451211: Bookstores

Then pick Show Report to see that there are 223 bookstores in Oregon and 358 in Washington in 1997.

Question: After successfully expanding your antique sink and tub replicas into the greater Boston area, you now set you sights on New York City. How many plumbing wholesalers do your account representatives need to service in just the five boroughs of New York City?

Answer: Using the Geography Quick Report link in American FactFinder (**http://factfinder.census.gov**), first select under type of area Economic Place. Then in the geographic area choose "New York, NY." After picking Show Report, you can see all the two-digit industries in the city of New York. To find plumbing wholesalers (NAICS 42172), use the Change Selections button to examine the table at the six-digit level. The resulting table shows your representatives need to cover 117 businesses.

Question: Searching every bookstore in Oregon and Washington for that special book about the Cascades is too large a task. How many bookstores are located in greater Portland?

Answer: Using the Geography Quick Report link in American FactFinder (**http://factfinder.census.gov**), first select under type of area Metropolitan Statistical Area. Then in the geographic area choose Portland-Salem, OR-WA CMSA. After picking Show Report, you can see all the two-digit industries in the greater Portland. To find bookstores (NAICS 451211) use the Change Selections button to examine the table at the six-digit level. The resulting table shows you need to contact 118 stores.

Chapter 9

Question: You are interested in contacting Polycom Inc., a company that makes video conferencing equipment. Unfortunately, you do not know where it is located. Use the Dun and Bradstreet online database to find the address of Polycom's headquarters.

Answer: Go to **http://dbreports.telebase.com** and pick the U.S. company profile button. In the name field type Polycom and check the button Limit to Headquarters. This returns with one company in Milpitas, California. Picking More Information provides the address, phone number, and line of business.

Question: You are interested in building custom bicycles for serious triathletes but want to outsource making parts like bicycle wheels. Use *Thomas Register* to find how many bicycle wheel manufacturers exist in the United States and Canada.

Answer: Open a printed copy of *Thomas Register* or log on to **http://www. thomasregister.com**. If using the online version, type the term *bicycle wheel* in the search window. This directory currently lists 13 different bicycle wheel manufacturers.

Question: How much cash did McDonald's hold last quarter?

Answer: Go to the SEC website (**http://www.sec.gov**), and pick Search for Company Filings. Then pick Quick Forms Lookup and enter McDonalds in the company name box and 10-Q in the form type. The most recent quarterly report when this book was written is August 10, 2001. This report shows McDonalds had $413.3 million as of June 30, 2001.

Question: How much did Michael Eisner, Chairman and CEO of Walt Disney Inc., get paid last year?

Answer: Pay for senior executives is found in DEF-14A forms. Go to the SEC website **http://www.sec.gov** and pick Search for Company Filings. Then pick Quick Forms Lookup and enter Walt Disney into the company name box and DEF-14A in the form type box. Mr. Eisner's pay is located in the table labeled Executive Compensation Summary Table. The table shows Eisner in 2000 got $813,462 in annual salary, $8.5 million in bonus, and $3 million in other compensation.

Chapter 10

Question: You work for the vitamin division of a pharmaceutical company. The marketing department suggests raising multivitamin prices while the sales force is adamantly opposed. Using the industry data series, check how much multivitamin prices changed over the last year.

Answer: The PPI industry ID code for multivitamins is 2834#711. The PPI value changed from 147.8 in 1999 to 150.1 in 2000, an increase of 1.6%. You can see these numbers by going to the PPI website (**http://www.bls.gov/ppi**) and picking Create Customized Tables followed by Industry Data. After the public data query application starts, choose 2834 Pharmaceutical preparations in the select an industry box and 2834#711 Multivitamins in the select one or more Products box.

Question: Vitamins are found in both the industry and commodity lists. Use the commodity data series to check how much adult multivitamins prices have changed. How different are answers from the commodity and industry databases?

Answer: The PPI for adult multivitamins changed from 141.4 in 1999, to 143.4 in 2000 an increase of 1.7%. You can see these numbers by going to the PPI website (**http://www.bls.gov/ppi**) and picking Create Customized Tables followed by Commodity Data. After the public data query application starts, choose 06 Chemicals and allied products in the select a group box and 06360111 Adult Multivitamins in the select one or more items box. The slight difference between the two series is due to the commodity series covering only adult multivitamins while the industry series covers both adults and children's vitamins.

Question: The original 1977 *Star Wars* movie gross receipts were $461 million. The 1999 Star Wars movie *The Phantom Menace* had gross receipts of $431 million. Comparing just the raw numbers suggests the two films were roughly equal box office hits. If the 1977 receipts are corrected for inflation which film did better?

Answer: Using the inflation calculator at **http://www.bls.gov/cpi** it is easy to convert 1977 receipts into 1999 dollars. Insert the values $431 and 1977 into the top half of the calculator and the year 1999 into the bottom. Pressing Calculate gives $1.27 billion. This means the original movie grossed almost three times *The Phantom Menace's* amount.

Question: The 1997 hit movie *Titanic* took in $601 million. How do its receipts compare after adjusting for inflation to the original 1977 *Star Wars* gross of $461 million?

Answer: Converting the 1977 value of $461 million into 1997 dollars shows that *Star Wars* grossed $1.22 billion, which is double *Titanic's* $601 million gross.

Question: Your broker just called and recommended buying stock in a video rental chain. The broker's research department just raised its forecast of the stock's future price by 25% based on expectations of much higher profit margins. You are skeptical. What has happened to video rental fees in the last few years?

Answer: Video rental fees are tracked in the CPI (**http://www.bls.gov/cpi**). To see how much video rental fees have changed, find Create Customized Tables (one screen) and select the link under this heading entitled Consumer Price Index—All Urban Consumers (Current Series). This brings up the public data query program, which needs three pieces of information. First, select U.S. city average for the area. Second, select Rental of video tapes and discs in the item box. Last, check the box labeled Not Seasonally Adjusted. Picking Get Data shows virtually no change in video rental fees from 1998 to 1999, followed by a drop of 1.5% from 1999 to 2000. Unless this video chain is either cutting costs dramatically or boosting its customer base, the CPI numbers suggest the revenue side will not produce a dramatic increase in earnings.

Question: Given you are not interested in purchasing stock in the video rental chain, your broker wants to know if he can recommend cable television companies. Intrigued, you want to know how cable television rates have changed over time.

Answer: Cable television rates are also tracked in the CPI (**http://www. bls.gov/cpi**). Select Consumer Price Index—All Urban Consumers (Current Series) under Create Customized Tables (one screen). This time fill in U.S. city average for the area, Cable television in the item box, and last check the box labeled Not Seasonally Adjusted. Picking Get Data shows cable television fees have soared during the 1990s, rising from 175.7 in 1991 to 266.8 in 2000, a change of 52%.

Chapter 11

Question: As soon as you finished giving the phone center staff a raise, the sales force asked how much of an increase it was getting. How much did wages increase for individuals in sales occupations last year?

Answer: To answer this question, go to Compensation Cost Trends homepage at **http://www.bls.gov/ect**. Select Create Customized Tables (one screen) and choose Wages and Salaries in step 1, Private industry in step 2, Index Number in step 3, 113 Sales Occupations in step 4, and Not seasonally adjusted in step 5. Pressing the Get Data button shows that the employment cost index rose from 143.3 in the 4th quarter of 1999 to 148.7 in the 4th quarter of 2000, a gain of 3.6 percent. To reduce ill feelings within the company, however, you provide the sales staff with a 4.4 percent raise to ensure parity with the call center.

Question: You need to hire some engineers in Denver for your mining operation. How much are mining engineers currently paid and how many are working in the Denver area?

Answer: The SOC number is 17-2151 for mining and geological engineers. To find information about this group in Denver, go to the OES website at **http://www.bls.gov/oes** and pick the link Tables Created by BLS. Then pick 1999 Metropolitan Area estimates and choose Denver, Colorado. Mining engineers are located under Architecture and Engineering Occupations. In 1999 there were 150 mining engineers working in the Denver area earning on average $68,050.

Question: The brochures and other sales material produced by your Texas-based company consistently look drab and outdated. You are thinking about hiring a graphic designer to improve these materials. How much are graphic designers paid per hour in Texas?

Answer: Graphic designers are SOC number 27-1024. In 1999 the median wage for Texas designers was $15.84 and the mean wage was $16.36. To find these numbers go to the OES homepage (**http://www.bls.gov/oes**) and choose Tables Created by BLS. Then pick 1999 State estimates and click on the map anywhere within the borders of Texas. Graphic designers are found under the Arts, Design, Entertainment, Sports, and Media Occupations heading.

Question: You just received a detailed bid from a general contractor to rebuild corporate headquarters. Overall, the bid is much higher than expected and certain parts do not make sense. One item that catches your eye is that the hourly rate for general plumbing work is only half the electrician's rate. You wonder whether plumbers are paid that much less per hour than electricians. Use the NCS to find the pay rate for plumbers and electricians.

Answer: Using pay information from the NCS, it is easy to find out how much plumbers and electricians are paid. Go to **http://www.bls.gov/ncs** and select Wages (NCS) under the Create Customized Tables (one screen) heading. In the first box, entitled Select an Area, choose All United States. In the second box, entitled Select an Occupation, choose Plumbers, pipefitters, and steamfitters. In the third box, entitled Select a Work Level, use Overall occupation average. Pressing Get Data reveals in 1999 this group made $20.37 per hour. Repeating the steps and changing the Select an Occupation box to Electricians shows that in 1999 the average worker in this category made $19.12 per hour. The NCS survey shows that plumbers are actually paid slightly more than electricians, not the other way around. Given this discrepancy, you should think about bringing in another general contractor to bid the job.

Question: Your company employs a small group of long-haul truckers to transport items from the factory to the distribution centers. Given this small group is the most crucial link in your supply chain, you want to ensure they are paid fairly. How much do junior and senior truck drivers earn?

Answer: Go to **http://www.bls.gov/ncs** and select Wages (NCS) under the Create Customized Tables (one screen) heading. In the first box, entitled Select an Area, choose All United States. In the second box, entitled Select an Occupation, choose Truck drivers. In the third box, entitled Select a Work Level, use Level 01. This time instead of pressing Get Data, press the Add To Your Selection button. Change the work level box to Level 02 and again press the Add To Your Selection button. Repeat this for all seven levels and then press Get Data. Results for 1999 show pay ranged from $7.73 for junior truck drivers (level 01) up to $17.28 per hour for senior drivers (level 07).

Question: You notice that your benefits costs have skyrocketed for your blue-collar workers in the last year. Are other companies having a similar problem?
Answer: To answer this question go to Compensation Cost Trends homepage at **http://www.bls.gov/ect**. Select Create Customized Tables (one screen) and choose Benefits in step 1, Private industry in step 2, Index Number in step 3, 120 Blue-collar Occupations in step 4, and Not seasonally adjusted in step 5. Pressing the Get Data button shows that the employment cost index rose from 146.4 in the 4th quarter of 1999 to 154.3 in the 4th quarter of 2000, a gain of 5.4 percent. These results show that benefit costs for blue-collar workers are rising steadily but are not skyrocketing.

Chapter 12

Question: Your best friend was laid off almost four months ago and is getting very discouraged about finding a good job. She believes almost no one looks as long as she has. Is she right? How many people have been unemployed 15 or more weeks?
Answer: Use the CPS table generator located at **http://www.bls.gov/cps** to answer this question. First select "Historical data for series in the monthly Employment Situation news release" under the Get Detailed Statistics heading. From the selection list, choose the sixth line labeled Duration of Unemployment. Then go to the section of the table for Percent Distribution and check the box in the Not seasonally adjusted column that is labeled "15 weeks and over." When Retrieve data is selected, the table created shows that currently on average between 1-in-5 and 1-in-4 unemployed individuals have been searching for more than 15 weeks. In the early 1990s the average was 1-in-3.

Question: How many workers hold multiple jobs?
Answer: Use the CPS table generator located at **http://www.bls.gov/cps** to answer this question. First select "Historical data for series in the monthly Employment Situation news release" under the Get Detailed Statistics heading. From the selection list choose the 10th line, labeled Persons not in the labor force and multiple jobholders by sex. Then check the box in the Total column (the left of the three selections) that is labeled "Percent of total employed" under the heading Total multiple jobholders. When Retrieve data is selected, the table created shows that on average almost 6% of the nation's work force holds multiple jobs in any given month.

Question: You need a quick estimate of the number of clergy. How many are there in the United States?

Answer: Use the FERRET system located at **http://ferret.bls.census.gov** to answer this question. First, select the CPS Public Basic Monthly from the list of surveys. Select March 2001 for the date and then from the list of major categories select just the Occupation category. Then, highlight the following variable:

Indus.&Occ.—(main job)occupation code…………..{PTI01OCD}[11422]

After selecting this variable set its range to 176 (Clergy 2042). FERRET estimates show that for March 2001 there were 367,442 clergy in the United States.

Question: You are responsible for hiring more teachers for the state of New York. How many teachers are currently employed or currently looking for work in the state?

Answer: The FERRET system located at **http://ferret.bls.census.gov** answers this question. Select the CPS Public Basic Monthly from the list of surveys. Select March 2001 for the date and then from the list of major categories select Labor Force Variables, Industry and Occupation, and Geography. Finally, highlight these three variables while holding down the CONTROL key.

Geography—FIPS state code…………………………..…......{GESTFIPS} [11511]

Indus.&Occ.—(main job)occupation, major groups-recode……….............................{PRDTOCC1}[11434]

Labor force—employment status………............................{PEMLR}[11287]

After selecting these three variables, set the range of the GESTFIPS variable to NY, limit PRDTOOC1 to 9 and 10, to capture both college and primary school teachers, and do not place limits on the PEMLR variable. FERRET produced the following output for March 2001:

SAS Data Set with 187 obs was created for your query

Labor force status, recode	Frequency	Percent
Employed at work	420,262	95.4%
Employed absent	8,932	2.0%
Unemployed on layoff	2,794	0.6%
Unemployed looking	3,088	0.7%
Other not in labor force	5,320	1.2%

This output means there were over 420,000 individuals working as teachers, 5,800 individuals looking for teaching positions, and 5,300 teachers out of the labor force for reasons like maternity leave. This means there are almost no additional teachers available to hire within the state and you should begin bringing teachers in from other locations.

Chapter 13

Question: You are interested in starting a business that helps people find renters for apartments, homes, and other property. What percentage of tax filers rented out their property? What percentage of total income did net rental payments constitute?

Answer: Go to **http://www.irs.gov** and pick Tax Stats. Then pick the Individuals link under the Statistics by Topic. Then pick the Complete Report Publications link, download 98INALCR.EXE and open the file 98IN14AR.XLS. Cell B221 shows that 4,338,888 returns reported net rental income out of 124,770,662 returns filed (cell b8), which is approximately 3.5 percent. Dividing total net rental income (cell C221) by total adjusted gross income (cell C8) shows that rents constitute less than 1 percent of adjusted gross income.

Question: Assume you itemize your deductions. Do you pay more or less tax than other people in your AGI bracket?

Answer: Go to **http://www.irs.gov** and pick Tax Stats. Then pick the Individuals link under the Statistics by Topic. Then pick the Complete Report Publications link, download 98INALCR.EXE and open the file 98IN21ID.XLS to see if you pay more or less tax than other itemizers in your AGI bracket. Columns J and K from line 271 to 296 contain the number of returns and amount paid by AGI bracket. For example, the AGI $35,000 to under $40,000 has the 2,006,362 under number of returns and 5,971,256 under amount. This means that roughly 2.0 million returns were filed with this AGI and the total income tax owed was almost $6 billion (the amount column is in $1,000 of dollars. Do not forget to add back in the missing 000s). To compute the average tax owed, divide the total tax by the number of returns, for an answer of $2,976.

Question: After years of fighting on the corporate battleground, you yearn to retire and open a small bar and grill. Before ditching your suit and tie, you want to know how much money sole proprietors earn from running, eating, and drinking establishments. What kind of income can you expect?

Answer: Go to **http://www.irs.gov** and pick Tax Stats. Then pick the Sole Proprietorships link under Statistics by Topic. Then pick Industry Statistics on the resulting page. Each year the quarterly magazine *Statistics of Income Bulletin* periodically publishes an article on sole proprietorship returns. Scroll down the list until you find the most recent article. When this book was written, the most recent article was in the Summer 2001 issue. Table 1 in the 2001 article shows in the 1999 tax year the gross profit margin before the proprietor took any income for Food Services and Drinking Places was 5.9 percent ($1.87 billion in net income / $31.4 billion in receipts). Given the average restaurant grossed $123,700 ($31.4 billion in receipts / 253.8 thousand returns) your expected income is only $7,300 per year. Maybe, the corporate world isn't so bad after all?

Question: Your general contractor consistently complains about how crushing taxes are ruining the building business. After listening for awhile you are curious and want to know whether general building contractors pay more taxes than other businesses.

Answer: Table 6 of the 1997 *Corporation Income Tax Returns* shows that all general contractors had net income subject to tax of $3.3 billion (cell K81 in the online 1997 excel file Tabl6.xls) and paid $986 million in federal income tax (cell K93), for an average tax of 29.9 percent. The second column of Table 6 shows that the all industry average tax rate is 26.9 percent since corporations in the United States sold $16.6 trillion worth of goods and services and earned for their efforts a net income subject to tax of $684 billion and paid $184 billion in taxes. While these numbers suggest builders' pay slightly more than other businesses in taxes, the burden does not seem particularly crushing.

Chapter 14

Question: You are thinking about buying a home. What were the highest and the lowest interest rates recorded by FRED for 30-year conventional mortgages?

Answer: Go to FRED (**http://www.stls.frb.org/fred**) and select Interest Rates followed by 30-Year Conventional Mortgage Rate. The peak was in October 1981 when rates were 18.45%, while the low point was in October 2001 when rates were 6.6%.

Question: You work for a large regional homebuilder whose leaders are perplexed about the current housing market. When the company first started building homes, interest rate changes had a big effect on customers. Now, no matter what happens to interest rates, people just keep buying. You suggest that instead of looking at current mortgage rates, the company should be examining real, or inflation-adjusted, rates. Your discussion is intriguing and the president wants to

Graph: 30-Year Conventional Mortgage Rate Adjusted For Inflation. Monthly 1978 to 1999

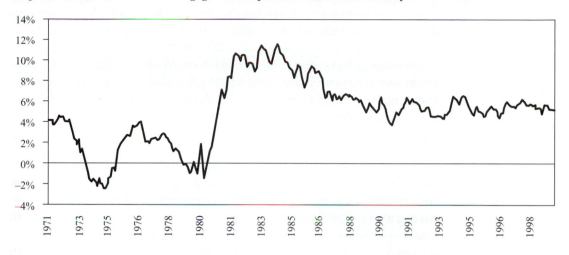

see a graph of inflation-adjusted 30-year mortgage rates right away. What does the graph look like?

Answer: Use FRED (**http://www.stls.frb.org/fred**) to find this answer by selecting Interest Rates followed by 30-Year Conventional Mortgage Rate. To find inflation information, go to the CPI homepage (**http://www.bls.gov/cpi**) and retrieve the Table Containing History of CPI-U From 1913 to Present. Using the CPI information you can calculate the inflation rate for the previous 12 months at every point in time. Then subtract this previous 12-month inflation figure from the 30-year mortgage rates and graph the result. You should get a picture like the one above.

The picture explains why, when the company first started building homes, interest rate changes had a big effect on customers and why now interest rates have no effect. Prior to 1990, real interest rates changed dramatically in the housing market. However, since 1990 real interest rates have been stable while nominal rates have changed quite a bit. The stability in real interest rates is why homebuilders perceive a disconnect between nominal rates and home-buying patterns.

Question: Travelers checks are big business for a number of financial firms, like American Express. How many dollars worth of travelers checks are currently outstanding?

Answer: Go to FRED (**http://www.stls.frb.org/fred**) and select Monetary Aggregates followed by Travelers' Checks Outstanding, which is under the M1 category. In the fall of 2001 there is over $8 billion U.S. of travelers checks outstanding.

Question: Your company builds major home appliances, like dishwashers and stoves, the vast majority of which are installed in new homes. You want to understand the potential size of the market. How many new homes are sold each month?

Answer: Go to FRED (**http://www.stls.frb.org/fred**) and select the Business/Fiscal link followed by New 1-Family Houses Sold: United States, which is under the New Home Sales category. In the summer of 2001 almost 900,000 new homes were sold each month.

Question: You are the credit manager for a large department store. You know a great deal about your customers' credit and income histories but know little about how your customers compare nationally. How much do typical consumers pay each month on their debts as a percentage of their income?

Answer: Go to FRED (**http://www.stls.frb.org/fred**) and select the Business/Fiscal link followed by Consumer Debt Service Payments as Percent of Disposable Personal Income %. In the second quarter of 2001 the ratio stood at 7.79%.

Question: Overall your company's sales growth is excellent. The only sales laggard during the late 1990s is the division selling products to state and local governments. The division head's standard response is that state and local governments are not expanding as quickly as other economic sectors. After hearing this explanation one too many times, you decide to investigate the issue yourself. Did state and local government spending lag the rest of the economy during the late 1990s?

Answer: FRED provides information on both GDP and GDP for selected sectors of the economy. Go to FRED's main page (**http://www.stls.frb.org/fred**) and pick Gross Domestic Product (GDP) and Components. Then select Real Gross Domestic Product in Chained 1996 Dollars under the 1 Decimal. Write down the first quarter's value for real GDP in 1995 ($7488.7 billion) and the fourth quarter's value in 1999 ($9037.2 billion). Then select "Real State and Local Government Consumption Expenditures and Gross Investment Gross" and write down the values for the same time periods ($863.3 billion and $1011.1 billion). Calculate the growth rates for both series (GDP: 20.7%; Gov. 17.1%), and you will see that state and local spending did lag the overall economy by 3.6% over five years, or 0.75% per year.

Chapter 15

Question: Motorcycles are no longer driven just by the young and restless. While the demographics of motorcycle owners are changing rapidly, the repairing and servicing of these machines is still reminiscent of the 1950s. You are writing a business plan to create a standardized chain of motorcycle repair shops, similar in concept to the national muffler replacement business. To find information about motorcycle imports, you need the relevant SITC code. What is it?

Answer: Go to the United States International Trade Commission's website (**http:// dataweb.usitc.gov**) and select Lookup for HTS/SIC/SITC/NAICS/ End-Use descriptions. Then select the four-digit SITC button and press List Items. Motorcycles are under the 1-digit group, labeled 7, which tracks machinery and transport equipment. The broad four-digit group identifier for motorcycles is 7851. Motorcycles are also broken down into a number of five-digit groups.

78511 Motorcycles with Capacity Not Exceeding 50 CC

78513 Motorcycles with Capacity Exceeding 50 CC But Not 250 CC

78515 Motorcycles with Capacity Exceeding 250 CC But Not 500 CC

78516 Motorcycles with Capacity Exceeding 500 CC But Not 800 CC

78517 Motorcycles with Capacity Exceeding 800 CC

Question: You have built a good business importing beer from Australia and are now thinking of expanding by importing wine. What is wine's four-digit SITC code?

Answer: Go to USTIC's website (**http://dataweb.usitc.gov**) and select Lookup for HTS/SIC/SITC/NAICS/End-Use descriptions. Then select the four-digit SITC button and press List Items. Wine is SITC 1121.

Question: In a previous practice question, you were creating a business plan targeting motorcycles and found the relevant SITC code. Using this code, determine how large the motorcycle import and export markets are currently.

Answer: Go to USTIC's website (**http://dataweb.usitc.gov**) and select ITC Trade DataWeb. Then press the U.S. Imports for Consumption button, the Quick Query button, and last Proceed. On the first page that comes up, fill in the Enter A Commodity Number box with 7851 and press the SITC button followed by Proceed to next step. On the next screen, leave the defaults alone and press Run Report. For 2000, the United States imported $2.1 billion worth of motorcycles and mopeds.

Question: In a previous practice question you were thinking of expanding your business by importing wine from Australia. How much wine does the United States import from this country?

Answer: Go to USTIC's website (**http://dataweb.usitc.gov**) and select ITC Trade DataWeb. Then press the U.S. Imports for Consumption button, the

Quick Query button, and last Proceed. On the first page that comes up, fill in the Enter A Commodity Number box with 1121 and press the SITC button. Then press the button next to Display All Countries Separately, followed by Proceed to next step. On the next screen, leave the defaults alone and press Run Report. For 2000, the United States imported $281 million worth of wine from Australia., ranking Australia as the United States' third largest foreign source of wine.

Question: What are U.S. tariff rates on motorcycle imports?
Answer: Go to USTIC's website (**http://dataweb.usitc.gov**) and select Tariff Database button. Type in the word "motorcycle" in the search box. Then select a specific motorcycle size. The exact size makes a difference since large and small motorcycles have different import duties. For bikes over 700 CC Mexican and Canadian imports pay nothing, nations with normal trade relations (NTR) or most favored nation (MFN) pay a rate of 2.4 percent, and all other countries pay an import duty of 10 percent.

Question: What are U.S. tariff rates on wine imports?
Answer: Go to USTIC's website (**http://dataweb.usitc.gov**) and select Tariff Database button. Type in the word "wine" in the search box. Then select a specific wine category. For this example, let's assume you want to import cases of 750 ml. bottles of red wine. Select from the list 22042150—Wine other than Tokay (not carbonated), not over 14% alcohol, in containers not over 2 liters— 01/01/2001. Nations with normal trade relations (NTR) or most favored nation (MFN) pay 6.3¢ per bottle, while all other countries pay 33¢ per bottle.

Question: Each month you ship hundreds of cases of French cheese by boat to New York. Citing rising transportation costs, your shipper has increased prices by roughly 2 percent each quarter. Are other importers facing the same cost increases?
Answer: Go to the International Price Indexes at **http://www.bls.gov/iep**. Pick Create Customized Tables (one screen). In the first step, select the Services International Index. In the second step, find EIUIU112 Ocean Liner Freight (Inbound). This item covers ocean freight for both Atlantic and Pacific traffic. Below this is the entry EIUIU11211 From Atlantic that tracks ocean freight primarily from Europe. Select the from Atlantic item and then pick Get Data. The resulting table shows that from March of 1991 until September of 2001 ocean freight prices do not exhibit any sharp upward or downward trend over time.

Question: How many British pounds does one Australian dollar buy today?
Answer: To find currency conversion rates, go to the IMF's website (**http://www.imf.org**). Then select IMF Finances followed by Current Rates. On October 26, 2001, each SDR was worth 0.89 British pounds while each SDR purchased 2.52 Australian dollars. Hence, one pound purchases (2.52 / 0.89), or 2.83 dollars.

Question: You are in deep discussions with a Brazilian produce company for importing acerolas (also called the Barbados cherry) into the United States. Acerolas are a small fruit that looks like a cherry, tastes very different, and has a very high vitamin C content. The company is quoting you a price of 40 Brazilian reais (also called reals) per case. How much is this in U.S. dollars?
Answer: To find currency conversion rates, go to the IMF's website (**http://www. imf.org**). Then select IMF Finances followed by Current Rates. On October 26, 2001, each SDR was worth 3.48 Brazilian reais while each SDR purchased 1.27 U.S. dollars. Hence, a 40 reais case of fruit costs 40 * (1.27/3.48), or U.S. $14.60 plus freight, insurance, and duties.

Appendix 1

Question: The CPI wine price index was 89 in 1980, 114 in 1990, and 147 in 1998. If the average bottle of wine cost $6 in 1998, how much did a bottle cost in 1980 and 1990?
Answer: If a bottle of wine costs $6 when the index is 147, then the conversion factor is ($6/147) = 0.041. Multiplying the conversion factor by the index values of 89 and 114 means the average bottle cost $3.65 and $4.67 in 1980 and 1990, respectively.

Index